Uncovering Calvin's God

Uncovering Calvin's God

John Calvin on Predestination and the Love of God

Forrest H. Buckner
Foreword by Oliver D. Crisp

LEXINGTON BOOKS/FORTRESS ACADEMIC
Lanham • Boulder • New York • London

Published by Lexington Books/Fortress Academic
Lexington Books is an imprint of The Rowman & Littlefield Publishing Group, Inc.
4501 Forbes Boulevard, Suite 200, Lanham, Maryland 20706
www.rowman.com

6 Tinworth Street, London SE11 5AL, United Kingdom

Copyright © 2020 by The Rowman & Littlefield Publishing Group, Inc.

All rights reserved. No part of this book may be reproduced in any form or by any electronic or mechanical means, including information storage and retrieval systems, without written permission from the publisher, except by a reviewer who may quote passages in a review.

British Library Cataloguing in Publication Information Available

Library of Congress Cataloging-in-Publication Data

Library of Congress Control Number: 2020942611

ISBN 978-1-9787-0384-1 (cloth)
ISBN 978-1-9787-0386-5 (pbk)
ISBN 978-1-9787-0385-8 (electronic)

Contents

Foreword *Oliver D. Crisp*		vii
Acknowledgments		xi
Abbreviations		xiii
1	One Disposition or Two? Framing the Question	1
2	The Knowledge of God: God's Revealed Nature	9
3	God's Disposition toward Humanity in Predestination	57
4	Integration: One Disposition and a Twofold Will	105
5	Calvin's Preaching: Testing Our Findings	111
6	Predestination and God's Love in Recent Calvin Scholarship	151
7	Calvin in Dialogue: Placing the Mystery	165
8	Predestination in the Key of Jesus Christ	191
Bibliography		207
Index		215
About the Author		221

Foreword

To be honest, Calvin didn't help himself: the beard, the severe cadaverous stare, the long black fur-trimmed robes. Even portraits painted from life seem, in Calvin's case, to condemn those who dare to look upon them. But then, magisterial Reformers were not church leaders given to theological moderation. As some recent scholarship has reminded us, theirs was a kind of prophetic calling.[1] The pictures of Calvin certainly fit that bill. But a calling to preach what, exactly? Surely to preach salvation understood according to the Christian gospel. And yet in the case of Calvin, the message that posterity has received (even if that is not what was communicated) often doesn't sound very much like good news. The words of the twentieth-century poet Phyllis McGinley describing the theology of Jonathan Edwards, the eighteenth-century New England successor to Calvin's project, could just as easily have been penned with the French Reformer in mind, to the effect that "small children, carried bedwards," should shudder at the prospect of meeting the wrathful "God of Mr. Edwards":

> Not God the Father or the Son
>   But God the Holy Terror.[2]

Even that modern literary apologist for the humanism of Calvinian theology, Marilynne Robinson, admits in one of her more trenchant essays that people today "know to disapprove" of Calvin "though not precisely why they should. . . . His misdeeds are somehow of a kind to forbid attention."[3] Perhaps his principal theological misdeed, often reported as something quite distasteful, is his understanding of predestination. Calvin conceives of God dividing humanity into two groups, some of whom are elect and saved according to his purposes, and some of whom are passed over and condemned in their sin. Who would believe that God would do *that*? In fact, as commentators often repeat, Calvin himself seems at times to have been rather embarrassed by his views on the subject. At one point in the final edition his *Institutes of the Christian Religion* he even confesses that the decree to ordain the fall of humanity was "dreadful indeed" ("*Decretum quidem horribile, fateor,*" *Institutes* 3.23.7). Hardly a ringing endorsement, we might think.

But is this really the case? Does the Calvin of history deserve the opprobrium he is often afforded by enlightened social historians? Perhaps more importantly, does Calvin shroud the gracious work of God in Christ in the darkness of a wrathful, transcendent deity unconcerned by the lives of the creatures whose fate he decides on a whim? Where does the God of love and the God who ordains all that comes to pass meet in Calvin's thought—*can* they even meet? These are not insignificant theological questions for those concerned to understand what Calvin actually taught, as well as the more general theological issue of how in principle one might give an account of God and his purposes in Christian doctrine that is able to connect the dots between predestination and divine love in such a way that the upshot is a coherent and plausible whole. Yet addressing this worry as it bears upon the thought of the great French Reformer is the task the Revd. Dr. Forrest H. Buckner has set himself in this volume. Drawing principally upon primary sources from Calvin's sermons and commentaries as well as the *Institutes*, and in dialogue with other thinkers in the tradition of the Protestant Reformation such as Martin Luther, Huldrych Zwingli, Heinrich Bullinger, Jacob Arminius, and Karl Barth, Buckner's study attempts a critical theological retrieval and assessment of Calvin's position. He does so fully engaged with the recent research on this vital question from a range of Calvin scholarship, and cognizant of the shortcomings and difficulties of Calvin's positive theological case.

Even if the reader is not wholly persuaded by the argument Buckner makes and the conclusions he reaches, what he does say is worthy of serious consideration and should give the naysayer pause for thought. Indeed, if he is right, then what Calvin (as opposed to Calvin's critics and would-be allies) says about the God of love and the God of the "dreadful decree" may yet surprise us.

Oliver D. Crisp
Professor of Analytic Theology
School of Divinity, University of St Andrews
Guy Fawkes Day, 2019

NOTES

1. See, for example, Jon Balserak, *John Calvin as Sixteenth Century Prophet* (Oxford: Oxford University Press, 2014).
2. Phyllis McGinley, "The Theology of Jonathan Edwards," *Times Three* (New York: Viking Press, 1961), 19.
3. Marilynne Robinson, "Marguerite De Navarre," in *The Death of Adam: Essays in Modern Thought* (New York: Picador, 1998), 174–75.

Acknowledgments

Although this book, like most, has a variety of tributaries that contributed to its emergence, the headwaters for the theological project at hand came through pastoral work with students in Colorado, USA. Having encountered over the years some of the biblical texts that appear to depict God's love in a restricted way and serving in a denomination rooted in the Reformed tradition, I remember standing in front of a room of hundreds of young people and telling them that God loved them. Although I was confident in the proclamation of God's love revealed in Jesus Christ, I could not ignore the nagging queries in the back of my mind, "Does Scripture really teach that God loves all the people in this room? Does the Reformed interpretation of Scripture do so? Do I need to add a disclaimer like 'if you respond in faith' or 'if you show signs of election'? Should I be saying, 'God loves *most* of you'?" Over time, these questions rested quietly in the back of my mind, rarely expressed but never resolved.

This book is the result of an extended examination of God's disposition toward humanity in the Reformed tradition, focusing particularly on the theology of John Calvin. My desire is that this book will benefit both academy and church. For the academy, I hope it provides a thorough, nuanced, and well-rounded reading of Calvin's teaching on predestination and what can be said about the God of predestination. In a time when much Calvin scholarship seems to be categorized into "Barthian" or "scholastic" interpretations, I have sought to avoid either pole and, as best as possible, let Calvin speak for himself from across his corpus.

For the church, I hope that Scripture readers, exegetes, pastors, lay leaders, and students discover a text that engages lingering questions regarding what they can faithfully say about God and about God's gracious work in election. Through careful engagement with Calvin's attempt to interpret Scripture as a faithful believer, pastor, and scholar, I hope that readers find insight into the key nodal points of this topic for their contemporary contextual exposition and understanding of Scripture. Not alone in their inquiries, readers wrestle with this important topic alongside Calvin and the universal church with the common task of worshipping God and witnessing to God's grace revealed in Jesus Christ.

This book could not have come together without the support of people too numerous to list, but I am compelled to name a few. First and most of all, I am grateful to my family; without the love, companionship, support, wisdom, and fun of Janelle, Esther, Bella, and River, this book never would have come to be. I am also grateful to Professor Alan Torrance for his wisdom and his model as a courageous, humble, and faithful scholar who offers his gifts for the sake of God's work in the world. Thanks to Joey Sherrard and many other scholar colleagues for allowing me to learn with and from you. Thanks to Dr. Gary Deddo for opening up to me the beauty of true theological study. Thanks to those who provided extremely helpful feedback on manuscripts, including Whitworth University colleagues Derek Taylor, Adam Neder, Greg Orwig, and most of all, Jim Edwards. I'm grateful to Michael Gibson and Neil Elliott at Lexington/Fortress Academic for their support. I am deeply appreciative to Oliver Crisp for his generosity in writing the foreword. Finally, thanks to Sandy and David for all you gave and modeled that finds fruit here, and thanks to the many others who provided intentional support and encouragement along this project's journey. Of course, although many have helped improve what follows, I am completely responsible for the final product.

Two other important preliminary notes are appropriate here. First, I am grateful to Banner of Truth Trust (www.banneroftruth.org) for permission to publish quotations from Calvin's *Sermons on Acts*; to Vandenhoeck & Ruprecht for permission to publish quotations from Calvin's *Sermons on Acts* from *Supplementa Calviniana*, vol. VIII; and to Westminster/John Knox Press for permission to publish quotations from Calvin's *Institutes*.

Second, in quotations from Calvin, I have retained his masculine pronouns for God and the masculine language (e.g., "mankind," "men") that appears in all of the English translations of his works. As a result, I have also found it more suitable to use masculine pronouns for God at times in my own descriptions and interactions with Calvin in the hope of providing minimal distraction to the reader.

Abbreviations

CD	Karl Barth, *Church Dogmatics*, 4 vols. in 13 parts, trans. G. F. Bromiley and T. F. Torrance (Edinburgh: T&T Clark, 1956–1975).
KD	Karl Barth, *Die kirchliche Dogmatik*. 4 vols. in 14 parts (Zurich: Evangelischer Verlag, 1932–1967).
ST	Thomas Aquinas, *Summa Theologica*, 5 vols., trans. Fathers of the Dominican Province (Notre Dame, IN: Ave Maria Press, 1948).
Tabula	Theodori Bezae, *Summa Totius Christianismi*, in *Tractationes theologicae*, 3 Vols. (Geneva, 1570–1582), 1:170–205; Theodore Beza, *A Briefe Declaration of the Chief Points of Christian Religion*, trans. William Whittingham (London: Tho, 1613).

Works by John Calvin

1538 Catechism	"Catechism 1538," trans. F. L. Battles, in *Calvin's First Catechism*, ed. I. John Hesselink, p. 1–38 (Louisville, KY: Westminster John Knox Press, 1997).
BLW	*The Bondage and Liberation of the Will: A Defence of the Orthodox Doctrine of Human Choice Against Pighius,* trans. G. I. Davies (Grand Rapids: Baker Books, 1996).
Congrégation	*Congregation sur l'élection éternelle de Dieu.*

CO	*Ioannis Calvini Opera quae supersunt Omnia*, ed. Wilhelm Braum, Edward Cunitz, and Edward Reuss, 59 vols. *Corpus Reformatorum*: vols. 29–87 (Brunswick: Schwetchke, 1863–1900).
CTS	*Calvin's Commentaries*, 45 vols. (Edinburgh: Calvin Translation Society, 1844–1856).
De Aeterna	*Concerning the Eternal Predestination of God*, trans. J.K.S. Reid (London: James Clark, 1961).
Harmony of Gospels	*Commentary on a Harmony of the Evangelists Matthew, Mark, and Luke.*
Harmony of Moses	Harmony of Exodus, Leviticus, Numbers, Deuteronomy.
Inst.	*Institutes of the Christian Religion*, ed. J.T. McNeill, trans. F.L. Battles, 2 vols. (Philadelphia: Westminster, 1960).
SC 5	*Supplementa Calviniana: Sermones de libro Michaeae*, ed. Jean Daniel Benoit. Vol. 5 (Neukirchen-Vluyn: Neukirchener Verlag des Erziehungsvereins, 1964).
SC 8	*Supplementa Calviniana: Sermones in Acta Apostolorum, cap. 1–7*, ed. Willem Blake and Wilhelms Moehn. Vol. 8 (Neukirchen-Vluyn: Neukirchener Verlag des Erziehungsvereins, 1994).
Selected Sermons from the Pastoral Epistles	*Selected Sermons from the Pastoral Epistles,* trans. Laurence Tomson (Vestavia Hills, AL: Solid Ground Christian Books, 2012).
Sermons on Acts	*Sermons on the Acts of the Apostles: Chapters 1–7*, trans. Rob Roy McGregor (Edinburgh: The Banner of Truth Trust, 2008), banneroftruth.org.
Sermons on Ephesians	*Sermons on the Epistle to the Ephesians,* trans. Arthur Golding (Edinburgh: Banner of Truth Trust, 1973).
Sermons on Galatians	*Sermons on Galatians,* trans. Kathy Childress (Edinburgh: Banner of Truth Trust, 1997).
Sermons on Micah	*Sermons on the Book of Micah,* trans. Benjamin W. Farley (Phillipsburg, NJ: P&R Publishing Co., 2003).

Sermons on Election and Reprobation	*Sermons on Election and Reprobation,* trans. John Field (Willowstreet, PA: Old Paths Publications, 1996).
Sermons on Job	*Sermons from Job,* trans. Leroy Nixon (Grand Rapids: Eerdmans, 1952).
Sermons on Ps. 119	*Sermons on Psalm 119,* trans. Thomas Stocker (Albany, OR: Books for the Ages, 1996).
Sermons on the Saving Work of Christ	*Sermons on the Saving Work of Christ,* trans. Leroy Nixon (Grand Rapids: Baker, 1950).
Sermons on the Ten Commandments	*Sermons on the Ten Commandments,* trans. Benjamin W. Farley (Grand Rapids: Baker, 1980).

Chapter One

One Disposition or Two? Framing the Question

On December 1, 1551, Swiss Reformer Heinrich Bullinger wrote his friend John Calvin, "Now believe me, many are offended by your statements on predestination in your *Institutes* . . . it is my opinion that the Apostles touched on this sublime matter only briefly, and not unless compelled to do so and even in such circumstances they were cautious that the pious were not thereby offended, but understood God to desire well for all people [*omnibus hominibus*] and in Christ to offer [them] salvation."[1] Bullinger highlights a topic that has been questioned in Christian theology since its inception and in Reformed theology since the 1500s, namely God's disposition toward humanity.[2] On the one hand, in light of the Reformed teaching that God's grace can only be received through God's gracious empowering, it appears that God has one disposition (of love) toward those who receive God's grace (the elect) and a different disposition (of just hatred) toward the reprobate who do not receive God's grace. On the other hand, the Bible's teaching on God's love for all people along with the Reformed commitment to preach the gospel to all seem to indicate that God is of one disposition toward all humanity, namely, paraphrasing Bullinger's words, desiring well for all people.

This question has practical implications for the scholar as well as the serious reader and teacher of Scripture, particularly those who find themselves interpreting Scripture in the Reformed tradition. Looking carefully at Scripture and the doctrine of predestination, the question arises, "What is it that I can say about God?" Further, can someone following Calvin's reading of Scripture stand in front of a group of people and proclaim, "God loves you!" without adding an explicit or implicit qualification such as, "if you respond in faith" or "if you are elect"? Can a Christian leader confidently preach and teach God's trustworthy and loving character? Can followers of Jesus trust God's love, justice, goodness, and power for themselves and their communities? As Christians consider complex contemporary social questions, do they have an obligation to regard all people as loved by God? These questions are present today in pulpits, classrooms, and seminary libraries, as well as in personal studies and small group discussions.

Some Reformed divines have determined that God has two separate and opposite dispositions toward human beings based on their identity as elect or reprobate. As a stark example, John Owen explains that God gives temporal good things "to the very people that He hates, whom He has a fixed determination to punish, and whom He has declared to be reserved for eternal punishment and destruction" not because God is trying to reveal his love to them; on the contrary, "as sovereign, [God] is fattening them up for the coming day of slaughter [*diem mactationis*]."[3]

Karl Barth responded to such teaching in the Reformed tradition by asserting that God is of one disposition toward humanity, as revealed in Jesus Christ. Barth says,

> We cannot say that God ordains equally and symmetrically as man's end both good and evil, both life and death, both his own glory and the darkening of this glory. . . . Without overlooking or denying the accompanying shadow we will, in fact, speak of God only as Creator, Reconciler and Redeemer; as the One from whom only a *good* gift [*nur g u t e Gabe*] can *only* be expected. The concept which so hampered the traditional doctrine was that of an equilibrium or balance in which blessedness was ordained and declared on the right hand and perdition on the left. This concept we must oppose with all the emphasis of which we are capable.[4]

Contemporary scholars and pastors continue to explore this question. For example, biblical scholar Matthew Levering, in his book on biblical, theological, and historical perspectives on predestination, describes the enduring dilemma regarding the doctrine of predestination as how to "balance God's superabundant love with his providence and permission of permanent rebellion."[5] In other words, Levering identifies the biblical tension regarding God's disposition toward humanity. In the course of his study, Levering asserts that Calvin's approach to predestination "undermines the innocence of God."[6] This conclusion resonates with Karl Barth's famous assertion that his "decisive objection" to the Calvin's doctrine of predestination is the way that the Reformed doctrine of predestination undercuts trust in the God revealed in Jesus Christ by positing a bare, hidden God (*deus nudus absconditus*) "behind and above" Jesus.[7]

In light of this ongoing dilemma, we set our sights on Calvin's understanding of God's disposition toward humanity. Although Calvin is just one voice in the variegated Reformed tradition, the lucid brevity of his writings, his nonspeculative and pastoral methodology, and his commitment to interpret carefully the whole witness of Scripture for the edification of the church have resulted in his ongoing prominence in contemporary biblical and theological reflection. Understanding his teaching on God's disposition toward humanity would thus be beneficial for contemporary Reformed scholars, pastors, and leaders, along with anyone who has wrestled with Scripture's witness to God's unmerited grace and the mystery of faith. Before providing a preview of what lies ahead, I shall explicate the scope of the project and provide a few important definitions.

SCOPE OF THE PROJECT

An examination of a theologian as prolific and as thoroughly studied as Calvin necessarily requires clarity as to the scope of one's research and exposition. Here I shall explain the key decisions regarding the scope of this project before defining two crucial concepts for our study.

First, in order to let Calvin's voice be heard, this analysis focuses primarily on Calvin's teaching itself. When Calvin clearly refers to another theologian, his reliance is noted, but since Calvin's use of sources is difficult to track,[8] we shall primarily rely upon Calvin's direct teaching. In chapter 7, we shall engage with a few other Reformers to provide perspective on and context for Calvin's account.

Second, as valuable as it would be, this is not an historical chronicle of the development of Calvin's thought but rather an integrated account of his theology via his extant writings. In agreement with recent developments in Calvin scholarship, we shall thus draw from Calvin's teaching across his corpus instead of giving primacy to the *Institutes* at the expense of his exegetical work. For Calvin, the *Institutes* are not a modern systematic theology or a comprehensive account of all of his theological commitments. He told his readers (Christians, particularly ministers in training) that the *Institutes* was a guide for reading Scripture as well as a place for Calvin to take up "doctrinal discussions" (*disputationes*) and "commonplaces" (*locos communes*).[9] Accordingly, we shall engage with Calvin's commentaries, sermons, and occasional writings alongside the 1559 mature Latin version of the *Institutes*.[10]

Third, we shall focus our efforts on primary sources. Within Calvin's broad corpus, we have necessarily selected writings in which Calvin specifically addresses the topics at hand. Besides Calvin's work, significant secondary literature has been consulted and noted throughout the project, and in chapter 6 we provide an overview of relevant secondary literature. However, no claims have been made that all existing secondary literature has been examined. Doing so would have overwhelmed the footnotes and likely distracted from our task of seeking *Calvin's* understanding of God's disposition toward humanity.

Fourth, this is primarily a project of theological retrieval, not historical or constructive theology. Although I shall draw upon Calvin's historical location while noting questions for further consideration and possible contradictions, the heart of the project is a synthetic exposition of Calvin's teaching itself. This includes giving Calvin the benefit of letting his teaching be heard, even when apparent contradictions result. Therefore, most theological and logical critiques are postponed or simply noted in chapters 2–5. After clearly establishing and understanding Calvin's teaching, we will critically examine his approach in chapters 6–8 and there provide some evaluative questions and critiques that arise from Calvin's account. Although I share my opinions in chapters 7 and 8, my desire for this theological retrieval and my subsequent reflections is that they would be primarily a source for scholars, pastors, students, and faithful learners to grapple with the key nodal points regarding predestination and God's disposition toward humanity in their own contexts.

Finally, this is neither an attempt to sanitize nor disparage Calvin's theology. Accordingly I shall attempt throughout to avoid reading Calvin through the lens of an imposed tradition, whether that be a Barthian, a Reformed scholastic, or a different tradition.[11] I do not see Calvin's theology as the ideal theology to which we long to return, but it represents one faithful, brilliant, influential, and fully human pastor's attempt to interpret the whole witness of Scripture for the purpose of equipping pastors, encouraging believers, and building up God's church.

Having established the scope of the project, we now define two fundamental terms for our use, namely *disposition* and *will*. First, we must examine some distinctions in the Reformed understanding of God's "will."

In Calvin's work, we see a distinction between God's hidden will (*voluntas arcana*) and God's revealed will (*voluntas revelata*) that are both included within God's one, simple will.[12] An example of this distinction in Calvin's teaching is his commentary on Matt. 23:37 when Jesus weeps over Jerusalem, thus exhibiting God's revealed will for the salvation of all alongside his secret will to save only the elect.[13]

The Reformed tradition after Calvin continued to hold and develop these distinctions in God's will. The Reformed orthodox distinguish between God's hidden will or good pleasure (*voluntas beneplacitum*) and God's preceptive will (*voluntas signum*).[14] John Frame, drawing upon Bavinck and others, summarizes the Reformed teaching of God's will in terms of God's "decretive will" and God's "preceptive will." God's decretive will, or the will of God's good pleasure (*beneplacitum*), is God's secret or hidden will. This is God's "eternal purpose, by which he ordains everything that comes to pass,"[15] including choosing of some people to pass over and leave in their sin and deserving condemnation. God's preceptive will, or God's "expressed will" or "signified will" (*signum*), refers to states of affairs that God "sees as desirable, but which he chooses not to bring about." This corresponds to Calvin's revealed will. An example is God's desire that not anyone should perish (2 Pet. 3:9, Ezek. 18:23) or God's desire for human repentance (e.g., Is. 30:18, 65:2).[16]

Building upon these historical concepts, in the course of this study we use slightly different terminology for contemporary conceptual clarity. Instead of God's preceptive, signified, or revealed will, we speak of God's disposition toward humanity. By *disposition*, we mean God's attitude, inclination, or orientation toward humanity.

We distinguish this from God's secret or decretive *will*, which is hidden in God's secret counsel and according to which God orders everything that comes to pass in time. In other words, in this study, God's will refers directly to God's purpose or intent that leads to action. God wills what he does.[17]

We make this distinction between God's disposition and God's will in order to remove any terminological confusion. God's will is what he accomplishes in his sovereign rule over everything that comes to pass (a doctrine to which Calvin is committed). God's disposition is his orientation toward something or someone, which may or may not result in decisive action. As we shall see, for Calvin, God can be of one disposition toward all while not willing and acting according to that disposition.

Note that we are not speaking about God's will in regard to his personal guidance (e.g., God's will for my next career decision). In addition, we are not discussing the variegated distinctions within God's one will that were intricately developed in the era of Reformed orthodoxy after Calvin.[18]

With this scope and these definitions in mind, we now provide an overview of the project ahead.

PREVIEW: GOD'S ONE DISPOSITION AND TWO-FOLD WILL TOWARD HUMANITY

Our task is to determine God's disposition toward humanity in Calvin's theology. We shall do so by examining his teaching on the knowledge of God and predestination. We start with the knowledge of God because we must determine our grounds for speaking meaningfully about God and determine how trustworthy that God-talk is. Once the grounds of that knowledge are established, we can discuss the content of what is known about God and what can be confidently said of God. We subsequently examine predestination itself as the doctrine that most explicitly reveals God's disposition and will toward humanity.

In chapter 2, we examine Calvin's teaching on the knowledge of God. We discover there that God can only be known by those with faith according to the ways he has accommodated himself to humanity in creation and providence, in Scripture, and most clearly in Christ. According to Calvin's nonspeculative and pastoral methodology, he teaches that believers can have limited, skeletal knowledge of God's essential attributes and fleshed-out knowledge of God's relative attributes, or "excellencies" (*virtutes*), which describe God's unchanging nature. Therefore, since there is no neutral knowledge of God, any question about God's disposition toward humanity can only be asked in relation to the God who has made himself known to the faithful as loving, righteous, judging (of evil), powerful, wise, good, and holy.[19]

In chapter 3, we discern God's disposition toward humanity in Calvin's explicit teaching on predestination. In short, we find that God's one, secret, and righteous will is accommodated to the elect in a twofold but asymmetrical way: (1) God's revealed electing will that corresponds directly with God's nature and displays God's one disclosed disposition toward humanity; (2) God's veiled, reprobating will that as a bare fact is inscrutably enacted in a manner that only corresponds with God's nature in part.

In chapter 4, we integrate our findings into a clear series of statements that describe Calvin's teaching on God's disposition toward humanity before testing our findings in chapter 5 by examining Calvin's preaching. Through a broad survey of Calvin's extant sermons, we evaluate the correspondence of our findings with Calvin's actual proclamation of Scripture in Geneva. We discover that Calvin's preaching does in fact clearly align with our findings regarding Calvin's understanding of God's one disposition toward humanity and God's one, righteous, decidedly asymmetrical, twofold will.

In chapter 6, we examine recent relevant Calvin scholarship and begin our explicit critical evaluation of Calvin's doctrine by acknowledging a few of the important strengths and weaknesses of Calvin's account.

In chapter 7, we continue the constructive and critical discussion of Calvin's teaching by placing Calvin's doctrine of predestination and God's disposition toward humanity in dialogue with three sixteenth-century Reformers, with Jacobus Arminius, and with Karl Barth. In so doing, we find that Calvin was not unique among sixteenth-century theologians in his exposition of God's disposition toward humanity and that his approach is also not the only tenable Reformed option. A commonality among these faithful theologians and exegetes is the elevation of the person and work of Jesus Christ as the primary foundation for discerning God's disposition toward humanity. At the same time, these variant approaches necessarily assert a mystery somewhere in their doctrinal system. Putting Calvin in context with others illuminates the necessity of making hermeneutical, exegetical, theological, and logical priority decisions that specify the locus of mystery in the doctrine of predestination and God's corresponding disposition. In chapter 8, I further critique a few of Calvin's specific choices and provide my own constructive description of a faithful doctrine of predestination in light of this study.

In the end, we find that for Calvin, God has made known his one disposition toward humanity. The only God who can be known, proclaimed, and trusted is God the Father, the God of creation, election, and redemption who relates to his people according to his fatherly love and revealed electing will. For reasons known only to him, according to his veiled reprobating will, he inexplicably creates some whom he does not rescue from their sinful state of rebellion against him. For Calvin, the asymmetrically twofold, secret will of God expressed in election and reprobation exists in harmony alongside God's one, disclosed, merciful disposition toward humanity. Although Calvin's conclusions evince some contradictions, any account of the doctrine of predestination will inevitably include incomprehensible elements somewhere. Any good account will always place those mysteries only after discerning God's primary disposition toward humanity in the gracious person and work of Jesus Christ, just as Calvin sought to do.

We begin our inquiry by exploring Calvin's teaching on what can be trustworthily known about God.

NOTES

1. *CO* 14:215. Translation from Bruce Gordon, *Calvin* (New Haven, CT: Yale University Press, 2009), 206–7.

2. As Heiko Oberman says, "The history of theology can well be written in terms of a constant effort to reconcile and relate God's love and God's wrath" (*The Harvest of Medieval Theology* [Grand Rapids: Baker Academic, 1983], 186).

3. John Owen, *Biblical Theology,* trans. Stephen P. Westcott (Pittsburgh, PA: Soli Deo Gloria Publications, 1994), 78–79. Latin: John Owen, *The Works of John Owen* (Edinburgh: 1850), 76.

4. *CD* II/2, p. 171; *KD*, p. 187. My translation in part. Emphasis original.

5. Matthew Levering, *Predestination: Biblical and Theological Paths* (Oxford: Oxford University Press, 2011), 197.

6. Levering, *Predestination*, 197. See chapter 7 for a closer analysis of Levering's argument and the tenability of his conclusions regarding Calvin's teaching on predestination.

7. *CD* II/2, p. 110–11; *KD*, p. 119. Cf. G. C. Berkouwer, *Divine Election* (Grand Rapids: Eerdmans, 1960), 12.

8. Cf. A. N. S. Lane, *John Calvin: Student of the Church Fathers* (Edinburgh: T&T Clark, 1999).

9. *Inst.* "Letter to the Reader," pp. 4–5; *CO* 2:1–4. Cf. David Gibson, *Reading the Decree: Exegesis, Election and Christology in Calvin and Barth* (London: T&T Clark, 2009), 155–56. Cf. Richard Muller, *The Unaccommodated Calvin: Studies in the Foundation of a Theological Tradition* (Oxford: Oxford University Press, 2000), 101–17. In short, the *Institutes* and the commentaries have a mutually informing, symbiotic relationship and will be engaged accordingly.

10. The Latin title is *Institutio Christianae Religionis in Libros Quator*. *Institutio* is in the singular and has the inherent meaning of foundation or groundwork, as in a building. Thus, a more appropriate English translation might be "The Foundation of the Christian Religion in Four Books." Although the Latin title is singular, as a result of its four volumes, *Institutes* has become the popular English rendering, which I shall utilize throughout.

11. I sincerely but humbly write this statement with the assumption that I have inevitably not always been aware of my limited interpretive lens through which I am reading Calvin, but this statement expresses my intent. None of us writes (or reads) from an Archimedean point outside of our own cultural context, training, and experience.

12. Richard Muller, *Post-Reformation Reformed Dogmatics: The Rise and Development of Reformed Orthodoxy, Ca. 1520 to Ca. 1725, Vol. 3* (Grand Rapids: Baker Academic, 2003), 438. Cf. *Comm Matt.* 6:10; *CO* 45:198.

13. *Comm Matt.* 22:37; *CO* 45:644. Calvin also points out that God's revealed will makes people responsible for their rejection of the gospel. Cf. Muller, *P.R.R.D., Vol. 3*, 440.

14. Muller, *P.R.R.D., Vol. 3*, 458.

15. John Frame, *The Doctrine of God* (Phillipsburg, NJ: P&R Publishing, 2002), 531.

16. Frame, *The Doctrine of God*, 533. Cf. Richard Muller's distinction of God's "revealed will" of the unlimited sufficiency of Christ's redemptive death and God's "eternal divine will" that limits the efficacy of Christ's death to the elect (*Calvin and the Reformed Tradition: On the Work of Christ and the Order of Salvation* [Grand Rapids: Baker Academic, 2012], 106). Cf. Paul Helm, "Calvin, Indefinite Language, and Definite Atonement," in *From Heaven He Came and Sought Her: Definite Atonement in Historical, Biblical, Theological, and Pastoral Perspective*, ed. David Gibson and Jonathan Gibson (Wheaton, IL: Crossway Books, 2013), 112.

17. Cf. Frame, *The Doctrine of God*, 528.

18. Cf. Muller, *P.R.R.Dr., Vol. 3*, 443–75. Muller asserts that the Reformed orthodox after Calvin do not engage in metaphysical speculation regarding the will of God. However, they "do draw Reformed doctrine into a far more consistent dialogue with the scholastic past and work far more concertedly than any of the Reformers, even Musculus, to adapt the medieval distinctions to Protestant use" (Muller, *P.R.R.D., Vol. 3*, 444).

19. As we shall see, this is not a comprehensive list.

Chapter Two

The Knowledge of God

God's Revealed Nature

> This is the rule of sound and legitimate and profitable knowledge, to be content with the measure of revelation, and willingly to be ignorant of what is deeper than this. We must indeed advance in the acquisition of divine instruction, but we must so keep in the way as to follow the guidance of God.[1]

In our quest to understand Calvin's teaching regarding God's disposition toward humanity, we begin with what Calvin called "the final goal of the blessed life . . . knowledge of God."[2] We seek here to discern, according to Calvin, what we can know about God and how we arrive at that knowledge. In short, who is this God being proclaimed and how is this God known? We shall find that the knowledge of God, though offered to all, is only accessible to those who have faith, which, in turn is inevitably connected to piety. Secondly, we shall discover how the majestic, invisible God provides knowledge of himself to finite human creatures, namely through God's accommodation of himself to human capacity. Finally, it will become clear that the content of the knowledge of God which is accessible to believers is a practical and experienced knowledge of God's nature (or character) alongside a limited, skeletal knowledge of God's essence. In sum, we come to see that for Calvin, reliable, practical knowledge of God's nature and skeletal knowledge of God's essence are available only to those who have faith in Christ as they receive God's accommodation of himself to humanity, primarily through God's works (most notably the person and work of Jesus) as interpreted and revealed in Scripture.

We shall examine the knowledge of God in Calvin's teaching in three parts, answering the questions: Who is able to receive knowledge of God? How does God communicate himself? What is the content of God's self-communication? We shall conclude by discussing a few key implications in regard to our question of God's disposition toward humanity.

WHO CAN KNOW: THE KNOWLEDGE OF GOD OFFERED TO ALL BUT ONLY RECEIVED BY THE FAITHFUL

In this section, we shall explore Calvin's interpretation of Scripture's teaching regarding who is able to access the knowledge of God and how they are able to appropriate that knowledge. First, we shall examine Calvin's assertions regarding universal access to the knowledge of God. Then we shall explore Calvin's explicit doorway to right knowledge of God, namely pious faith in the Mediator.

Universal Access to Knowledge of God: Receptive Capabilities Corrupted by the Fall

Although Calvin entitles the first book of the *Institutes* "Knowledge of God the Creator," it becomes quickly apparent that the knowledge of God that is mediated through God's creation and sustenance of creation is not in and of itself sufficient for creaturely apprehension of God. In *Institutes* 1.3–5, Calvin directly addresses the knowledge of God the Creator that can be obtained without faith and apart from Scripture; "Now I have only wanted to touch upon the fact that this way of seeking God is common both to strangers and those of his household [*exteris et domesticis*]."[3] Besides a few brief subsections,[4] these are the only chapters in the *Institutes* that describe the knowledge of God outside the interpretive lens of Scripture as apprehended by faith.

In pursuing our question of God's disposition toward humanity, we shall examine Calvin's argument in 1.3–5 in order to discern the extent to which Calvin teaches that those without faith can access knowledge of God. We shall find that although God has made himself known to all people directly and also through his works of creation and sustenance of that creation, such knowledge can only be rightly interpreted through Scripture and received by faith via the work of the Spirit.

In 1.3 and 1.4, Calvin discusses the knowledge of God that is native to human existence. In God's first action toward humanity, he created humans to know him. Through the awareness of divinity (*sensus divinitatis*),[5] which God placed in every human being, "men[6] one and all perceive that there is a God."[7] Similarly, all people contain the seed of religion (*semen religionis*),[8] which, "if Adam [and Eve] had remained upright" (*si integer stetisset Adam*), would have led humanity to right knowledge of God from his works in the created order.⁹ Instead, because of the sinful corruption of human nature, the *sensus divinitatis* and *semen religionis* only lead humans to curiosity and empty speculations. Thus, "They do not therefore apprehend [*non apprehendunt*] God as he offers himself, but imagine him as they have fashioned him in their own presumption,"¹⁰ resulting in various forms of idolatry or direct attempts to deny God's existence.¹¹ When life gets difficult, some people halfheartedly seek God in order to appease their fear of God's judgment, yet they still fundamentally trust in themselves instead of God. Thus, the "seed remains . . . that there is some sort of divinity; but this seed is so corrupted that by itself it produces only the worst fruits."¹² In sum, according to Calvin, God has placed a witness to himself in the heart of all people that informs them of God's majesty and partially reveals to them their sinfulness, but because of sin that seed never sprouts to true knowledge of God.

Calvin then turns in 1.5 to God's revelation of himself through his creating and ruling the universe. Affirming the fact that the blessed life (*beata vita*) is situated in the knowledge of God, Calvin offers a second way that God has made knowledge of himself available to all: "Lest anyone, then, be excluded from access to happiness [*felicitatem*], [God] not only sowed in men's minds that seed of religion of which we have spoken but revealed himself and daily discloses himself in the whole workmanship of the universe. As a consequence, men cannot open their eyes without being compelled to see him."¹³ Further, in his comments on Rom. 1:20, Calvin says, "God is in himself invisible; but as his majesty shines forth in his works and in his creatures everywhere, men ought in these to acknowledge [*agnoscere*] him, for they clearly set forth their Maker."¹⁴ Thus God's wisdom is available even to the "most untutored and ignorant persons," and through the magnificence of the heavens and the beauty, symmetry, and articulation of the human body, "there is no one to whom the Lord does not abundantly show his wisdom."¹⁵

Not only has God revealed himself in his works of creating the universe as a "theater of his glory,"¹⁶ he also discloses himself in his providential care for the created order. Calvin says that the cause of God's creating and preserving his creation "is his goodness [*bonitatem*] alone. But this being the sole cause, it ought still to be more than sufficient to draw us to his love, inasmuch as there is no creature, as the prophet declares, upon whom God's mercy has not been poured out."¹⁷ God's revelation of himself in his providential rule is not limited to sustenance of the natural order, but he also reveals his power and wisdom in his administration of human society and providential care for sinners that recalls them to his "fatherly kindness" (*paterna indulgentia*).¹⁸

However, just as in the case of the inner revelation of God through the sense of divinity, God's external revelation of himself to humanity through his creation, though more than sufficient in itself, is unable to find reception in human hearts and minds. Instead of rightly seeking God, all people "became instantly vain in their imaginations, so that they groped in the dark, having in their thoughts a mere shadow of some uncertain deity, and not the knowledge of the true God."[19] Therefore, "the manifestation of God, by which he makes his glory known in his creation, is with regard to the light itself, sufficiently clear [*satis evidentem*]; but that on account of our blindness, it is not found to be sufficient [*non adeo sufficere*]. We are not however so blind that we can plead our ignorance as an excuse for our perverseness."[20] Thus, because of the sinful state of humanity, God's revelation in creation does not in actuality "signify such a manifestation as men's discernment can comprehend; but, rather, shows it not to go farther than to render them inexcusable."[21]

Moving forward from the failure of general revelation to bear fruit, Calvin teaches that sinful humans can only rightly access that knowledge through faith and Scripture by the illuminating work of the Spirit. Calvin summarizes his argument in his *Commentary on Hebrews*, "Men's minds therefore are wholly blind, so that they see not the light of nature which shines forth in created things, until being irradiated by God's Spirit, they begin to understand [*intelligere*] by faith what otherwise they could never grasp [*caperent*]."[22] Similarly, in the *Institutes* as he nears the end of his exploration of the knowledge of God outside of faith, Calvin says, "The invisible divinity is made manifest in [God's creative works], but . . . we have not the eyes to see this unless they be illumined by the inner revelation of God through faith."[23]

Along with faith, we need Scripture to come to right knowledge of God. Calvin points out that although God has "set forth to all without exception" his presence in his creation, "it is needful that another and better help [*adminiculum*] be added to direct us aright to the very Creator of the universe." Thus, just as spectacles (*specilla*) allow an old man with weak eyes to read, "so Scripture, gathering up the otherwise confused knowledge of God in our minds, having dispersed our dullness, clearly [*liquido*] shows us the true God."[24] Scripture, which receives its authority from God by the Spirit,[25] is the only source "of right and sound doctrine" (*rectae sanaeque doctrinae*), and from it "emerges the beginning of true understanding when we reverently embrace what it pleases God there to witness of himself."[26]

For Calvin, Scripture and faith have a symbiotic relationship. Although God's majesty is on display in Scripture for all to see, only believers, "who have been enlightened by the Holy Spirit have eyes to perceive." Calvin proceeds to say that the primary content of what we are to learn from the Scriptures is faith.[27] Therefore, Scripture rightly witnesses to faith in Christ while being accessible only by faith in Christ to those who have been given eyes to see by the Spirit.

In sum, Calvin argues that God has sufficiently put forth knowledge of himself to all people through the *sensus divinitatis* and *semen religionis* in all humans and through his works of creation and providential rule over creation. However, sin has so blinded the eyes of all humanity that God's self-witness only leads to idolatry or the denial of God's existence as humans chase their vain religious speculations. Only through the Spirit's working in the inner revelation of God through faith and by means of the spectacles of Scripture do people come to true knowledge of God. In the *Institutes*, Calvin thus completes his exploration of the knowledge of God outside of faith in 1.5 and proceeds to discuss what can be known from Scripture as seen with eyes of faith, namely God's self-witness to himself through his works as Creator and Redeemer. Therefore, the twofold knowledge of God that Calvin puts forth as a possibility for humans is not a general revelation to all people through creation and a special revelation to the elect through Christ's work of redemption. On the contrary, although God has revealed himself to all humanity, it is only those with faith who are able to receive any revelation of God aright.

With this in mind, we now turn to explore more closely this means of obtaining knowledge of God.

Human Access to the Knowledge of God

As only those with faith are able to apprehend aright the knowledge of God that he offers all people, we shall now briefly examine Calvin's characterization of this faith. Discussing the foundations of human knowledge of God, Calvin says, "Here indeed is pure and real religion [*pura germanaque religio*]: faith so joined with an earnest fear of God that this fear also embraces willing reverence, and carries with it such legitimate worship as is prescribed in the law."[28] Thus Calvin lays out the two key human elements in the right reception of God's revelation of himself, namely faith in Christ and piety. We shall briefly explore them here.

Faith in the Mediator: The Doorway to Knowledge of God

In his exposition of John 1:18 ("No one has ever seen God, but God the One and Only has made him known"), Calvin says, "The knowledge of God is the door [*ianua*] by which we enter into the enjoyment of all blessings [*bonorum*]; and it is by Christ alone that God makes himself known [*patefaciat*], hence too it follows that we ought to seek all things from Christ. This order of doctrine is to be carefully observed."[29] Using *patefacio*[30] as a word picture, Calvin describes God as throwing open the door of the knowledge of himself through Christ's mediation alone. For Calvin, true knowledge of God is only possible through faith in Christ the Mediator.[31]

Calvin's comments on 1 Pet. 1:21 illustrate the two key roles that faith in Christ the Mediator plays in our knowledge of God: Christ provides a concrete object of faith through whom we rise to God,[32] and Christ the Mediator assures us that we sinners can confidently approach the majestic God as his children, instead of cowering before him.[33] In sum, for Calvin, faith in Christ is the only means of approaching God and gaining right knowledge of God.[34]

Having seen that faith in Christ is the entryway to proper knowledge of God, we now turn to explore faith's partner in one's approach to God, namely the fear of God, or piety.

Lived Knowledge: The Necessity of Piety

For Calvin, piety necessarily accompanies faith in the acquisition of right knowledge of God as an embodied manifestation of that knowledge. Calvin says, "We shall not say that, properly speaking, God is known where there is no religion or piety [*pietas*]."[35] He there defines *pietas* as "that reverence joined with love of God which the knowledge of his benefits induces [*conciliat*]."[36] In his 1545 Geneva Catechism, Calvin similarly defines the love for God as "recognizing him as at once our Lord, and Father, and Preserver," which is to be joined with a "reverence for him, a willingness to obey him, trust to be placed in him."[37] Right knowledge of God as apprehended by faith necessarily results in trust in, love for, and obedience toward God subsequently expressed in love for other human "neighbors."

Although it can appear at times that Calvin teaches piety as a prerequisite for right knowledge of God,[38] a close look at the reformer's writings reveals that Calvin is explicating the insoluble connection between right knowledge of God and a worshipful, obedient life in a manner that highlights their correct order, namely that the knowledge of God is received by grace alone and necessarily results in piety.[39]

Calvin's piety is not only individual but has communal ramifications as well, as evidenced in his teaching on the Lord's Supper, in which believers are united with Christ and thus with each other as part of his one body.[40] As they experience the benefits of Christ, they properly express their piety in thanksgiving to God and in love for others.[41] Elsie McKee summarizes Calvin's approach well: "For Calvin . . . the larger pattern of Christian devotion to God can only be lived out fully when worship and justice, liturgy and love for the neighbor, go hand in hand."[42]

Dowey summarizes: "For [Calvin] the religious or existential response is not something that may or may not come in addition to knowledge of God, but is part of its very definition."[43] For Calvin, true knowledge of God is inseparable from obedient reverence toward, trust in, and love for God and thus love for others.

In sum, for Calvin, although God extends the witness of himself to all people, the knowledge of God is accessed only by faith in Christ the Mediator which inevitably results in piety. Seeing who is able to grasp the knowledge of God, we now turn to examine *how* God reveals himself to those human creatures.

HOW WE KNOW: GOD'S ACCOMMODATED COMMUNICATION OF HIMSELF TO HUMANITY

As we continue to seek Calvin's teaching on the knowledge of God as it relates to God's disposition toward humanity, we now consider *how* God communicates the knowledge of himself. A longer quotation from Calvin summarizes his teaching on human apprehension of God:

> For how can the human mind measure off [*definiat*] the measureless essence of God [*immensam Dei essentiam*] according to its own little measure, a mind as yet unable to establish for certain the nature of the sun's body, though men's eyes daily gaze upon it? Indeed, how can the mind by its own leading come to search out God's essence when it cannot even get to its own? Let us then willingly yield to God his knowledge [*sui cognitionem*]. For as Hilary says, he is the one fit witness to himself [*idoneus sibi testis*], and is not known except through himself [*per se*]. But we shall be 'yielding it to him' if we conceive him to be of such a kind as [*talem . . . qualem*] he reveals himself to us, without inquiring about him elsewhere than from his Word.[44]

For Calvin, the knowledge of God is not obtainable through human reason or inquiry. God can only be known because God has made himself known in a manner that humans can grasp. As Calvin says, "In short, God now presents himself to be seen [*conspiciendum*] by us, not such as he is [*non qualis est*], but such as we can comprehend [*qualem modulus noster eum capit*]. Thus is fulfilled what is said by Moses, that we see only as it were his back (Ex. 33:23), for there is too much brightness in his face."[45]

God accomplishes this self-revelation to humans through what Calvin often calls accommodation (*accommodare*).[46] As Kurt Richardson summarizes:

> Calvin's view of revelation is that the knowledge imparted by any means to human beings is always an act of condescension on God's part in which he accommodates his own self-knowledge, or knowledge of creation as he made it and governs it, so that human beings may understand according to the conditions and contingencies of their knowing as human. God is otherwise and on his own terms incomprehensible according to the natural cognitive and speculative means and apertures of the body and mind.[47]

We shall first explain Calvin's logic for the necessity of accommodation, namely God's majesty and human limitations. Then we shall briefly examine the hierarchically structured means God uses to reveal himself to humanity: the created order, Scripture using human language, and most clearly, Jesus Christ.

The Majestic God and the Necessity of Accommodation

Accommodation is necessary because of God's majesty and human limitations. As Calvin says in his commentary on Romans, "God in his greatness can by no means be fully comprehended by us, and . . . there are certain limits within which men ought to confine themselves, inasmuch as God accommodates [*attemperat*] himself to our small capacities what he testifies of himself. Insane then are all they who seek to know of themselves what God is [*quid sit Deus*]."[48] Although we shall elaborate later on the content of the knowledge of God that Calvin teaches, here we briefly examine Calvin's teaching on God's majesty in relation to human limitations in order to understand why accommodation is necessary.

For Calvin, God's majesty is beyond human comprehension. Regarding God's majesty, Calvin commonly recalls 1 Tim. 6:16, "God dwells in unapproachable light, whom no one has ever seen or can see."[49] For Calvin, God is infinite and spiritual (*immensus et spiritualis*) and thus inaccessible to creaturely knowing. As an infinite being, God exceeds the possibility of human senses or imagination. Because God is spiritual, humans are not allowed to imagine anything physical about God. He does not dwell on earth, "and yet as he is incomprehensible he also fills the earth itself."[50] Commenting on Ps. 104:1–2, Calvin says, "If men attempt to reach the heights of God, although they fly above the clouds, they must fail in the midst of their course. Those who search for God in his naked majesty [*in nuda sua maiestate*] are certainly very foolish."[51] In short, human limitations preclude their grasping God's majesty.[52]

These limitations on human access to God's majesty exist both because of Calvin's assumed ontological hierarchy and because of human sinfulness.[53] Highlighting Calvin's assumed hierarchy of being which elevates God above the spiritual angels who are in turn superior to embodied humanity, Huijgen points out according to Calvin's Genesis teaching, even before sin came into the world, God had to accommodate himself to corporeal humanity.[54] Thus, for Calvin, by nature of their corporeal being, humans cannot fully know God in his majesty.

Beyond the ontological barrier, the immense obstruction of human sinfulness also prevents humans from rightly perceiving God. When sinful humans apprehend God's life and light, the death and darkness that is within them is exposed.[55] For example, Calvin chastises Moses for asking too much in his request to see God's glory; even though Moses asked with good intentions, his desire was "for more than is lawful or expedient" because if God granted Moses his desire, "it would be injurious and fatal to Moses."[56] In sum, for Calvin, God's immense glory cannot be comprehended, or even experienced, by limited and sinful human creatures.

However, even though we cannot know God in his glorious majesty, God has graciously chosen to accommodate the light of his glory to match our humble capacity so that we might gradually attain to the knowledge of God for which we were created.[57]

In order to unfold Calvin's teaching on accommodation, we shall draw upon Huijgen's analogy of concentric circles that depict the levels of accommodation and the extent to which they reveal God (see figure 2.1): seeing the universe (outer circle), hearing the Word of God (more inward), touching (my addition) Christ the Mediator (inner circle). At the core is God who dwells in unapproachable light. Humans commune with God by the Spirit through Christ the Mediator as God's ultimate accommodation of himself.[58] When considering this model of accommodation, it is important to recognize the interdependence of the circles as they all witness to God at the center. We shall now briefly explore these three levels of accommodation to develop Calvin's understanding of how God has made himself known to humanity.

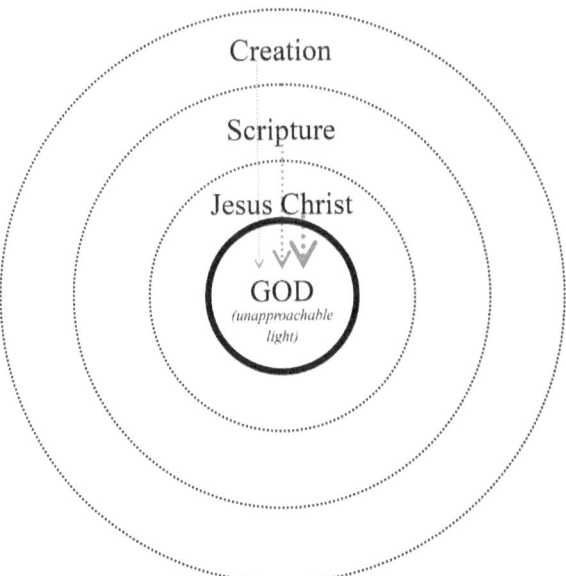

Figure 2.1. God Made Known: Calvin's Levels of Accommodation

Accommodation in and through Creation

As we have already seen, for Calvin, God has put forward in his works in the universe a clear witness to himself that can only be accessed by faith in Christ and through the spectacles of Scripture. Therefore, although God's accommodation of himself in the creation and sustenance of the universe is the most broadly accessible revelation of God to humans, it is inseparably linked to the inner circles of Scripture and Christ. In short, the universe is a theater of God's glory which reveals God accurately when perceived by faith via Scripture and Christ, by the Spirit.[59] As Calvin says in his comments on Psalm 104, God's essence is inaccessible, "but as he irradiates the whole world by his splendor, this is the garment in which He, who is hidden [*absconditus*] in himself, appears [*apparet*] in a manner visible [*visibilis*] to us." He goes on to say that to enjoy the sight of God, "we must cast our eyes upon the very beautiful fabric of the world in which he wishes to be seen by us."[60] We shall explore more fully below *what* God communicates through his accommodation of himself through his works in the universe.

Accommodation in and through Scripture Using Human Language

Scripture is the next inner circle in Huijgen's accommodation diagram through which God makes himself known to limited humans. Calvin explains, in Scripture "also emerges the beginning of true understanding when we reverently embrace what it pleases God there to witness of himself."[61] Again referring to God's unapproachable light, Calvin says, "The splendor of the divine countenance [*vultus*] . . . is for us like an inexplicable labyrinth unless we are conducted into it by the thread of the Word [*verbi linea*]."[62] In Scripture, God makes himself known.

Since Calvin holds that all Scripture is directly inspired by God and self-authenticating,[63] an exegete may not divide Scripture as if some elements witness to God and others do not. Thus Huijgen describes, "We have to note that Calvin does not provide a theory of religious language, and the possibility of God-talk. He pictures the reverse movement: God employs human language to reveal himself." Thus biblical language is not an account of experiences of God communicated in human language but actually "the way God presents Himself to human [*sic*] who otherwise cannot grasp Him."[64]

Thus, in God's self-presentation in Scripture, God employs human language and concepts. Randall Zachman elucidates Calvin's understanding of the role of human language in God's accommodation in Scripture through a study of Calvin's use of analogy and anagoge: "The method of divine accommodation, and hence of divine self-revelation, is understood by Calvin in terms of the analogy and anagoge between the sign and the reality signified, and . . . Calvin is therefore best understood when he is seen as an analogical and anagogical theologian." Zachman then defines the terms, saying, "Analogy stresses the similarity amid difference between the sign and the reality signified, whereas anagoge stresses the elevation from the temporal sign to the spiritual reality it represents."[65] God has given humanity visible images that are meant to be analogies by which we come to know God, which happens when we anagogically connect the earthly image to the eternal reality it depicts.

An example of Calvin's teaching about analogy and anagoge comes from his comments on Jeremiah 23, where, speaking about Christ's role as a wise and prudent king, he says, "And we know that Christ is often compared to earthly kings, or set forth to us under the image of an earthly king, in which we may see him; for God accommodates [*attemperat*] himself to our ignorance." Thus, Calvin offers an analogy between earthly kings, which we know, and Christ as the heavenly king. Calvin goes on to point out that even though the analogy in human language and concepts is inadequate, "the comparison ought not to be deemed improper; for God speaks to us according to the measure of our capacities, and could not at once in a few words fully express what [sort] Christ is [*qualis esset Christus*]." After acknowledging the use of analogy, Calvin points out the anagoge, inviting elevation from the human analogy to the spiritual reality, "But we must bear in mind that from earthly kings we must ascend [*tenenda est anagoge*] to Christ; for though it is compared to them, yet there is no equality; after having contemplated in the type what our minds can comprehend, we ought to ascend farther and much higher."[66] Calvin recognizes and affirms the use of human language and concepts in Scripture as God has accommodated himself there and leads us upward from the human concepts to the spiritual realities to which they point.

Utilizing Alan Torrance's discussion of theological language in light of Wittgenstein's work, it becomes clear that Calvin's doctrine of accommodation could be seen to align with some of the major developments in language theory in the twentieth century. Torrance highlights the way that modern language theory since Wittgenstein has posited that the meaning of a word arises from its use. Therefore, to understand a word correctly, one must approach words a posteriori with the flexibility necessary to understand words within their given semantic reference.[67] Calvin's teaching on accommodation hints at a similar understanding of theological language. Calvin recognizes the human familiarity with a term or concept and then invites the reader to ascend from what they know of the term to the spiritual meaning. In other words, the term must be commandeered by the Spirit. Thus the language is neither univocal nor equivocal but dynamically interpreted through the Spirit based upon its Scriptural use.[68]

Further, drawing upon Eberhard Jüngel's work on the inherent meaning in metaphor, Torrance asserts that scriptural metaphors "should not be seen as serving to obscure the specific Reality of God (and, therefore, as theologically peripheral), nor as unwarrantable forms of anthropomorphic projection (similes), but as essentially creative means through which the *dissimilar* God comes to us in an *assimilating* or 'theopoietic' event, articulating his own reality for our understanding (expanding and deepening our conceptual categories to this end)."[69] Similarly, when Calvin describes scriptural metaphors as accommodation, he implies that God is finding a way to make known his reality to our limited human capacities. In this way, humanity is thus invited to an engagement with God that transcends previously held definitions of terms.

God utilizes a variety of metaphors to accommodate himself to human understanding in Scripture. For example, Scripture describes God with physical body parts or human emotions. About such anthropomorphic statements, Calvin famously states,

> For who even of slight intelligence does not understand that, as nurses commonly do with infants, God is wont in a measure to 'lisp' [*balbutire*] in speaking to us? Thus such forms of speaking do not so much express clearly what God is like [*exprimunt qualis sit*] as to accommodate [*accommodant*] the knowledge of him to our slight capacity.[70]

This accommodation is also displayed when Scripture describes God as angry or repenting, which, according to Calvin's commitment that God is beyond all disturbance of the mind,[71] do not refer to the same human phenomena occurring in God but describe our experience of God.[72] Calvin points out various other examples of God's accommodation in Scripture, including the way God communicates about himself differently in the Old Testament as compared with the New Testament,[73] Jesus' discussion of the manna as spiritual food,[74] and the gospel which acts as the bridge between God's accommodation of himself in Scripture and his accommodation in Christ, who is the lone *scopus* (goal) of Scripture.[75] Calvin says that the beauty of the gospel is that, as opposed to the law which only blinded, in the gospel, "Christ's glorious face is clearly beheld . . . the majesty of the Gospel is not terrific, but amiable—is not hid, but is manifested familiarly to all [*familiariter omnibus patefiat*]."[76] Thus, God's accommodation of himself to humanity in Scripture is most clearly accomplished in Christ, God's "lively image"[77] and the innermost ring around God's unapproachable light in the diagram. It is to God's accommodation of himself in Christ to which we now turn.

Accommodation in and through Christ

God's ultimate act of accommodation is the incarnation of Jesus Christ, through whom God reveals as much of his nature as believers can appropriate, providing reliable and saving knowledge of God in a manner fit for embodied humans.

Calvin teaches that in Christ, God reliably makes himself known. As Calvin speaks about this revelation in Christ throughout his corpus, I shall highlight just a few instances here. Commenting upon Col. 1:15, Calvin points out that "Christ is the image of God because He makes God in a manner visible to us."[78] Christ does not reveal God's essence to us, but Christ's *homoousion* with the Father guarantees the reliability of Christ's revelation of God, "for Christ would not truly represent God if He were not the essential Word of God;" Calvin proceeds, "The sum is, that God in Himself, that is, in His naked majesty [*in nuda sua maiestate*], is invisible; and that not only to the physical eyes, but also to human understanding; and that He is revealed [*revelari*] to us in Christ alone, where we may behold Him as in a mirror [*in speculo*]."[79] Calvin even proceeds to say, regarding Col. 2:9, that in contrast with God's previous, partial accommodation of himself through "figures or power and grace," in Christ, God "communicates himself to us wholly [*totum*] . . . and has appeared [*apparuit*] to us essentially [*essentialiter*]."[80] At this point, it is important to remember that Calvin repeatedly teaches that humans cannot know God's unknowable essence or immanent life,[81] even in Christ.[82] Therefore, Calvin is here making the point that what we see in Christ is wholly consistent with what we see in God; there is no variance from God's revelation in Christ, nor is there any ground for seeking knowledge of God outside of what he offers us in Christ, including seeking knowledge of God's unknowable essence.[83] In sum, for Calvin, God is "no other but he who is made known in Christ [*qui in Christo cogniscitur*]."[84]

For Calvin, not only is Christ the best witness of God that we have, he is the only way God is known.[85] "As God dwells in inaccessible light, He cannot be known [*cognosci*] but in Christ, who is his lively image [*viva sua imagine*]."[86] Similarly Calvin notes regarding Matt. 11:27, "the Father, who dwells in inaccessible light, and is in himself incomprehensible, is revealed to us by the Son, because he is the lively image of Him, so that it is in vain to seek for Him elsewhere."[87] In Christ, the problem of God's inaccessible majesty is resolved: "For the naked majesty of God would, by its immense brightness, ever dazzle our eyes; it is therefore necessary for us to look on Christ. This is to come to the light, which is justly said to be otherwise inaccessible."[88]

Calvin summarizes his view of God's reliable, salvific accommodation of himself in Christ when he says, "Apart from Christ the saving knowledge of God does not stand. . . . In this sense Irenaeus writes that the Father, himself infinite, becomes finite in the Son, for he has accommodated himself to our little measure lest our minds be overwhelmed by the immensity of his glory."[89] Calvin goes on to say that the saving knowledge of God as merciful Father is only made possible through Christ. Therefore, God's accommodation to us in Christ as Mediator between God and humanity allowed believers to "truly taste God's mercy, and thus be persuaded that he was their Father."[90] In Christ, God has made himself known as a loving Father so that believers might trust in him for salvation.

Not only does Christ provide a reliable revelation of God to those who believe, he is himself the anagoge, or means of ascent to knowledge of God, through his work as Mediator. Zachman summarizes, "Christ is therefore the image of the invisible God, in whom God becomes somewhat visible to us, so that we might come to know the unknown God by analogy with what we know, and so that we might ascend to God by means of the anagoge between Christ and God."[91] Commenting on Thomas's delayed acknowledgment of Jesus as the resurrected Lord, Calvin says, "That our faith may arrive at the eternal Divinity of Christ, we must begin with that knowledge which is nearer and more easily acquired. Thus it has been justly said by some, that by Christ Man we are conducted to Christ God."[92] In Christ, God accomplishes his ultimate accommodating act in the Incarnate Son, making himself known to limited humanity, providing reliable and salvific knowledge of himself.[93]

In summary, although humans cannot come to know the God who dwells in unapproachable light by their own means, God has made himself known at the level of human comprehension through his works in creation and providence, through Scripture, and most of all through the incarnate Christ.[94] As we have seen, the three levels of Huijgen's accommodation diagram are interdependent and founded upon Christ. Only through faith in Christ the Mediator can God be known at all, but Scripture, as perceived by faith and illuminated by the Spirit, is the primary means by which we come to know God's nature as it is revealed and confirmed in Christ. Further, God's works in the universe can only be rightly interpreted with the eyes of faith and the spectacles of Scripture; with those in place, God's providential work in the created order further confirms and illuminates God's accommodation of himself in Scripture and in Christ. For Calvin, God's accommodation provides grounds for human language about God that is securely rooted in God himself as both from God and reliably witnessing to God.

Having seen how we come to knowledge of God and speak rightly about him, we now turn to explore the content of this revealed knowledge of God. *What* is it that we can say about God?

THE CONTENT OF OUR KNOWLEDGE: PRACTICAL KNOWLEDGE OF GOD'S NATURE THROUGH HIS WORKS

The content of our knowledge of God is commonly described via God's attributes or perfections. Some interpreters of Calvin have held that his distinct antispeculative aversion to metaphysical discussions of the divine attributes stands in contrast with much of the medieval and Reformed scholastic tradition.[95] Others, like Calvin scholars Todd Billings and Richard Muller, have sought to correct this claim, asserting catholicity and continuity in Calvin's doctrine of God.[96] However, in the midst of their helpful corrective, Billings and Muller have overstated their case by focusing on material continuity with the classical tradition, and in so doing, obscuring Calvin's nonspeculative, pastoral methodology in his doctrine of God.[97]

In this section, we shall examine Calvin's teaching on the content of the knowledge of God, particularly recognizing the distinction in Calvin's teaching between knowledge of the absolute (essential) attributes of God and knowledge of the relative (personal) attributes of God. We shall find that believers have access to limited knowledge of God's essence and ample practical knowledge of God's nature (or character) as described by God's excellencies (*virtutes*) and made known through God's works. We shall address each of these elements in turn.

Knowledge of God's Essence: A Skeleton

First, Calvin teaches that humans cannot obtain comprehensive knowledge of God's essence, nor should they speculate about that essence. However, God has accommodated himself in Scripture to provide limited, "skeletal" knowledge of God's essential attributes.[98]

No Comprehensive Knowledge of or Speculation about God's Essence

Calvin forwards a partially negative, or apophatic, approach to the absolute attributes of God, asserting that humans cannot comprehend, nor should they speculate concerning, God's incomprehensible essence.[99] Calvin says, "We know that the most perfect way of seeking God, and the most suitable order is not for us to attempt with bold curiosity [*audaci curiositate*] to penetrate to the investigation of his essence, which we ought more to adore than meticulously to search out."[100] Again he asserts that God's essence (*essentia*) "is incomprehensible [*incomprehensibilis*]; hence, his divineness [*numen*] far escapes all human perception."[101] Even in Christ, through whom we receive the most complete revelation of God, God's essence is not revealed. Commenting on Jesus' words in John 14:10, "I am in the Father and the Father is in me,"

Calvin says, "I do not refer these words to Christ's divine essence [*divinam . . . essentiam*], but to the mode of revelation. For Christ, so far as His secret divinity [*arcanam . . . deitatem*] is concerned, is no better known to us than is the Father."[102] Only in the eschaton, when we are clothed in "heavenly and blessed immortality," shall we have direct access to God; "The majesty of God, now hid, will then only be itself seen, when the veil of this mortal and corruptible nature shall be removed."[103] Even then, "our vision shall not grasp [*comprehendat*] the whole of God [*totem Deum*]."[104]

While generally accepting the broadly orthodox essential attributes of God (e.g., God's immutability, omniscience, aseity, simplicity, etc.), Calvin also contends that since humans cannot access knowledge of God's essence, they should refrain from any type of speculation about God or God's being beyond what God has provided through his accommodation in Scripture and in Christ.[105] Calvin says, "So, humans of themselves cannot approach God, but it is necessary that He approaches us, and that we conceive Him as He offers Himself in His word [*parole*], and be content with what is written in it [*contenu*]."[106] Calvin defines speculation as ungrateful[107] and impious inquiry[108] that pompously ignores God's gracious self-witness in Scripture and in his works[109] and which results in cold, worthless knowledge[110] "flitting around in the brain."[111] He thus says regarding Ezekiel's throne room vision, "Nothing is more useful in such matters than wisdom tempered with sobriety and discretion"; we must not "do as scholastic theologians [*scholastici theologi*] do—philosophize with subtlety concerning God's essence, and know no moderation in their dispute!"[112]

From a more positive perspective, as Huijgen points out, knowledge of God for Calvin is not meant to be speculative because it must be personal, revealing to us knowledge of God and ourselves (*Dei cognitione et nostri*).[113] Huijgen says, "The correlation of the knowledge of God, and the knowledge of ourselves, focuses theology, and reduces its task in comparison to scholastic forms of theology. For true theology is useful, and edifying, because she stays within the bounds of the knowledge of God and of ourselves."[114] We shall further address this personal perspective below, but here we simply acknowledge that Calvin considers speculation regarding God's essence as outside of the realm of proper theological inquiry.[115]

Having observed Calvin's teaching regarding God's incomprehensible essence and Calvin's condemnation of speculation, it would be easy to conclude that Calvin is a nonspeculative theologian who is disinterested in many of the classical attributes of God. However, even though Calvin considers God's essence to be inaccessible to human inquiry, Calvin still finds warrant in Scripture for limited knowledge of God's essence, to which we now turn.

Limited Knowledge of God's Essential Attributes

Calvin finds in Scripture the grounds for limited, skeletal knowledge of God's essence that he directly links to occasional and pastoral ends. By "skeletal," I mean knowledge of God that provides a basic framework for talking about God in himself without claiming comprehensive knowledge of God's essence. In short, it is knowledge *that* God is (e.g., spiritual), not knowledge of *what* God is (e.g., what makes up God's spiritual being metaphysically). We shall first discuss what Calvin does teach concerning God's essence before highlighting Calvin's unique approach to these essential attributes of God.

In accordance with the Christian tradition of his day, Calvin affirms all of the classical attributes of God and teaches that, among other things, God is infinite, spiritual, simple, eternal, *a se*, immutable, and omnipresent.[116] None of these attributes of God provides constructive knowledge of what God's essence actually is or how it is that God can be infinite, spiritual, and simple. For example, in his discussion of the Trinity in the *Institutes*, Calvin points out that God is infinite, spiritual, and simple, providing skeletal descriptions that set boundaries regarding our understanding of God as incomprehensible, immaterial, and noncomposite. Calvin does not provide a material description of God's essence; a philosophical explanation of how it is that God can be infinite, spiritual, and simple; or a discussion of the logical ordering of the perfections. Notably, instead of being prompted by metaphysical speculation on the Trinity, the occasion here is Calvin's refutation of false teaching, which is typical of Calvin's teaching regarding the absolute attributes.[117]

It is also worth noting how infrequently and little Calvin teaches about the essential attributes in the *Institutes*. For example, he provides no extensive lists of the essential attributes.[118] Although such a list may be amalgamated through careful searching,[119] each instance is typically driven by a dispute, false teaching, or doctrinal need. Formally, Calvin does not set aside a locus or even a subsection in the *Institutes* to discuss the essential attributes, even in his two books that are entitled "The Knowledge of God." This contrasts with the initial locus "About God" (*de Deo*) in Melanchthon's 1535 and 1543 *Loci Communes*. According to Muller, Melanchthon's *Loci* (specifically the 1535 edition) was an important influence on Calvin's organization of the *Institutes*.[120] Instead of following Melanchthon here, Calvin kept his particular order without a specific locus on God's essence, further confirming his theological and pedagogical methodology regarding the essential attributes.

Regarding God's essential attributes elsewhere in his commentaries, Calvin similarly teaches a skeletal knowledge of God's being and links the teaching about God's essence to occasional and pastoral needs.[121] For example, in his commentary on Exod. 3:14, when God reveals his name to Moses, Calvin points out God's aseity (that God is not dependent upon anyone for existence and is the source of all that exists) and omnipotence (that God is not under the power of any) and immediately shows the pastoral import of the passage, namely to embolden Moses in his task of leading the Israelites out of Egypt.[122] In a passage from Numbers 23, when Balaam asks Balak if he would make God a liar, Calvin affirms God's immutability but does so without engaging in any metaphysical speculation about how or why God cannot change. Instead, for Calvin, God's immutability reminds us that God's word is true and unchangeable, worthy of our unhesitating trust.[123] Similar examples occur in both the *Institutes* and the commentaries.[124]

Thus when Muller claims that if Calvin had compiled the *Institutes* out of his commentaries, "we can easily imagine a rather vast discussion of divine attributes,"[125] we must seriously qualify that statement. As a Biblical and exegetical theologian, Calvin carefully engaged each text, including those that speak of God's being. However, even though a list of attributes could be built by searching through all the commentaries and lectures, they do not include vast discussions of God's attributes, nor do they incorporate extensive speculation regarding God's absolute perfections.

Therefore, it is clear that Calvin affirms the classical attributes, in material agreement with the medieval, sixteenth-century Reformed, and Reformed scholastic traditions. However, Calvin's methodology regarding the divine attributes is distinct as he provides nonspeculative, skeletal knowledge of God's essence directly linked to doctrinal and pastoral needs of the church.

We now turn to explore the primary constructive, material content of Calvin's teaching on what humans *can* know of God.

What Believers Can Know: Practical Knowledge of God's Nature through God's Works

Referring to God's self-revealing words to Moses as he passed by him in Exod. 34:6–7, Calvin points out that after God's eternity and self-existence are announced simply in the Divine Name (יהוה), "thereupon his excellencies [*virtutes*] are mentioned, by which he is shown to us not what he is in himself [*non quis sit apud se*], but what he is like toward us [*qualis erga nos*]: so that this recognition of him consists more in living experience than in empty and high-flown speculation [*speculatione*]."[126] This passage captures the central thrust of Calvin's doctrine of God. As Cornelis van der Kooi says, "Calvin's interest lies more with God's acts than with God's essence."[127]

Alongside the skeletal knowledge of God's essence (here, God's eternity and self-existence), Calvin teaches that believers can materially know God's nature, or what sort God is (*qualis sit*), as described by his excellencies (*virtutes*) that are revealed through his works as interpreted and disclosed in

Scripture.[128] The result is practical, personal knowledge of God that leads to a pious life of trust.

In short, Calvin teaches extensively about the profitable understanding of God's nature and excellencies depicted in Scripture, to which we now turn.

Qualis Sit (God's Nature) — What Sort God Is

Calvin's primary, positive teaching about God consists in his explication of God's unchanging nature and character, or what sort God is. In the *Institutes*, Calvin opposes those who ask the question, "What is God? [*quid sit Deus?*]" by responding, "It is more important for us to know of what sort he is [*qualis sit*] and what is consistent with his nature [*eius naturae*]."[129] In a similar statement in his teaching about faith, Calvin says, "For it is not so much our concern to know who God is in himself [*quis in se sit*], as what he wills to be toward us [*qualis esse nobis velit*]."[130] In these examples, as well as in his words regarding Exod. 34:6–7 above, Calvin distinguishes between what/who God is himself (*quid/quis sit*) and God's nature or character, what sort God is (*qualis sit*).[131]

Calvin's extended comments in 1.10.2 most clearly display this usage. There Calvin points out God's nature in his, "kindness, goodness, mercy, justice, judgment and truth." He proceeds to use *qualis* again, saying, "In Jeremiah, where God declares in what character [*qualis*] he wants us to know him [*agnosci*]," God highlights his mercy, judgment, and justice, the three of which Calvin says imply God's truth, power, holiness, and goodness.[132] In this passage, Calvin correlates God's character or nature (*qualis*) with God's powers or excellencies (*virtutes*) which are revealed through God's concrete actions.[133] Calvin's comments on John 17:4 show how God's nature relates to the incarnation of Christ. Calvin says, "God had been made known to the world both by the doctrine of Christ, and by his miracles; and the glory of God is, when we know what sort he is [*qualis sit*]."[134] In God's works, including the person and works of Christ, he concretely reveals *qualis sit*, his nature or character, as far as creatures can comprehend.

For Calvin, God's revealed nature is unchanging because God is unchanging.[135] As Calvin says in his comments on Ps. 77:11–12, "Because God's heart [*animum*] and nature [*ingenium*] change not [*non mutat*], he cannot but show himself at length merciful to his own."[136] Similarly, in his comments on Num. 23:18, Calvin highlights the difference between human nature (or character) and God's nature, asserting that God's word can be trusted because God himself is true and unchanging. He says, "We in our consideration of His nature [*natura*], should remember that He is liable to no changes [*conversionibus*], since He is far above all heavens."[137] Similarly, regarding James 1:16–18, Calvin links God's unchanging goodness with his unchanging nature.[138] Thus, Huijgen identifies God's nature as a roughly accommodated version of God's essence, saying "God's nature is 'proper' to God, as His essence is," and therefore believers should not think that God "could act contrary to his merciful character—even if that seems to be the case."[139]

Although God makes his nature known, humans cannot have comprehensive knowledge of that nature. Calling upon his doctrine of accommodation, Calvin thus says regarding 1 John 3:2, again referring to Exod. 33–34, that "God now presents himself to be seen [*conspiciendum*] by us, not such as he is [*non qualis est*], but such as we can comprehend [*qualem modulus noster eum capit*]."[140] Therefore God accommodates his nature only to the extent that limited humans can apprehend it. God's revealed nature is consistent and objectively true of God but only partially known by human creatures.

We now turn to examine the content of Calvin's teaching regarding God's nature, namely God's excellencies revealed through his works.

The Excellencies: Calvin's Attributes of God

Calvin famously says that we are to concern ourselves with who God is toward us (*erga nos*) instead of who God is in himself (*apud se*).[141] Warfield summarizes Calvin's approach well, "[Calvin] is refusing all *a priori* methods of determining the nature of God and requiring of us to form our knowledge of Him *a posteriori* from the revelation He gives us of Himself in His activities."[142] In his comments about the knowledge of God's nature "toward us," Calvin is describing the *only way* that fallen humans come to know God, namely through faith as God accommodates himself to humanity in his concrete works in the world. Therefore, in his constructive teaching about God, instead of listing "perfections" or "attributes"[143] of God, Calvin identifies the "excellencies"[144] (*virtutes*) of God as they are expressed through God's specific actions.[145]

Calvin's 1538 Catechism outlines his teaching on what those with faith can know of God from his works, highlighting six characteristics of God recognized through of his works: immortality (beginning of all), power (creator and sustainer of all), wisdom (governor of all), goodness (cause of all that exists), righteousness (defending the godly and condemning the ungodly), and mercy (gently dealing with our sin).[146] Thus, for Calvin, God's nature is concretely made known to us in his works and expressed via his excellencies.

Calvin describes his understanding of the relationship of God's works to his excellencies, and the purpose of both, in *Institutes* 1.5.10. There Calvin says that God's works, individually and especially as a whole, depict to us God's excellencies "not different from a painting [*non secus atque in tabulis*]." This painting is on display for all humanity (*universum hominum genus*) to see and thus be drawn into true happiness (*felicitatem*). As God's works reveal God's excellencies, humans are responsible to ponder these excellencies and contemplate how God reveals his "life, wisdom, and power" and thus exercises toward us (*erga nos*) "his righteousness, goodness and mercy."[147] Therefore, through God's works in creation, providence, and redemption, God displays his excellencies for all to see, so that through them all people might come to recognize him.[148] In short, "God is known [*cogniscitur*] by means of his excellencies [*virtutibus*], and his works [*opera*] are evidences of his eternal divinity [*divinitatis*]."[149] As Parker says, Calvin's *virtutes* are the expression of God's Godhood (God's glory) in action.[150]

One way Calvin organizes his discussion of God's excellencies is the division in the *Institutes* between what God reveals about himself from the vantage point of faith and through the lens of Scripture in his works as Creator (Book 1) vis-à-vis what he reveals in his works as Redeemer (Book 2). Here we follow that same structure, while drawing from across his corpus to get a glimpse of what we learn of God from his works as Creator and Redeemer.

Excellencies Revealed through God's Creative Works

As Creator and Ruler over creation, God displays his excellencies such as glory, kindness, goodness, mercy (love), righteousness (justice), judgment, truth, holiness, power, and wisdom in the created order, the "most glorious theatre" (*splendidissimo theatro*)[151] of his works.[152] God manifests his wisdom in forming all that exists in its intricacy and grandeur, his power in sustaining all that he has made, his loving generosity in creating humanity in his image to live the happy life in communion with him, and his goodness, mercy, and love as he bears with sinful, rebellious humanity while sustaining the whole human race. God is also the active governor and preserver of the whole created order, driving the celestial frame, sustaining, nourishing, caring for everything in creation as an expression of his special care which reveals "his fatherly favor [*paternus eius favor*]."[153] His earthly rule also shows forth his righteousness and judgment in his preservation of his church and condemnation of evil.[154] Drawing upon his passion for astronomy, Calvin forces himself to cut short his commentary on the majesty of God on display in the heavens, saying, "For there are as many miracles of divine power, as many tokens of goodness, and as many proofs of wisdom, as there are kinds of things in the universe."[155]

Before examining the ways that God confirms and reveals his excellencies through his works as Redeemer, it is worth noting some translation problems that can cause confusion regarding God's perfections. Although Calvin consistently employs *virtutes*, English translators often take liberty to use the word "attributes" or "perfections" instead of "powers" or "excellencies."

For example, in the Jeremiah commentary, the translator substitutes "power and perfections" for the singular *virtute*.[156] The most glaring example of a misleading translation is in Calvin's comments upon Rom. 1:20 when he says that humans can have knowledge of God's eternal power and divinity, and God's divinity has become known to us, "which cannot exist except accompanied with all attributes of God [*singulis Dei virtutibus*], since they are all included under that idea."[157] Muller uses this verse to support his claim that Calvin clearly sees the attributes of God as "indivisibly and irreducibly belonging to the divine essence" as part of Muller's broader argument that Calvin stands in general continuity with the later Reformed tradition in his teaching of God's attributes.[158] However, one verse later in the Romans commentary, Calvin continues his argument regarding what is included in God's divinity: "No idea can be formed of God without including his eternity, power, wisdom, goodness, truth, righteousness, and mercy." Calvin proceeds to demonstrate how each of these excellencies can be observed from God's works in the world, such as the way God's wisdom is seen in how "he has arranged things in such an exquisite order." Calvin concludes, "Since men have not recognized these attributes [*virtutes*] in God, but have dreamt of him as though he were an empty phantom, they are justly said to have impiously robbed him of his own glory."[159] From Calvin's use of *virtutes* here, it is clear that he is primarily referring to God's relative, or communicable, attributes, not God's essential attributes.[160] Contrary to what the translation (and Muller's comments) suggests, Calvin is not primarily speaking about the classification of or ordering of God's essential attributes. Instead, he is addressing the trustworthy, positive knowledge we can have of the one true God, namely his nature as described by his excellencies and revealed through his works.

As seen through the lens of Scripture by faith, in his works as Creator, Sustainer, and Ruler of the universe in general and humankind in particular, God reveals himself to be powerful, wise, good, merciful, just, glorious, and merciful. However, Calvin does not teach that one can fully understand and experience God's fatherly love, a central concept for Calvin's doctrine of God, outside of God's work as Redeemer.[161]

Excellencies Revealed through God's Redemptive Works

God's work in redemption, culminated in the person and actions of Jesus Christ the Redeemer, confirm, elucidate, and expand upon the excellencies exemplified through God's works as Creator and Ruler.[162] We have already shown in detail the ways that Calvin affirms God's accommodation of himself to humanity in the person of Christ, thus revealing his powers as displayed in his comments on Col. 1:15, "in Christ [God] shows us His righteousness [*iustitiam*], goodness, wisdom, power [*virtutem*], in short, His entire self [*se denique totum*].[163] We shall see in our exposition of God's work of election in chapter 3 that Calvin also sees God's paternal love for the elect displayed through God's gracious work in election to salvation.[164]

God's excellencies are also broadly and clearly made known in the grand narrative of redemption that runs from the fall in the Garden of Eden to the work of Jesus and on to the redemption of God's people. Although much more could be said, here we highlight God's excellencies revealed in God's gracious giving of the law, in God's wrath, and in God's gracious, multifaceted reconciling work through Jesus' life, death, resurrection, and ascension.

In providing Israel with the law, God reveals his righteousness, faithfulness, goodness, and mercy. The law perfectly reveals God's righteousness[165] and invites humans to live the happy life in God's ways.[166] The law also reveals God's faithfulness, goodness, and mercy by setting before his rebellious people the blessings and curses that are intended to lead people to repentance and obedience.[167] Finally, the law also reveals God's judgment and goodness in the fact that the law, though intended to bring life, results in condemnation because of God's inherent opposition to evil and to those who persevere in evil.

In the incarnation, life, death, resurrection, ascension, and ongoing intercession of Jesus, God even more dramatically illuminates his excellencies.[168] Calvin is clear that although speaking of the cross as shorthand is permissible, the complete and unified work of Christ was necessary and sufficient for the work of redemption of humanity according to God's plan. The Triune God accomplished this work of redemption in the one person of Christ, divine and human, in his offices of prophet, priest, and king. Here we note the way Calvin concludes his extended discussion in *Institutes* 2.16 of Christ's redemptive work:

> Our whole salvation and all its parts are comprehended [*comprehensas*] in Christ. We should therefore take care not to derive the least portion of it from anywhere else. If we seek salvation, we are taught by the very name of Jesus that it is 'of him' (1 Cor. 1:30). If we seek any other gifts of the Spirit, they will be found in his anointing. If we seek strength, it lies in his dominion; if purity, in his conception; if gentleness, it appears in his birth. For by his birth he was made like us in all respects (Heb. 2:17) that he might learn to feel our pain. If we seek redemption, it lies in his passion; if acquittal, in his condemnation; if remission of the curse, in his cross (Gal. 3:13); if satisfaction, in his sacrifice; if purification, in his blood; if reconciliation, in his descent into hell; if mortification of the flesh, in his tomb; if newness of life, in his resurrection; if immortality, in the same; if inheritance of the Heavenly Kingdom, in his entrance into heaven;

if protection, if security, if abundant supply of all blessings, in his Kingdom; if untroubled expectation of judgment, in the power given him to judge. In short, since rich store of every kind of good [*omne genus bonorum*] abounds in him, let us drink our fill from this fountain, and from no other.[169]

In his incarnation, Christ displayed God's power, goodness, and faithfulness;[170] in his life of obedience, Christ displayed God's mercy, patience, and righteousness.[171] At the cross, Jesus most clearly displayed God's love, righteousness, and judgment (of evil), while further illuminating all of God's excellencies.[172] In the resurrection, God reveals his power (over evil and death), holiness, and glory.[173] In the ascension and ongoing mediation of Christ as high priest, God elucidates his faithfulness, goodness, and power.[174] In the double grace of justification and sanctification, both of which are given to believers by faith as God subsequently forms them into Christ's image by the Spirit,[175] we see God's love brilliantly displayed as well. This is just to highlight a few of the ways Jesus reveals God's excellencies in his person and work!

While Christ clearly confirms and magnifies all of God's excellencies, he most clearly reveals God as a loving father toward his children, Calvin's central metaphor for describing God.[176] Van der Kooi summarizes,

> Precisely in the school of Christ can creation, providence and the hidden work of the Spirit be called upon. In fact the school of Christ includes classes and grades where initially a faint notion of God is given, then a more powerful impression of his majesty and role as judge is imparted, and finally Christ appears as the image of the loving Father as the centre and goal of the knowledge of God.[177]

According to Calvin, in God's concrete actions of creation, providence, and redemption, God has revealed his excellencies, the constructive content of Calvin's doctrine of God. These excellencies generally reveal God's nature or character. However, Calvin specifically highlights a few excellencies which display the core of what believers can know about God's nature. It is to that core we now turn.

The Synopsis of God's Revealed Nature

Although all of God's attributes and excellencies are interrelated,[178] Calvin summarizes God's revealed nature as God's mercy, justice, and righteousness, while elevating God's mercy revealed in Christ as the most important element of God's nature for humans to know. Regarding Jeremiah's depiction of God's exercising mercy, judgment, and justice on earth, Calvin says that God "declares in what sort [*qualis*] he would have us know him." Calvin goes on, "Certainly these three things are especially necessary for us to know:

mercy [*misericordia*], on which alone the salvation of us all rests; judgment [*iudicium*], which is daily exercised against wrongdoers, and in even greater severity awaits them to their everlasting ruin; justice [*iusititia*] whereby believers are preserved, and are most tenderly nourished." For Calvin, all of God's excellencies are summed up in these three.[179] At the center of God's revealed nature, God expresses his fatherly love as he mercifully cares for his children in his righteousness while judging all that stands opposed to him. This synopsis of God's excellencies corresponds with Calvin's consistent description of God as Judge and Father throughout his writings.[180]

Among God's excellencies, Calvin asserts that God's mercy is the single most important to know.[181] For Calvin, as in his comments upon Jer. 9:23–24 above, this mercy is a reference to God's חֶסֶד (*hesed*), God's steadfast, covenant lovingkindness revealed in Scripture.[182] In his comments on Ps. 145:8, Calvin says about Exod. 34:6 that the description there of God as "compassionate and gracious . . . abounding in love and faithfulness" gives us "more clear and familiar [*clarius vel familiarius*] a description of the nature of God . . . than can anywhere be found."[183] Calvin goes on to explain that God's mercy is the most important *virtus* of God to know because God's power placed before us apart from his mercy would overwhelm us with terror; instead God reveals his mercy to us so that we might "fly to him without delay."[184] Calvin here identifies the center of God's nature, namely his mercy and faithfulness. Of course, as we have also observed, God's nature is most clearly revealed in Christ, through whom we come to know God as loving Father.[185] Christ the Mediator is not only the means by which God's love is exhibited but also the means by which people receive God's love for them.[186] In Christ, therefore, we find the clearest, concrete expression of what God revealed in his name to Moses, namely God's abundant fatherly love and mercy.

Calvin's definition of *iusititia* (justice or righteousness) is particularly notable and possibly surprising. He elucidates it further in his Jeremiah lectures, in which he particularly asserts that God's righteousness/justice (*iustitia*) is not the opposite of mercy: "The justice of God is not to be taken according to what is commonly understood by it; and they speak incorrectly who represent God's justice as in opposition to his mercy."[187] At times, Calvin also defines righteousness in relation to morality demanded by the law, but here (and consistently in his Psalms Commentary), Calvin describes righteousness as God's faithfulness to his people.[188]

For Calvin, God's judgment is "the rigor which he exercises against the transgressors of his law."[189] In other words, since the law is the embodiment of righteousness, God's judgment is his condemnation of all evil. God's judgment is expressed toward both believers and unbelievers, but it is received quite differently and accomplishes distinct ends. For the believer who is reconciled with God and clothed in Christ's righteousness, God's chastisement (*castigatio*) is the correction or admonition of a father that reveals God's paternal love, invites believers to recognize their deserts outside of Christ, and leads them to self-reflection, repentance, and avoidance of evil. God tempers his chastisement so as not to overwhelm believers. Toward the unbeliever who remains God's sinful enemy, God pours out his vengeance (*ultio*) as a judge and reveals his wrath (*ira*). Although they could take his judgments as a warning and flee to Christ, the non-elect harden their hearts instead and only come to know God as Judge and Avenger. In short, God's judgment is experienced differently depending upon one's relation to Christ.[190]

For Calvin, God's nature can be summarized by referring to God's righteousness, God's judgment (of evil), and centrally, God's mercy.

Excursus on God's Wrath toward Humanity

Because God's judgment and wrath toward the reprobate is quite important for understanding God's disposition toward humanity, we take a brief excursus here to explore Calvin's teaching on God's wrath on humanity. We shall first address two possible misinterpretations of Calvin's teaching on God's wrath before describing Calvin's actual account of God's wrath on sinful humans and providing two brief reflections on Calvin's teaching on wrath.

First, we must briefly address two potential misunderstandings, namely wrath as God's emotional anger and the contrast between the Old Testament God of wrath and the New Testament God of love.

For Calvin, God's wrath is not like the human emotion of rage but an accommodated expression of God's judgment on sin and evil. Calvin puts it plainly, "By wrath [*iram*], understand God's judgment [*iudicio*], which meaning is had everywhere [*passim*]."[191] Defining what it means to be "children of wrath," Calvin similarly points out, "Wrath [*ira*] means the judgment of God [*iudicium Dei*]; so that the children of wrath are those who are condemned [*damnati*] before God."[192]

In a more extended description, Calvin teaches,

> The word wrath [*ira*], according to the usage of Scripture, speaking after the manner of men [ανθρωποπαθως], means the vengeance of God [*pro ultione Dei*]; for God in punishing, has, according to our notion, the appearance [*faciem*] of one in wrath. It imports, therefore, no such emotion [*motum*] in God, but only has a reference to the perception and feeling [*ad sensum*] of the sinner who is punished.[193]

In parallel with his teaching on accommodation in the *Institutes* in which he describes the anthropomorphisms in the Bible as God's accommodation of himself to human capacity,[194] God's wrath is an accommodation to describe humanity's experience of God's judgment. In sum, God's wrath expressed toward humanity is not a bottled-up emotion within God that must be somehow exhausted; it is simply the righteous God's judgment upon evil.

Calvin is also quite clear that God's wrath is present in both the Old and New Testaments.[195] He is not a neo-Marcionite (or Manichee) who could speak of the God of the Old Testament as the God of wrath and the New Testament God as the God of love.[196] Instead, Calvin teaches continuity between the Old and New Covenants, noting that there are some differences in the "manner of administration" (*modum administrationis*) without any distinction in substance because both covenants are founded on the same promises of Christ.[197] Again calling on God's accommodation to human capacity and needs, Calvin likens God's self-presentation in different times to the way in which a "head of household" (*paterfamilias*) parents differently as his children grow older. God has not changed, "rather, he has accommodated himself to men's capacity, which is varied and changeable."[198] Therefore, for Calvin, there is one God of the Old and New Testaments, the covenant-making God made known in Christ; God's wrath is not to be ignored or forgotten after God graciously takes on human flesh in the incarnation.

Having cleared up those two potential misunderstandings of Calvin's teaching on God's wrath, we now turn to Calvin's positive teaching. Here we see that God's wrath emerges from the conflict between evil and God's perfect righteousness and goodness; we see how God's wrath as judgment is enacted; and we see how even God's wrath is infused with mercy. God's wrath, like all of his actions, is executed according to his unchanging righteous, judging, and merciful nature.

First, for Calvin, God's wrath is the inevitable result of unrighteousness in the presence of God's inherent righteousness (as witnessed to in the law, as we observed above). In the same way that light cannot mix with darkness, God, who is the fount of all goodness, righteousness, and love, necessarily condemns that which is diametrically opposed to him, namely evil and unrighteousness.[199] Thus, "God, who is the highest righteousness [*summa iustitia*], cannot love the unrighteousness that he sees in us all."[200] Simply, God's wrath is God's opposition to that which is contradictory to him. To be able to *not* condemn unrighteousness, God would have to cease to be God. Since Calvin teaches that the stain of sin infiltrates the whole fallen human person,[201] there is no part of a human that God cannot hate. Thus, "As God hates sin, we are also hated by him as far as we are sinners."[202]

Second, God actively condemns all human unrighteousness in his wrath. Calvin says, "We are so vitiated and perverted in every part of our nature that by this great corruption we stand justly condemned [*damnati*] and convicted [*convicti*] before God."²⁰³ Similarly, "The one who is a just Judge [*iustus iudex*] does not allow his law to be broken without punishment [*impune*], but has been equipped for vengeance [*ad vindictam*]."²⁰⁴ God's condemnation takes various forms, including temporal suffering,²⁰⁵ death,²⁰⁶ the loss of the happy life for which God created us,²⁰⁷ and the abandonment of humanity into further sin as they continue to reject him.²⁰⁸ Thus, as an expression of God's judgment on evil and according to God's veiled reprobating will, God condemns any who remain in their unrighteousness.

Third, for Calvin, even God's wrath on sinful humanity includes echoes of God's mercy according to his nature. For example, death itself reminds us of God's punishment of the fall, admonishing us to seek life in God alone.²⁰⁹ Similarly, earthly sufferings are "tokens of God's wrath" that are meant not only to punish but are primarily to lead to Christ and dependence upon God's fatherly love.²¹⁰ The corruption of and condemnation of the earth that proceeds from the fall is meant to incite us to "groan" (*ingemiscamus*) over our sin²¹¹ and lead us to the mercy of God.²¹² In God's discussion with Adam and Eve immediately after their decision to eat of the fruit, Calvin comments that God acted more "as a physician than as a judge," giving them a chance to confess their sin (which they unfortunately rejected).²¹³ God's mercy is even on display in the curse of Adam, first in the fact that God subjects humanity "only to temporal punishment, that, from the moderation of divine anger, they might entertain hope of pardon" and in refuting Adam's excuses in order to "more easily lead him to repentance."²¹⁴ God expresses merciful wrath upon humanity by using his judgment to invite people to him. Even God's judgment is informed by mercy.

This leads us to two reflections regarding Calvin's teaching on God's wrath. First, God's wrath on sin is not a measurable entity that must be exhausted prior to God's being able to look upon people with favor again. In light of God's righteousness and human unrighteousness, God's wrath will never end until humanity is made righteous before God by the removal of their sinful nature and the condemnation of their sin. God's wrath is the righteous God's inherent judgment upon anything or anyone unrighteous.²¹⁵

Second, God's wrath is an expression of his nature. Here, Jeremy Wynne's work on the wrath of God as a divine perfection provides insight into Calvin. Wynne, drawing significantly on Barth's account, argues that in Scripture, wrath is "proper to God's character, not in the same manner as the righteousness that overflows from eternity in the triune life of God, but nonetheless as the righteous God who is present in opposition to all human opposition."²¹⁶ Similarly, Barth teaches that God's wrath is subservient to God's love as a redemptive opposition to all human opposition to God. This is particularly displayed in Barth's doctrine of election. Because all humanity is elect in

Christ, God declares that every individual person is his child. When people resist that declaration by rejecting God's grace in Christ, God, in an expression of his love, rejects their rejection by affirming that they are his children. In their resistance, they experience the wrathful fire of God's love.[217] Thus God's wrath is teleologically driven: God's loving opposition to all human rejection of God and God's loving purposes.

Calvin's account is slightly different. For Calvin, God's wrath is also not in conflict with his other powers, but it is an expression of his loving, righteousness, and judging nature[218] as God judges wickedness in a manner that invites people to repentance. Calvin's account differs from Barth's and Wynne's in that for Calvin, God's wrath is less about the creature's *telos* and attitude toward God and more about God's inherent condemnation of evil. God who is the source of all righteousness and goodness is inherently opposed to all that is unrighteous and evil, as expressed in his judgment (or wrath). Since all humanity is saturated with hateful sin, God can only look on humanity with wrath. When people come to trust in Christ, they are considered in God's sight according to Christ's righteousness, but those who remain outside of Christ stand condemned in their sin, objects of God's wrath.

In both Barth's and Calvin's accounts, reconciliation is driven by God's love for people. In both accounts, God hates and condemns evil. To summarize the difference, for Barth, God's wrath falls upon anything that stands in the way of God's loving purposes for humanity; God's wrath is an expression of his love. For Calvin God's wrath is God's direct condemnation of all that is evil and unrighteous, including humans who remain saturated in their own unrighteousness. The difference is that Barth's primary reference point is God's purposes for humanity whereas Calvin's primary reference point is God's inherent opposition to evil. Although not mutually exclusive, these accounts of God's wrath are notably distinct.

To recapitulate, for Calvin, God's wrath is not a human-like emotion of anger but an expression of God's judgment upon evil that is a demonstration of God's nature and is thus observed in both the Old and New Covenants. Wrath is God's innate and active opposition to all that is evil and includes echoes of God's mercy in its execution. In wrath, God, who is the source and definition of all goodness, condemns evil.

Having explored God's wrath and its connection to God's excellencies, we continue our exposition of what believers can know of God by examining the character of the knowledge of God available to them.

Practical, Personal, and Pious Knowledge of God

As we have seen, Calvin consistently condemns empty speculative knowledge of God. In its place, Calvin espouses practical knowledge of God that directly leads to a faithful and pious life. In the *Institutes*, Calvin describes the practical purpose of his exegetical work:

> "Furthermore, in the reading of Scripture we ought ceaselessly to endeavor to seek out and meditate upon those things which make for edification [*aedificationem*]. Let us not indulge in curiosity or in the investigation of unprofitable things. And because the Lord willed to instruct us, not in fruitless questions, but in sound godliness [*pietate*], in the fear of his name, in true trust and in the duties of holiness, let us be satisfied with this knowledge."[219]

As seen in this passage and expanded on below, for Calvin right knowledge of God is pastorally edifying, is experienced, and results in pious faith.

Pastoral Knowledge

First, for Calvin, teaching about God must be pastorally edifying, or useful (*utilis*).[220] Van der Kooi defines usefulness as "that which does justice to the correct relation between God and man, or which promotes fellowship between man and God, and which motivates man to obedience and worship."[221] We offer a few examples here of Calvin's explicit connection between the knowledge of God and its pastoral usefulness. We have already observed that God reveals his mercy to allow us to approach him without fear[222] and that Scripture depicts the Father's love for the Son to the end that believers would know they are loved.[223] Knowledge of God's fatherly love and power also have direct pastoral utility in the believer's confidence to approach God and trust him in prayer.[224] More broadly, Calvin calls believers to meditate on God's works continually in order to know God's grace and be edified in their faith.[225] Not only is the knowledge of God's excellencies meant to be edifying, but as noted above, when Calvin provides skeletal knowledge of God's essential attributes, he also consistently relates the attributes to the edification of the people, whether in refuting a false teaching or in pointing toward the pastoral benefits of an essential attribute attested to in Scripture. As Selderhuis explains, "Calvin always applies doctrine to the practice of faith."[226] For Calvin, right knowledge of God is pastorally edifying and useful in leading believers closer to God.

Experienced Knowledge

Consistent with his focus on the knowledge of God's nature as revealed through his actions, Calvin also teaches that right knowledge of God is obtained "more in living experience than in vain and high-flown speculation."[227] Calvin believes that God provides the faithful with grounds to know him concretely through experience. He says, "The Lord wishes to be acknowledged to be true, not by a bare and naked imagination, but by actual experience, that is, by preserving the people whom he has adopted."[228] In his 1538 Catechism, Calvin writes that even if God's excellencies are clearly manifest in heaven and earth, "yet we at last comprehend their real goal, value, and true meaning for us only when we descend into ourselves and ponder in what ways the Lord reveals his life, wisdom, and power in us, and exercises toward us his righteousness, goodness, and mercy."[229] However, Calvin is not promoting subjective religious experience as the sole grounds for knowing God. Instead, he is advocating a move away from simple cognitive knowledge to personally certified knowledge of God's excellencies, thus affirming our embodied humanity in relation with God. As Hesselink says, "Though Calvin defines faith as knowledge, it is more a knowledge of the heart than the head, more of the affections than the understanding."[230] Thus, Calvin asserts, "We cannot deny God's claim to praise in all his excellencies [*virtutibus*], but we are most sensibly affected by such proofs of his fatherly goodness [*bonitas*] as we have ourselves experienced."[231]

Another way Calvin emphasizes experience in his teaching of the knowledge of God is in his doctrine of the sacraments. As he says regarding the mystery of the reality of Christ's presence in the bread of the Lord's Supper, "I rather experience [*experior*] it than understand [*intelligam*] it."[232] Calvin further declares, "In the sacraments, the reality is given to us along with the sign; for when the Lord holds out a sacrament, he does not feed our eyes with an empty and unmeaning figure, but joins the truth with it, so as to testify that by means of them he acts upon us efficaciously [*efficaciter*]."[233] He goes on to point out that in receiving the Lord's Supper, the truth of Christ's presence is not separated from the physically experienced sign. Thus, by faith and through the physical manifestation of the bread, we enjoy the body of Christ in fellowship with him.[234] Sacraments are another example of the role that experience plays in Calvin's doctrine of God. Right knowledge of God is experienced knowledge of God, as received by faith.

The End of Knowledge of God: Pious Faith

Finally, Calvin teaches that right knowledge of God results in pious faith, the same place that knowledge of God begins.[235] However, this is not circular reasoning but an ascension by faith into the knowledge of God via union with Christ by the Spirit.[236] Calvin defines faith as "a firm and certain knowledge of God's benevolence [*benevolentiae*] toward us, founded upon the truth of the freely given promise in Christ, both revealed to our minds and sealed upon our hearts through the Holy Spirit."[237] Thus faith for Calvin is not primarily about cognitive assent to doctrinal truths but about confidence in God's nature and assurance of God's attitude toward us, God's disposition toward us. Because God has shown himself to be trustworthy, merciful, powerful, wise, just, judging, and most of all merciful,[238] we have been given grounds and impetus for faith in this God who has revealed himself. If pious faith does not result, then the knowledge of God has not been rightly comprehended.[239] As we saw above, for Calvin, justification and sanctification are distinct but inseparable gifts of God's grace in Christ that is received by faith. Therefore, the faith that emerges from the proper knowledge of God enables and demands a pious life of obedience to God as empowered by and graciously perfected in Christ.

Therefore, we have come full circle, but now we see that, staying consistent with his nonspeculative, pastoral theological methodology, the knowledge of God about which Calvin is concerned is pastorally edifying, is experienced, and results in a pious life.

Through God's concrete revelation of himself in his works as interpreted and revealed in Scripture, those with faith can have absolute confidence in God's benevolent will toward them according to God's nature. This nature has been made known most clearly in Christ; it can be described in short as God's mercy, or slightly longer as God's mercy, righteousness, and judgment. Through trust in God's disposition toward us as revealed in his nature and excellencies, we are assured of our identity as the children of our loving Father that permeates Calvin's teaching. Therefore, as we soon move forward to consider directly the doctrine of predestination, Calvin assumes that the believers who hear of this doctrine will already be convinced of God's fatherly love for them; the content of Calvin's doctrine of the knowledge of God provides a specific foundation for discussing predestination.

This leads to the question of the relation of God's nature to his essence, to which we now turn.

The Relation between God's Nature and Essence

Although Calvin does not speak extensively on the relation between God's nature and essence, he is quite clear that God's nature is constant because it is rooted in God's constancy.[240] Commenting on Ps. 25:6, Calvin links God's merciful nature and essence saying, God "cannot divest himself of the feeling of mercy which is natural to him, and which can no more cease than his eternal existence."[241] Similarly, Calvin comments that David, in the midst of affliction and a dearth of God's presence, holds close "the consideration that although God, who from his very nature is merciful [*qui natura misericors est*], may withdraw himself, and cease for a time to manifest his power, yet he cannot deny himself; that is to say, he cannot divest himself of the feeling of mercy which is natural to him, and which can no more cease than his eternal existence [*aeterna eius essentia*]."[242]

In his lectures on Jonah, Calvin again asserts that God's merciful nature is not accidental to God but is true of God's very self and is thus consistent. Calvin points out that even though Jonah was tasked by God to preach God's judgment on Nineveh, Jonah knows from the "living representation of God" (*viva effigies Dei*) to Moses in Exodus 33–34 that God was wont to be merciful and would forgive the Ninevites as soon as they repented because "he would otherwise deny his own nature: God cannot be unlike himself [*Deus non potest esse sui dissimilis*], he cannot put off that disposition of which he has once testified to Moses."[243] Therefore, although there is an epistemological distinction between God's nature and God's essence, both are unchangeably rooted in the invariable God.

The secondary literature on the relation of God's nature and essence is divided. Horton emphasizes the subjective experience of the human regarding the knowledge of God, saying that only through Christ's mediation of revelation "are we assured that we will encounter a gracious and welcoming God instead of a terrifying judge." According to Horton, God's accommodation in Christ does not show us who God really is in himself but simply who God has chosen to be toward his people.[244]

However, as we have previously demonstrated, Calvin's concern with who God is "toward us" does not reflect a duality in God that changes based on the subject in view. Instead, Calvin teaches that God's unchanging nature is revealed through his concrete works in the world, thus enabling confident talk about God. Horton is right to say that believers can only know God's welcome through Christ, but (as we saw above) this distinction is not based on variability in God's nature but upon God's inherent judgment upon evil. To those who remain in sin, God is seen as a judge, but to those who are clothed in Christ's righteousness, God is known as a Father. God does not simply choose to act differently toward different people as Horton indicates, but he acts in accordance with who he is in himself, in accordance with his unchanging nature.

Holmes, Parker, and van der Kooi all clearly indicate a direct connection between God's accommodation of himself to humanity and God in himself.[245] Holmes contends that in Calvin, God's accommodation provides truth but not complete truth. Holmes points out that God has accommodated himself to us in Christ, allowing the immeasurable God to be known in the measurable person of Christ.[246] Parker asserts that "God reveals Himself to us for His Glory and for our salvation; and hence he reveals, not His *essentia* which no man can see and live, but His *gloria* and His *virtutes*; i.e. that He is God and that He will be God toward us." God's revelation through his excellencies does not reveal all of God, but "God does not reveal Himself as different from what He is in Himself. He who is revealed is He who reveals Himself. . . . We know God truly, but we do not know God wholly."[247] Finally, van der Kooi asserts that God is other and above us in such a way that humans cannot have knowledge of God's essence but do receive knowledge of God that is consistent with who God is.[248] Simply put, although believers do not know God's essence, they do truly know God and his unchanging nature that is rooted in his unchanging essence.

IMPLICATIONS: KNOWLEDGE OF GOD BY FAITH ALONE

As we conclude, let us review our path thus far. We have sought a foundation for discussing God's disposition toward humanity by examining Calvin's teaching about what we are able to know about God and how we are able to access that knowledge. We first analyzed how human beings come to any accurate knowledge of God. We discovered that knowledge of God is offered to all but is only rightly discernible to those who have faith in Christ the Mediator. In light of human sinfulness and creaturely limitations before God's overwhelming majesty, we have found that all knowledge of God comes through God's accommodation of himself to humanity. This accommodation occurs primarily through the created order (rightly interpreted), through Scripture, and ultimately through the incarnate Christ. Next we examined what we can know about God. There, we discovered that for Calvin, humanity cannot know or speculate about God's incomprehensible essence, but they can have limited, skeletal knowledge of God's essence, which Calvin relates to useful, pastoral ends. The constructive content of Calvin's teaching on the knowledge of God consists in God's revelation of what sort he is (*qualis sit*), or his unchanging nature, through his actions in the world. This nature is described by God's excellencies, which constitute the constructive content of Calvin's teaching on the doctrine of God. This knowledge of God is meant to have practical usefulness, be experienced, and lead to pious faith that is certain of God's disposition toward us.

In addition, there is no neutral place from which to study God's disposition toward humanity. Outside of the perspective of faith, no right knowledge of God can be accessed. In other words, for Calvin, there is no Archimedean point from which one could access and evaluate God (or any Christian doctrine). Only through trust in the Mediator can one have accurate knowledge of God as he has accommodated himself to humanity. This is not because those with faith have inherent, superior capabilities but because faith is the only way to receive the knowledge of God that Christ mediates to humanity by the witness of the Spirit. Therefore, as we consider God's disposition toward humanity in Calvin's teaching, Calvin assumes that we come already knowing the trustworthy, unchanging nature of the merciful, righteous, and judging God who has made himself known most clearly and highlighted his mercy in the person and work of Christ.

Finally then, what are the implications of this knowledge of God's nature for the rest of this study and for our question regarding God's disposition toward humanity? Simply put, although we cannot yet forward answers to the question regarding God's disposition toward humanity in Calvin's teaching, we now possess two essential building blocks for examining our question: we know that we can confidently speak about God in ways that correspond to who God really is, and we know the fundamental nature of the God who predestines.

For Calvin, there is only one God to proclaim, namely the merciful, righteous, and judging Father revealed most clearly in Jesus Christ. This is the God of predestination. Therefore, with God's unchanging nature in mind, we turn to examine God's disposition toward humanity in Calvin's teaching on predestination.

NOTES

1. *Harmony of Moses*, Ex. 33:18; *CO* 25:108.
2. *Inst.* 1.5.1, p. 51; *CO* 2:41.
3. *Inst.* 1.5.6, p. 59; *CO* 2:46. Within these chapters, we also discover a concentration of Calvin's overt appeals to the pagan philosophers, including Plato, Cicero, Statius, Aristotle, and Plutarch, as opposed to his typical appeals to Scripture.
4. For example, *Inst.* 2.7.8, 10–16; *CO* 2:259–265, regarding the way the law terrifies and restrains unbelievers.
5. *Inst.* 1.3.1, p. 43; *CO* 2:36. Calvin also uses *sensus deitatis*, as in *Inst.* 1.3.3, p. 46; *CO* 2:38.
6. Although I shall maintain the noninclusive language of the English translations of Calvin's works throughout, *men* and *man* typically connote humankind.
7. *Inst.* 1.3.1, p. 44; *CO* 2:36.
8. *Inst.* 1.3.1, p. 44; *CO* 2:36. Cf. *Inst.* 1.4.1, p. 47; *CO* 2:38.
9. *Inst.* 1.2.1, p. 40; *CO* 2:34.
10. *Inst.* 1.4.1, p. 47; *CO* 2:38. Cf. *Comm. John* 1:5; *CO* 47:6.
11. *Inst.* 1.4.2–3, pp. 48–49; *CO* 2:39–40.
12. *Inst.* 1.4.4, p. 51; *CO* 2:41. Calvin identifies some of these fruits as vice and superstition in *Comm. John* 1:5; *CO* 47:6.
13. *Inst.* 1.5.1, p. 52; *CO* 2:42. Cf. *Comm. Heb.* 11:3; *CO* 55:145–146.
14. *Comm. Rom.* 1:20; *CO* 49:23.
15. *Inst.* 1.5.2, p. 53; *CO* 2:43.

16. *Comm. Heb.* 11:3; *CO* 55:146. Cf. *Inst.* 1.6.1, 1.14.20, p. 180; *CO* 2:131. Cf. *Inst.* 2.6.1; *CO* 2.247–248.

17. *Inst.* 1.5.6, p. 59; *CO* 2:46.

18. *Inst.* 1.5.7, p. 60; *CO* 2:46.

19. *Comm. Heb.* 11:3; *CO* 55:145.

20. *Comm. Rom.* 1:20; *CO* 49:24. Cf. *Comm. Heb.* 11:3; *CO* 55:146. Cf. B. B. Warfield, "Calvin's Doctrine of the Knowledge of God," *The Princeton Theological Review* (1909), 234–35.

21. *Inst.* 1.5.14, p. 68; *CO* 2:52. Cf. *Comm. Heb.* 11:3; *CO* 55:146.

22. *Comm. Heb.* 11:3; *CO* 55:145. My translation. There Calvin also simply states, "It is by faith alone we know that it was God who created the world." Cf. *Comm. John* 1:9; *CO* 47:9. Cf. Warfield, "Calvin's Doctrine the Knowledge of God," 237.

23. *Inst.* 1.5.14, p. 68; *CO* 2:52. Cf. *Comm. 2 Cor.* 4:4; *CO* 50:51. Cf. *Inst.* 2.6.1; *CO* 2:247–248.

24. *Inst.* 1.6.1, pp. 69–70; *CO* 2:53. Cf. *Comm. Gen.*, "Argument"; *CO* 23:9–10. Cf. *Inst.* 1.14.1; *CO* 2:117.

25. Cf. *Inst.* 1.7, pp. 74–81; *CO* 2:56–61.

26. *Inst.* 1.6.2, p. 72; *CO* 2:54.

27. *Comm. 2 Tim.* 3:16; *CO* 52:383–384.

28. *Inst.* 1.2.2, p. 43; *CO* 2:35.

29. *Comm. John* 1:18; *CO* 47:19.

30. Literally, "to throw open."

31. As Barbara Pitkin says, for Calvin "all true knowledge of God is through knowledge of God's saving activity in Christ" (*What Pure Eyes Could See: Calvin's Doctrine of Faith in Its Exegetical Context* [Oxford: Oxford University Press, 1999], 33).

32. Cf. *Comm. John* 14:1; *CO* 47:321–322. Cf. *Inst.* 3.2.6, p. 548; *CO* 2:401. Cf. *Comm. John* 17:3; *CO* 47:376–377. Cf. *Inst.* 2.6.4, pp. 346–47; *CO* 2:251–252. Cf. Augustine, *The City of God Against the Pagans,* trans. R. W. Dyson (Cambridge: Cambridge University Press, 1998), 11.2.

33. *Comm. 1 Pet.* 1:21; *CO* 55:227. Cf. *Harmony of the Gospels*, Matt. 6:9; *CO* 45:196. Cf. *Comm. John* 1:16; *CO* 47:16–18. Cf. *Comm. John* 15:9; *CO* 47:342.

34. Even human relationship with God in the Old Testament was mediated through Christ, though the visible means of relationship were the sacrifices and the Law (*Inst.* 2.6.2, p. 343; *CO* 2:248–249).

35. *Inst.* 1.2.1, p. 39; *CO* 2:34.

36. *Inst.* 1.2.1, p. 41; *CO* 2:34.

37. John Calvin, "Catechism of the Church of Geneva, 1545," in *Tracts, Vol. 2*, ed. Henry Beveridge and Jules Bonnet, Calvin Translation Society, Q218. *CO* 6:78.

38. For example, *Inst.* 1.6.2, p. 72; *CO* 2:54–55; *Inst.* 1.2.1, p. 39; *CO* 2:34; *Inst.* 1.4.4, p. 50; *CO* 2:40.

39. The same concept can be observed in Calvin's teaching on sanctification, which is both a completed gift in Christ *and* lived out through a lifelong process of regeneration by the Spirit. Cf. *Inst.* 3.15.5–6; *CO* 2:582–584.

40. *Inst.* 4.17.38; *CO* 2:1041. Cf. Cornelis van der Kooi, *As in a Mirror: John Calvin and Karl Barth on Knowing God: A Diptych*, trans. Donald Mader (Leiden: Brill, 2005), 30.

41. *Inst.* 4.17.40; *CO* 2:1042.

42. Elsie Anne Mckee, *John Calvin: Writings on Pastoral Piety*, ed. Elsie Anne Mckee (New York: Paulist Press, 2001), 249. Cf. Elsie Anne McKee, *John Calvin on the Diaconate and Liturgical Almsgiving* (Geneva: Librairie Droz, 1984), 13. Cf. my chapter, "Pietas and Caritas: John Calvin's Preaching on Love for Neighbor," in Karin Maag and Arnold Huijgen (eds), *Calvinus Frater in Domino: Papers of the Twelfth International Congress on Calvin Research* (Göttingen: Vandenhoeck & Ruprecht, 2020).

43. Edward A. Dowey, *The Knowledge of God in Calvin's Theology* (New York: Columbia University Press, 1964), 26.

44. *Inst.* 1.13.21, p. 146; *CO* 2:107. My translation in part. Cf. *Inst.* 1.4.1, p. 47; *CO* 2:41.

45. *Comm. 1 John* 3:2; *CO* 55:331.

46. With a similar meaning, Calvin also uses *attemperare*. Cf. *Comm. Rom.* 1:19; *CO* 49:23.

47. Kurt A. Richardson, "Calvin on the Trinity," in *John Calvin and Evangelical Theology: Legacy and Prospect*, ed. Sung Wook Chung (Colorado Springs, CO: Paternoster, 2009), 33. As Arnold Huijgen describes it, "Divine accommodation does not enlarge human capacity, but embraces humans in their limited capacity to lead them to the knowledge of God through the work of the Holy Spirit" (*Divine Accommodation in John Calvin's Theology: Analysis and Assessment* [Göttingen: Vandenhoeck & Ruprecht, 2011], 292). Cf. van der Kooi, *As in a Mirror*, 42. Cf. T. H. L. Parker, *The Doctrine of the Knowledge of God* (Edinburgh: Oliver and Boyd, 1952), 51. Cf. Dowey, *Knowledge of God*, 17. Cf. F. L. Battles, "God Was Accommodating Himself to Human Capacity," *Interpretation* 31, no. 1 (1977), 33.

Regarding the rhetorical dimensions of accommodation, see J. Todd Billings, *Calvin, Participation, and the Gift: The Activity of Believers in Union with Christ* (Oxford: Oxford University Press, 2007), 36. Cf. E. David Willis, "Rhetoric and Responsibility in Calvin's Theology," in *The Context of Contempory Theology*, ed. Alexander McKelway and E. David Willis (Atlanta: John Knox Press, 1974), 48.

48. *Comm. Rom.* 1:19; *CO* 49:23. We shall address below Calvin's distinction between what God is (*quid sit Deus*) as unknowable to humans and God's nature (*qualis sit Deus*) as knowable.

49. Cf. *Inst.* 1.6.3, p. 73; *CO* 2:55; *Inst.* 1.18.3, p. 234; *CO* 2:171; *Inst.* 3.2.1, p. 543; *CO* 2:398.

50. *Inst.* 1.13.1, p. 121; *CO* 2:89.

51. *Comm. Ps.* 104:1; *CO* 32:85. My translation. Cf. *Comm. 1 John* 2:23; *CO* 55:325. Cf. *Comm. Jer.* 50:25; *CO* 39:418.

52. Cf. Huijgen, *Accommodation*, 290.

53. Cf. *Comm. 1 Tim.* 6:16; *CO* 52:332.

54. Huijgen, *Accommodation*, 214–15.

55. *Comm. Is.* 6:5; *CO* 36:131. Cf. *Inst.* 1.1.3, p. 39; *CO* 2:33.

56. *Harmony of Moses*, Ex. 33:18; *CO* 25:108.
57. *Harmony of Moses*, Ex. 33:20; *CO* 25:111. Cf. *Inst.* 2.6.4, pp. 346–47; *CO* 2:252.
58. Huijgen, *Accommodation*, 305–12.
59. *Inst.* 1.6.2, p. 72; *CO* 2:54. Cf. *Inst.* 1.14.20; *CO* 2:131. For a magnificent summary of Calvin's understanding of the interrelation of the knowledge of God as revealed in Christ and confirmed in God's works in the universe, see *Comm. Gen.* "Argument"; *CO* 23:9–12.
60. *Comm. Ps.* 104:1–2; *CO* 32:85. Of course, this knowledge is only accessible by faith (*Comm. Ps.* 104:3–4; *CO* 32:86).
61. *Inst.* 1.6.2, p. 72; *CO* 2:54. Cf. *Comm. Is.* 40:18; *CO* 37:19.
62. *Inst.* 1.6.3, p. 73; *CO* 2:55.
63. *Inst.* 1.7.5, p. 80; *CO* 2:60.
64. Huijgen, *Accommodation*, 271.
65. Randall C. Zachman, "Calvin as Analogical Theologian," *Scottish Journal of Theology* 51, no. 2 (2009), 162.
66. *Comm. Jer.* 23:5–6; *CO* 66:410. Cf. *Sermons on Election and Reprobation*, no. 12, p. 265; *CO* 58:174.
67. Alan J. Torrance, *Persons in Communion: An Essay on Trinitarian Description and Human Participation* (Edinburgh: T&T Clark, 1996), 332–35.
68. This is contra Paul Helm, who asserts that Calvin sees language about God as analogical and accommodated, "with elements of univocity but also with elements of equivocity" (*Calvin's Ideas* [Oxford: Oxford University Press, 2004], 31).
69. Torrance, *Persons in Communion*, 354.
70. *Inst.* 1.13.1, p. 121; *CO* 2:90.
71. An assumption rooted in the classical definition of perfection, but one that is not a foregone conclusion in today's biblical and theological discussions.
72. *Inst.* 1.17.13, p. 227; *CO* 2:165–166. For example, *Comm. Rom.* 1:18; *CO* 49:23. Cf. Zachman, "Calvin as Analogical Theologian," 171.
    Huijgen points out that Calvin's hermeneutical key regarding the passages of God's changing is based primarily on metaphysical assumptions, namely that all change is relegated to the creaturely realm. If Calvin had been more consistent in his methodology, he would have allowed God's accommodation as one repenting to provide knowledge of God equally as much as God's accommodation in Scripture that he does not change. In this way, since we humans cannot know God's unchanging essence, "we should hold to God's accommodated revelation, which means that in practice God shows Himself as changing" (Huijgen, *Accommodation*, 275).
73. *Inst.* 2.11.13–14, pp. 462–64; *CO* 2:338–340.
74. *Inst.* 2.10.6, p. 433; *CO* 2:316.
75. *Comm. 2 Cor.* 3:16; *CO* 50:45. In light of the dynamic nature of Calvin's use of language discussed above, Christ is also the semantic *scopus* of Scripture's language. The ultimate meaning of Scripture's language finds its root and fulfillment in Christ.
76. *Comm. 2 Cor.* 3:12; *CO* 50:44.
77. *Comm. John* 1:18; *CO* 47:19.

78. *Comm. Col.* 1:15; *CO* 52:84–85.
79. *Comm. Col.* 1:15; *CO* 52:85.
80. *Comm. Col.* 2:9; *CO* 52:104. "In [Christ] we find also God the Father, as he truly communicates himself to us by him" (*Comm. 2 Cor.* 5:19; *CO* 50:71. Cf. *Comm. Heb.* 1:3; *CO* 55:12).
81. Cf. *Comm. 1 Tim.* 6:16; *CO* 52:332. Cf. *Inst.* 1.5.1, p. 52; *CO* 2:41. Cf. *Harmony of Moses*, Ex. 3:14; *CO* 24:44.
82. *Comm. John* 14:10; *CO* 47:326.
83. In light of Calvin's teaching about God's inscrutable essence, his use of the adverb *essentialiter* instead of the noun *essentia* in his comments on Col. 2:9 also highlights the way Calvin is describing *how* God has appeared in Christ—in a manner that is congruent with his essence—instead of saying that we see God's essence *directly* in Christ. This contrasts with Huijgen's reading (and translation) of the passage in which he concludes, albeit with later qualifications, "God's essence can be known, and is known, but only in Christ" (*Accommodation*, 283–84).
84. *Comm. 1 John* 2:23; *CO* 55:325.
85. "God is comprehended in Christ alone [*Deum in Christo solo comprehendi*]" (*Inst.* 2.6.4, p. 347; *CO* 2:252. Cf. *Comm. Isaiah* 6:1; *CO* 36:126. Cf. *Comm. Ezek.* 1:25–26; *CO* 47:56).
86. *Comm. John* 1:18; *CO* 47:19. Cf. *Comm. Isaiah* 35:9; *CO* 36:421.
87. This revelation only occurs as the Spirit opens one's eyes to the glory of Christ (*Harmony of the Gospels*, Matt. 11:27; *CO* 45:320. Cf. *Comm. Heb.* 1:3; *CO* 55:12).
88. *Comm. 1 John* 2:23; *CO* 55:325.
89. *Inst.* 2.6.4, p. 347; *CO* 2:252. Cf. *Comm. 1 Pet.* 1:21; *CO* 55:227.
90. *Inst.* 2.6.4, p. 347; *CO* 2:252. Cf. *Comm. 1 John* 2:23; *CO* 55:325.
91. Zachman, "Calvin as Analogical Theologian," 179.
92. *Comm. John* 20:28; *CO* 47:444. Cf. *Comm. Gen.* 28:12; *CO* 23:391. Cf. Augustine, *City of God*, 11.2.
93. God's ongoing accommodation of himself in Christ also continues in the Sacraments, through which believers ascend from the signs of Christ and his work to a greater reality, namely union with Christ by the Spirit (*Inst.* 4:17.33, pp. 1407–8; *CO* 2:1035. Cf. Zachman, "Calvin as Analogical Theologian," 185).
94. Included in this accommodation is the way that the preached Word and the sacraments flow from and witness to God's accommodation in Scripture and Christ by the Spirit.
95. Cf. William Stacy Johnson and John H. Leith, *Reformed Reader: A Sourcebook in Christian Theology* (Louisville: Westminster/John Knox Press, 1993), 75.
96. "Whatever speculation Calvin was advising against, he was certainly not against an affirmation of key classical attributes of God. Indeed Calvin unequivocally affirms the classical attributes of God in a basic form" (J. Todd Billings, "The Catholic Calvin," *Pro Ecclesia* 20, no. 2 [2011], 128–29). Cf. Muller, *P.R.R.D., Vol. 3*, 206. Cf. Oliver Crisp, "Calvin on Creation and Providence," in *John Calvin & Evangelical Theology: Legacy and Prospect*, ed. Sung Wook Chung (Colorado Springs, CO: Paternoster, 2009), 61.

97. For details of this argument, see my chapter, "Calvin's Non-Speculative Methodology: A Corrective to Billings and Muller on Calvin's Divine Attributes," in *Calvinus Pastor Ecclesiae. Papers of the Eleventh International Congress on Calvin Research*, ed. Arnold Huijgen and H. J. Selderhuis (Göttingen: Vandenhoeck & Ruprecht, 2016).

98. In line with Calvin's nonspeculative theological methodology and reliance upon the creedal Christian tradition, Calvin does not attempt to define God's essence or describe how we know that God has an essence.

99. J. Todd Billings, *Union with Christ: Reframing Theology and Ministry for the Church* (Grand Rapids: Baker Academic, 2011), 68, 74. Cf. Buckner, "Calvin's Non-Speculative Methodology."

100. *Inst.* 1.5.9, p. 63; *CO* 2:47.

101. *Inst.* 1.5.1, p. 52; *CO* 2:41. Cf. *Harmony of Moses*, Ex. 3:14; *CO* 24:44. Cf. Huijgen, *Accommodation*, 268. Cf. van der Kooi, *As in a Mirror*, 126.

102. *Comm. John* 14:10; *CO* 47:326.

103. *Comm. 1 John* 3:2; *CO* 55:332. Cf. *Comm. 1 Tim.* 6:16; *CO* 52:333.

104. *Comm. 1 John* 3:2; *CO* 55:331–332. My translation. Huijgen attributes this to Calvin's assumed hierarchy of being (*Accommodation*, 258).

105. Cf. *Inst.* 1.13.19, p. 144; *CO* 2:106. Cf. *Inst.* 1.5.1, p. 52; *CO* 2:41. Cf. *Harmony of Moses*, Ex. 3:14; *CO* 24:44. This is in contrast with Thomas Aquinas's definition of speculation in which he, following Aristotle, asserts that both practical and speculative sciences are innately noble but with different ends (*Commentary on the Metaphysics of Aristotle*, trans. John P. Rowan [Chicago: Henry Regnery, 1961], 2.2.290. Cf. *ST*, I–I, q. 1, a. 4–5).

Calvin, who likely had little to no direct contact with Aquinas's work, exclusively speaks of speculation pejoratively.

106. *Serm. Job* 22:12–17; *CO* 34:300; translation from Huijgen, *Accommodation*, 300. Cf. *Comm. Is.* 6:4; *CO* 36:130.

107. *Comm. Col.* 2:10; *CO* 52:104. Cf. *Harmony of Moses*, Ex. 33:18; *CO* 25:108.

108. *Inst.* 1.4.1, p. 47; *CO* 2:38. Cf. van der Kooi, *As in a Mirror*, 118.

109. *Inst.* 1.4.1, p. 47; *CO* 2:38.

110. *Comm. John* 1:3, *CO* 47:4.

111. *Inst.* 1.5.9, p. 61; *CO* 2:47.

112. *Comm. Ezek.* 1:25–26; *CO* 47:57. Cf. *Comm. 1 Peter* 1:20; *CO* 55:226. Cf. Herman J. Selderhuis, *Calvin's Theology of the Psalms* (Grand Rapids: Baker Academic, 2007), 45–46.

113. *Inst.* 1.1.1; *CO* 2:32. Cf. Huijgen, *Accommodation*, 305.

114. Huijgen, *Accommodation*, 295. Cf. I. John Hesselink, *Calvin's First Catechism* (Louisville: Westminster John Knox Press, 1997), 52.

115. Huijgen contends that Calvin violates this rule when he allows the metaphysical presuppositions of his day to significantly influence his doctrine of God, particularly regarding God's immutability (*Accommodation*, 317–18). Likewise, van der Kooi rejects Calvin's view of God's changelessness as a by-product of Calvin's geocentric cosmology that interpreted change and relations as imperfections (van der Kooi, *As in a Mirror*, 147).

116. It is likely that the prevailing theological assumptions of Calvin's day included these perfections. Calvin does not object to those assumptions.

117. His occasion here is the panentheism of Seneca, the dualism of the Manicheans, and the antitrinitarian teaching of Servetus (*Inst*. 1.13.1–2, pp. 120–23; *CO* 2:89–90. Cf. *Inst*. 2.14.2–8, pp. 483–93; *CO* 2:353–361).

118. The longest list Calvin provides is in *Inst*. 1.14.3 where he mentions God's glory, eternity, self-existence, omnipotence, wisdom, and righteousness in response to the false teaching of the Manichees. Calvin quickly exhorts his readers toward teaching that has value for edification and away from "speculating more deeply than what is expedient" and thus wandering "away from the simplicity of faith [*fidei simplicitate*]" (*Inst*. 1.14.3, p. 163; *CO* 2:119).

119. For example, B. B. Warfield, "Calvin's Doctrine of God," *The Princeton Theological Review* (1909), 417–18. Cf. Muller, *P.R.R.D., Vol. 3*, 206.

120. Muller, *The Unaccommodated Calvin*, 125. Calvin was also familiar with the 1543 revision, as he wrote a preface to the 1546 French translation of the 1545 edition (Wulfert de Greef, *The Writings of John Calvin: An Introductory Guide*, trans. Lyle D. Bierma [Grand Rapids: Baker, 1993], 205).

121. Cf. Selderhuis, *Calvin's Theology of the Psalms*, 49.

122. *Harmony of Moses*, Ex. 3:14; *CO* 24:43. Cf. *Inst*. 1.10.2, p. 97; *CO* 2:73. Cf. *Harmony of Moses*, Ex. 6:2–4; *CO* 24:78.

123. *Harmony of Moses*, Num. 23:18; *CO* 25:283. Cf. *Comm. James* 1:16–18; *CO* 55:391–392. Cf. *Comm. Ps.* 102:25–27; *CO* 32:73.

124. For example, *Comm. Josh*. 7:22–23; *CO* 25:479. Cf. *Inst*. 1.13.8, p. 130; *CO* 2:96. Cf. *1538 Catechism*, p. 22, s. 20i; *CO* 5:337–338.

125. Muller, *P.R.R.D., Vol. 3*, 207.

126. *Inst*. 1.10.2, p. 97; *CO* 2:73. My translation. Cf. 3.2.6, p. 549; *CO* 2:402.

127. van der Kooi, *As in a Mirror*, 125. Cf. *Comm. Ps.* 86:8; *CO* 31:794.

128. This commitment to a limited knowledge of God's being and more extensive knowledge of God through his activities was common in patristic thinking as well. For example, Basil of Caesarea particularly forwarded the important distinction that humans speak rightly of God without having comprehensive knowledge of God's essence in his *Against Eunomius*. Lewis Ayres summarizes that for Basil, no *ousia* is ever fully known but God can be known by his diverse activities (*energeiai*) toward us (*Nicaea and Its Legacy: An Approach to Fourth Century Trinitarian Theology* [Oxford: Oxford University Press, 2004], 196). Cf. Basil of Caesarea, *Against Eunomius*, trans. Mark DelCogliano and Andrew Radde-Gallwitz (Washington, DC: Catholic University of America Press, 2011), 1.8.

It is difficult to discern how much direct influence Basil's teaching had on Calvin. Although Battles claims that Basil was a significant influence on Calvin, including being the source for Calvin's twofold knowledge of God, Lane asserts that Basil had a relatively minor impact on Calvin through the Latin translation of Basil's works published in 1540, which Lane contends Calvin only read once (*Calvin: Student of the Church Fathers*, 82–83). None of Calvin's three citations of Basil in the *Institutes* refers to theological language or the description of God's essence and energies.

129. *Inst*. 1.2.2, p. 41; *CO* 2:34–35.

130. *Inst.* 3.2.6, p. 549; *CO* 2:402.

131. It is difficult to determine an appropriate English equivalent for *qualis*, particularly because Calvin was not always consistent in his use of the term. We shall refer to God's "nature," "character," or "what sort God is" depending upon context.

132. *Inst.* 1.10.2, pp. 97–98; *CO* 2:73. My translation.

133. See following subsection for our analysis of Calvin's teaching on God's *virtutes*.

134. *Comm. John* 17:4; *CO* 47:378. The CTS translation mistakenly finishes the sentence with "what God is." That would be a more appropriate translation of *quid sit.* Cf. *Inst.* 2.15.2, p. 496; *CO* 2:362.

135. *Inst.* 1.2.2, p. 41; *CO* 2:34–35.

As in the case of Calvin's nonprecise use of *qualis*, Calvin is not always consistent in his differentiation between God's essence and nature (e.g., Calvin can speak of God's *natura* as simple and spiritual [*Comm. Is.* 44:15–17; *CO* 37:116]).

136. *Comm. Ps.* 77:11–12; *CO* 31:717. My translation.

137. *Harmony of Moses*, Num. 23:18; *CO* 25:283.

138. *Comm. James* 1:16–18; *CO* 55:391.

139. Huijgen, *Accommodation*, 285. Cf. "The Relation between God's Essence and Nature" on page 40 in this book.

140. *Comm. 1 John* 3:2; *CO* 55:331.

141. *Inst.* 1.10.2, p. 97; *CO* 2:73.

142. Warfield, "Calvin's Doctrine of God," 402. Cf. Dowey, *Knowledge of God*, 6. Cf. Helm, *Calvin's Ideas*, 13.

143. In the only use of *attributa* in the *Institutes* of which I am aware, Calvin uses it pejoratively regarding the way Sabellius spoke of the persons of the Trinity not as distinctions but as *attributa Dei* (*Inst.* 1.13.4, p. 125; *CO* 2:92).

144. "Powers" or "virtues" would be other possible translations.

145. Parker, *Knowledge of God*, 53–54. Cf. Randall C. Zachman, *Reconsidering John Calvin* (Cambridge: Cambridge University Press, 2011), 9.

146. *1538 Catechism*, p. 8, s. 3; *CO* 5:325.

147. *Inst.* 1.5.10, p. 63; *CO* 2:48. Cf. *Comm. Ps.* 111:2–4; *CO* 32:167–168.

148. Cf. *Comm. Ps.* 77:11–12; *CO* 31:716.

149. *Comm. Phil.* 2:6; *CO* 52:26. My translation. For Calvin, even God's excellencies are never fully understood by limited humanity: "Incomprehensible as is the immensity of the wisdom, equity, justice, power, and mercy of God, in his works, the faithful nevertheless acquire as much knowledge of these as qualifies them for manifesting the glory of God" (*Comm. Ps.* 111:2; *CO* 32:168).

150. Parker, *Knowledge of God*, 53–54. Cf. *Comm. John* 17:4; *CO* 47:378.

151. *Inst.* 1.6.2, p. 72; *CO* 2:54.

152. Cf. *Inst.* 1.5.10, p. 63; *CO* 2:48. Cf. *Inst.* 1.10.2, pp. 97–98; *CO* 2:73. Cf. *Inst.* 1.14.20, p. 180; *CO* 2:131. Cf. *Inst.* 2.6.1, p. 341; *CO* 2:247. Cf. *Harmony of Moses*, Ex. 34:6–7; *CO* 24:44. Cf. *Comm. Ps.* 145:4–6; *CO* 32:413. Cf. Zachman, *Reconsidering John Calvin*, 10.

153. *Inst.* 1.16.1, p. 198, *CO* 2:145. Cf. *Inst.* 1.2.1, p. 40; *CO* 2:34.

154. *Inst.* 1.17.1, p. 210; *CO* 2:154.

155. *Inst.* 1.14.21, p. 181; *CO* 2:133.

156. *Comm. Jer.* 9:23–24; *CO* 38:51.

157. *Comm. Rom.* 1:20; *CO* 49:24. The more recent translation makes the same mistake, utilizing "attributes" here (John Calvin, *The Epistles of Paul the Apostle to the Romans and to the Thessalonians,* trans. Ross MacKenzie [Grand Rapids: Eerdmans, 1995], 31).

158. Muller, *P.R.R.D., Vol. 3,* 206. Cf. Buckner, "Calvin's Non-Speculative Methodology."

159. *Comm. Rom.* 1:21; *CO* 49:24.

160. It is worth pointing out that although Calvin is predominantly concerned with God's excellencies as known through his acts here, he is not averse to including God's eternity in the list. He does not make the strict delineation between essential and personal attributes that modern theologians typically make.

161. *Inst.* 1.2.1, p. 40; *CO* 2:34. Cf. *Inst.* 2.6.1, p. 341; *CO* 2:247.

162. This statement is true when we reason chronologically regarding how God has made himself known. However, in light of the order of knowing, Calvin reverses this and says that God's works in creation actually confirm and elucidate the true knowledge of God that we have already received in Christ (*Comm. Gen.* "Argument"; *CO* 23:9–12).

163. *Comm. Col.* 1:15; *CO* 52:85. Cf. *Comm. John* 14:10; *CO* 47:326.

164. *Comm. John* 15:9; *CO* 47:342. Cf. The "sweet fruit" of knowing God's free mercy through the God's work in election (*Inst.* 3.21.1, p. 921; *CO* 2:679).

165. *Comm. Js.* 2:10; *CO* 55:401. Cf. *Harmony of the Gospels,* Matt. 5:17; *CO* 45:171.

166. *Harmony of the Gospels*, Matt. 5:22; *CO* 45:174.

167. *Harmony of Moses*, Deut. 7:9; *CO* 25:19.

168. Cf. *Comm. Rom.* 4:25; *CO* 49:87.

169. *Inst.* 2.16.19, pp. 527–28; *CO* 2:385–386.

170. Cf. *Comm. 1 John 4:9*; *CO* 55:353. Cf. *Inst.* 2.12.2, p. 465; *CO* 2:341. Cf. *Inst.* 2.14.6, p. 489; *CO* 2:358. Cf. *Inst.* 4.17.2, p. 1362; *CO* 2:1003. Cf. Irenaeus, *Against the Heresies,* trans. F. R. M. Hitchcock (London: Society for Promoting Christian Knowledge, 1916), 3.18.7. Cf. *Inst.* 2.22.4.

171. Cf. *Comm. Rom.* 8:4; *CO* 49:140. Cf. *Comm. 2 Cor.* 5:16; *CO* 50:68. Cf. *Comm. Gal.* 4:4; *CO* 50:227.

172. Cf. *Comm. John* 13:31; *CO* 47:316–317. Cf. *Comm. Rom* 1:17; *CO* 49:20. Cf. *Inst.* 2.17.4, p. 531; 2:389. Cf. *Comm. Rom.* 4:3; *CO* 49:69. Cf. *Comm. 2 Cor.* 5:21; *CO* 50:73–74. Cf. *Comm. 1 Pet.* 2:24; *CO* 55:251–252. Cf. *Comm. 2 Cor.* 5:21; *CO* 50:74. Cf. Billings, *Calvin, Participation, and the Gift,* 188.

173. Cf. *Comm. Rom.* 4:25; *CO* 49:87. Cf. *Comm. Rom.* 6:9–10; 49:109. Cf. *Inst.* 2.12.2, p. 466; *CO* 2:341.

174. Cf. *Comm. Heb.* 10:22; *CO* 55:129. Cf. *Inst.* 2.16.14, pp. 522–23; *CO* 2:381–382. Cf. *Inst.* 2.16.15, p. 524; *CO* 2:382. Cf. *Comm. 1 Pet.* 3:22; *CO* 55:269.

175. *Comm. Rom.* 6:14; *CO* 49:113. Cf. *Harmony of Moses,* Deut. 30:19; *CO* 25:56. Cf. *Comm. Rom.* 3:31; *CO* 49:67.

176. Hesselink, drawing upon a survey of Calvin scholarship, concludes that divine Fatherhood is Calvin's central way of discussing God's nature and character (*Calvin's First Catechism*, 117). Cf. Julie Canlis, "The Fatherhood of God and Union with Christ in Calvin," in *'In Christ' in Paul* (Tübingen: Mohr Siebeck, 2014).

177. van der Kooi, *As in a Mirror*, 83.

178. Cf. Selderhuis, *Calvin's Theology of the Psalms*, 49.

179. *Inst.* 1.10.2, p. 98; *CO* 2:73. Cf. van der Kooi, *As in a Mirror*, 131.

180. Cf. van der Kooi, *As in a Mirror*, 117–77.

181. Cf. Huijgen, *Accommodation*, 284–86.

182. Calvin says that God relates to his people based on his "gratuitous liberality. For *hesed* is equivalent to kindness or beneficence [*mansuetudo aut beneficentia*]; but when it is applied to God, it generally signifies mercy [*misericordiam*] or paternal favor [*paternum favorem*], and the blessings [*beneficia*] which flow from it" (*Harmony of Moses*, Deut. 5:9; 24:379).

183. *Comm. Ps.* 145:8; *CO* 32:414. My translation. Calvin also says that "God's nature [*natura*] is described" when the prophet says that God is "gracious and merciful, slow to anger, and abounding in steadfast love" (*Comm. Joel* 2:13; *CO* 42:545).

184. *Comm. Ps.* 145:8; *CO* 32:414. Cf. *Inst.* 3.2.30, p. 576; *CO* 2:422.

185. *Inst.* 1.2.1, p. 40; *CO* 2:35.

186. *Comm. John*, "The Argument to the Gospel of John," *CO* 47:vi. Cf. *Comm. 1 John* 3:16; *CO* 55:340. Cf. chapter 4.

187. *Comm. Jer.* 9:23–24; *CO* 38:51–52. Cf. "No Tension between Love and Justice" in chapter 4.

188. Regarding God's *iustitia*, Selderhuis summarizes Calvin's view in his commentary on the book of Psalms, "Calvin interprets the righteousness of God as his faithfulness and mercy whereby he protects believers" (*Calvin's Theology of the Psalms*, 157). Cf. *Comm. Ps.* 5:8; *CO* 31:69.

189. *Comm. Jer.* 9:23–24; *CO* 38:51–52.

190. This brings up the question that if God is merciful toward all and sovereign over all, why, according to Calvin, are not all people reconciled to God in Christ. We shall address that question in chapter 3, on predestination, where we find that from our human perspective, God's acts in election correspond directly with his revealed nature whereas his acts in reprobation only correspond with God's nature in part, as far as humans can understand.

191. *Comm. Rom.* 4:15; *CO* 49:78.

192. *Comm. Eph.* 2:3; *CO* 51:162.

193. *Comm. Rom.* 1:18; *CO* 49:23. Calvin's commitment to God's immutability and foreknowledge undergirds this definition of wrath. Since God already knows everything and does not change based on our actions, he is not surprised by our sin and thus forced into an emotional state of anger. It is a valid question whether Calvin's specific doctrine of immutability is exegetically defensible today; as noted above, both Huijgen and van der Kooi assert that it is not. Cf. Huijgen, *Accommodation*, 275–78. Cf. van der Kooi, *As in a Mirror*, 144–48.

194. *Inst.* 1.13.1, p. 121; *CO* 2:89.

195. Since *testamentum* can mean "testament" or "covenant," it is often unclear which English word is most appropriate. In *Inst.* 2.11, context indicates that "covenant" is a better option, contra Battles's translation.

196. *Inst.* 2.11.3, p. 452; *CO* 2:331.

197. *Inst.* 2.11.1, pp. 449–50; *CO* 2:329. One of the differences that Calvin notes is that in the Old Testament, "God manifested himself more fully as a Father and Judge by temporal blessings and punishments than since the promulgation of the gospel," *Harmony of Moses*, Lev. 26:3; *CO* 25:14. Cf. Willem Balke, *Calvin and the Anabaptist Radicals,* trans. William Heynen (Grand Rapids: Eerdmans, 1981), 309–13.

198. *Inst.* 2.11.13, pp. 462–63; *CO* 2:339.

199. *Inst.* 2.17.2, p. 530; *CO* 2:387.

200. *Inst.* 2.16.13, p. 505; *CO* 2:369.

201. *Comm. Rom.* 6:12; *CO* 49:110–111. Cf. *Inst.* 2.3.1, p. 290; *CO* 2:209–210. Cf. *Comm. Rom.* 7:14; *CO* 49:128. Cf. Augustine, *City of God*, 19.4, p. 921.

202. *Comm. Rom.* 5:10; *CO* 49:94. Cf. *Comm. Rom.* 1:17; *CO* 49:20. Cf. *Comm. Rom.* 5:6; *CO* 49:92. Cf. *Comm. 2 Cor.* 5:11; *CO* 50:70.

203. *Inst.* 2.1.8, p. 251; *CO* 2:182. This condemnation increases with one's awareness of the law because rejection of the law is a sign of even greater unrighteousness (*Comm. Rom.* 4:15; *CO* 49:79).

204. *Inst.* 2.16.1, p. 504; *CO* 2:368. My translation.

205. *Comm. Rom.* 8:31; *CO* 49:162.

206. *Comm. Gen.* 5:5; *CO* 23:106.

207. *Comm. Gen.* 3:19; *CO* 23:74.

208. *Comm. Rom.* 4:15; *CO* 49:79.

209. *Comm. Gen.* 5:5; *CO* 23:106. Of course this does not make death itself merciful. Death and alienation from God are opposed to God's intent for humanity, but God works mercifully by using the prospect of death to call people to him.

210. Believer and unbeliever experience suffering which is meant to lead to Christ, but believers who know God's fatherly mercy can receive the suffering as discipline, while unbelievers only know it as wrath (*Comm. Rom.* 8:31; *CO* 49:162. Cf. *Comm. Rom.* 8:36; *CO* 49:166. Cf. *Comm. Gen.* 3:19; *CO* 23:77. Cf. *Comm. Gen.* 3:23; *CO* 23:80).

211. *Comm. Gen.* 3:18; *CO* 23:73.

212. *Comm. Gen.* 3:17; *CO* 23:73. Fallen creation still retains "tokens of his goodness," not nearly as abundant as before the fall, but still witnessing to God's mercy.

213. *Comm. Gen.* 3:14; *CO* 23:68.

214. *Comm. Gen.* 3:17; *CO* 23:72. Cf. Noah in *Comm. Gen.* 6:3; *CO* 23:114 and *Comm. Gen.* 6:5; *CO* 23:117. In Calvin's account of the fall, in which one might expect significant exposition on the condemnation merited by Adam and Eve, Calvin speaks very little of God's wrath.

215. Cf. *Inst.* 3.11.11, p. 740; *CO* 2:543.

216. Jeremy J. Wynne, *Wrath among the Perfections of God's Life* (London: Continuum, 2010), 13.

217. *CD* IV/1, p. 173; *KD*, p. 189.

218. As we saw above, we could include a more extended list here, such as wisdom, power, goodness, truth, and so on.

219. *Inst.* 1.14.4, p. 120; *CO* 2:120. Cf. *Comm. Ps.* 145:4; *CO* 32:413.

220. Cf. *Comm. Ez.* 1:25–26; *CO* 40:58.

221. van der Kooi, *As in a Mirror*, 120.

222. *Comm. Ps.* 145:8; *CO* 32:414.

223. *Comm. John* 17:26; *CO* 47:390–391.

224. *Harmony of the Gospels*, Matt. 6:9; *CO* 45:195. Cf. *Comm. 2 Tim.* 3:16; *CO* 52:332.

225. *Comm. Ps.* 77:12; *CO* 31:717.

226. Selderhuis, *Calvin's Theology of the Psalms*, 56.

227. *Inst.* 1.10.2, pp. 97–98; *CO* 2:73.

228. *Comm. Is.* 49:8; *CO* 37:198.

229. *1538 Catechism*, p. 9, s. 3; *CO* 5:325.

230. Hesselink, *Calvin's First Catechism*, 52.

231. *Comm. Ps.* 145:7; *CO* 32:414. My translation. Cf. *Comm. John* 1:14, 47:15. Cf. *Comm. Heb.* 1:3; *CO* 55:12.

232. *Inst.* 4.17.32, p. 1403; *CO* 2:1032.

233. *Comm. Is.* 6:7; *CO* 36:133.

234. *Comm. Is.* 6:7; *CO* 36:133. Calvin then says that unbelievers can also receive the sign, but because they lack faith, "they have no experience of the truth," and therefore they do not "partake of Christ." Faith, experience, and the knowledge of God are bound together.

235. See "Human Access to the Knowledge of God" above.

236. van der Kooi, *As in a Mirror*, 107. Cf. *Inst.* 3.2.24, pp. 570–71; *CO* 2:418. Cf. *Harmony of the Gospels*, Matt. 11:27; *CO* 45:320.

237. *Inst.* 3.2.7; *CO* 2:403. Cf. *Inst.* 3.2.16; *CO* 2:411.

238. *Inst.* 3.2.29, p. 575; *CO* 2:421.

239. As Calvin says, "Now, the knowledge [of God's mercy, judgment and justice] mentioned here produces two fruits, even faith and fear" (*Comm. Jer.* 9:23–24; *CO* 38:52). Cf. Calvin, "Catechism of the Church of Geneva, 1545," Q6. *CO* 6:10. Cf. Dowey, *Knowledge of God*, 26.

240. Cf. *Comm. Is.* 6:1; *CO* 36:126. Cf. *Comm. 1 John* 3:2; *CO* 55:331. Cf. *Inst.* 1.2.2, p. 41; *CO* 2:35.

241. *Comm. Ps.* 25:6; *CO* 31:253.

242. *Comm. Ps.* 25:6; *CO* 31:253. Cf. *Inst.* 3.4.34, p. 663; *CO* 2:426.

243. *Comm. Jonah* 4:2; *CO* 43:265–266. Cf. Huijgen, *Accommodation*, 286.

244. Michael Horton, "Knowing God: Calvin's Understanding of Revelation," in *John Calvin and Evangelical Theology: Legacy and Prospect*, ed. Sung Wook Chung (Colorado Springs, CO: Paternoster, 2009), 4.

245. Helm also links God's essence and nature, saying, "God's activities . . . partly reveal his nature and are, so to speak, endorsed or guaranteed by his immutable essence" (*Calvin's Ideas*, 12). However, he does so using a speculative methodology that claims more knowledge of God's essence than Calvin would espouse. He also seeks to affirm God's freedom in a manner that aligns with a teaching of the *potentia*

absoluta of God, something that Calvin vehemently opposed (*Inst.* 3.23.2, p. 950; *CO* 2:700. Cf. David C. Steinmetz, *Calvin in Context* [Oxford: Oxford University Press, 1995], 40–50. Cf. "God Is Just, Therefore God's Will Is Just" in chapter 4).

246. Stephen R. Holmes, "Calvin on Scripture," in *Calvin, Barth, and Reformed Theology*, ed. Neil B. MacDonald and Carl Trueman (Colorado Springs, CO: Paternoster, 2008), 158–59.

247. Parker, *Knowledge of God*, 54. Cf. Huijgen, *Accommodation*, 285.

248. van der Kooi, *As in a Mirror*, 126.

Chapter Three

God's Disposition toward Humanity in Predestination

Calvin begins his four chapters set apart to describe the doctrine of predestination at the end of Book 3 of the 1559 *Institutes* with these words,

> A baffling question this seems to many. For they think nothing more inconsistent than that out of the common multitude of men some should be predestined to salvation, others to destruction. But how mistakenly they entangle themselves will become clear in the following discussion. Besides, in the very darkness that frightens them not only is the usefulness [*utilitas*] of this doctrine made known but also its very sweet fruit. We shall never be clearly persuaded, as we ought to be, that our salvation flows from the wellspring of God's free mercy [*ex fonte gratuitate misericordieae Dei*] until we come to know his eternal election, which illumines God's grace by this contrast [*comparatione*]: that he does not indiscriminately adopt all into the hope of salvation but gives [*dat*] to some what he denies [*negat*] to others.[1]

A few years later, in his final lectures before his death, Calvin made this statement regarding Ezekiel 18:23:

> If any one again objects – this is making God act with duplicity, the answer is ready, that God always wishes the same thing [*semper idem velle*], though by different ways, and in a manner inscrutable to us. Although, therefore, God's will is simple [*simplex est Dei voluntas*], yet great variety is involved in it, as far as our senses are concerned.[2]

Calvin's doctrine of predestination[3] has long been identified as a central element of Calvin's theological project.[4] As Cornelis van der Kooi writes, "If ever a doctrine has become notorious, if ever a person has become identified with and vilified for a doctrine, if a movement named for that person has ever become isolated through a doctrine, then that has been Calvin and his doctrine of predestination."[5] Although recent scholarship has rightly moved away from identifying predestination, or any single doctrine, as the central doctrine of Calvin's theological project,[6] predestination is still a key concept for Calvin's understanding of God's relation with humanity, and, on a popular level, predestination is often considered synonymous with the (sometimes derogatory) term "Calvinist."[7] In his time, Calvin was aware of the controversial nature of predestination. During his leadership of the church in Geneva, his doctrine of predestination received resistance from within Geneva and from neighboring Reformed communities. Albert Pighius, Jerome Bolsec, and Georgius of Sicily were a few outspoken opponents of the doctrine, in response to whom Calvin wrote his *Concerning the Eternal Predestination of God*, published less than a year after the Genevan City Council ruled in Calvin's favor against Bolsec's challenges.[8] In Calvin's attempts to unify the early Reformed churches, predestination also proved to be a point of disagreement between him and the key Swiss leader Heinrich Bullinger, who primarily espoused the teaching of single predestination.[9]

Although we shall expand further below, for Calvin, predestination is God's gracious work that is made known in Scripture that aligns with human experience and stands in continuity with the traditional teaching of the church. Calvin most commonly draws upon Augustine for support. As Christian Link asserts, Calvin's doctrine of predestination was not new, but had all of the same primary features as Luther's and Augustine's (and possibly Paul's) doctrines of election.[10] At the heart of Calvin's teaching on predestination is the certainty and gratuity of salvation in Christ for those with faith (the elect).[11] However, the bare facts of predestination can be summed up relatively simply, "before men are born their lot is assigned to each of them by the secret will of God."[12] The triune God as active subject chooses some people from before time to rescue from their state of sin and others to leave in the just deserts of their sinfulness.[13]

The question that faces us is what this doctrine of predestination reveals regarding God's disposition toward humanity. It would be easy to provide proof-texts from Calvin's writings to support either a one-disposition or a two-disposition hypothesis. An often quoted two-disposition proof-text drawn from the *Institutes* is:

> "We call predestination God's eternal decree [*aeternum Dei decretum*], by which [God] compacted with himself [*apud se*] what he willed to become of each man. For all are not created [*creantur*] in equal condition; rather, eternal life is foreordained for some, eternal damnation for others. Therefore, as any man has been created [*conditus est*] to one or the other of these ends [*finem*], we speak of him as predestined to life or to death."[14]

On the other hand, one could choose an example like Calvin's commentary on John 3:16: "Christ brought life because the Heavenly Father loves the human race [*genus humanum*], and wishes that they should not perish [*perire nolit*]."[15] As another example, Calvin comments on Is. 42:6, "He calls all men to himself, without a single exception, and gives [*destinat*] Christ to all, that we may be illuminated by him."[16] However, because of Calvin's commitment to exegete the diverse texts of Scripture, no single quote will settle the matter.[17]

Instead of carefully selecting proof texts to support a one-disposition or two-disposition hypothesis regarding God's stance toward humanity, we shall seek to understand Calvin's doctrine of predestination across the breadth of his theological project, acknowledging the various ways he (and the Bible) discusses the doctrine.[18] In the end, we shall see that in Calvin's account of predestination, God's one, secret, and righteous will is accommodated to the elect in a twofold but asymmetrical way: (1) God's revealed electing will that corresponds directly with God's nature and displays God's one disclosed disposition toward humanity; (2) God's veiled, reprobating will that is inscrutably enacted in a manner that only corresponds with God's nature in part. To show this, we begin by briefly defining key terms. Then we describe the content and results of God's revealed electing will and corresponding one disclosed disposition before recounting what Calvin teaches regarding God's veiled reprobating will. We then explore the relationship between the two parts of God's one, but asymmetrically related, twofold will that is only known by faith prior to finally exploring a few critical questions regarding Calvin's doctrine of predestination in light of our findings.

To reiterate, our primary goal in this chapter is to explicate Calvin's doctrine of predestination. Questions of logical consistency which could arise from his exposition are for the most part held for the questions at the close of this chapter or held to be addressed in chapter 8. We want to let Calvin's doctrine be clearly seen in toto before critically reflecting upon it.

KEY DEFINITIONS

To begin our examination of God's disposition toward humanity in Calvin's doctrine of predestination, we must define what we mean by God's revealed electing will and God's veiled reprobating will. In chapter 1, we defined *disposition* as God's attitude, inclination, or orientation toward humanity.[19] We distinguish that from God's *will* which refers to God's purpose or intent that always leads to action; God wills what he does.[20]

For Calvin, because God dwells in unapproachable light, his secret will is not something that can be scrutinized by limited humans,[21] but because God has revealed his nature and God always acts according to his nature, believers can by faith be confident that God's one, simple will[22] corresponds with God's righteous nature, even if they are not able to fully discern how it does so.[23] This one righteous will can be known in part as God reveals it.

Calvin's comments on 2 Pet. 3:9 illustrate the relation between God's disposition, revealed will, and veiled will. There, Calvin asks that if God wills that all should come to repentance, why are all not saved? He answers, "No mention is here made of the hidden purpose of God [*arcano Dei consilio*], according to which the reprobate are doomed to their own ruin, but only of his will as made known to us in the gospel [*de voluntate quae nobis in evangelio patefit*]. For God there stretches forth his hand without a difference to all, but lays hold only of those, to lead them to himself, whom he has chosen before the foundation of the world."[24]

All three of our key terms are illustrated here. God's disclosed disposition toward humanity is demonstrated in the call to preach the gospel to all people (sometimes called God's preceptive will). God's election of those whom God chose before the foundation of the world is God's *revealed electing will*. Those with faith in Christ can know both God's disclosed disposition and God's electing will. For example, "We must begin with what is revealed in Christ concerning the love of the Father for us and what Christ Himself daily preaches [*praedicet*] to us through the Gospel."[25] The third category is the way that the reprobate are "doomed to their own ruin" according to the "hidden purpose of God." For Calvin, the only humanly known reason for God's reprobating will is God's secret plan.[26] This hidden purpose (or secret counsel) is God's *veiled reprobating will* in our project. We use "veiled" instead of "hidden" because, although much about God's reprobating will is hidden, as we shall see below, it is still partially disclosed in Scripture and experience, as through a veil.

Now that the terms and basic definitions are in place, we shall begin our closer study of God's disposition toward humanity as expressed in Calvin's doctrine of predestination by briefly describing God's revealed electing will.

GOD'S REVEALED, ELECTING WILL: UNMERITED GRACE EXTENDED TO ALL AND RECEIVED BY THE ELECT

For though God invites all people indiscriminately [*totum populum promiscue*] to himself, yet he does not inwardly draw [*trahit*] any but those whom he knows to be his people, and whom he has given to his Son, and of whom also he will be the faithful keeper to the end.[27]

Introducing his commentary on the letter to the Ephesians, Calvin provides a glimpse into God's revealed electing will. Calvin there says that Paul begins the letter by discussing election, which allows Paul to state,

> that [the Ephesians] were now called into the kingdom of God, because they had been appointed to life before they were born. And here occurs a striking display of God's wonderful mercy [*admirabilis Dei misericordia*], when the salvation of men is traced to its true and native source [*vero et nativo fonte*], the free act of adoption. But as the minds of men are ill fitted to receive so sublime a mystery [*sublime arcanum*], he betakes himself to prayer, that God would enlighten the Ephesians in the full knowledge of Christ [*plenam Christi cognitionem*].[28]

In short, God's revealed electing will is expressed in the gospel of unmerited grace that is extended to all and received by the elect.

The Gospel: Sola Gratia

First, God's revealed electing will is made known in God's unmerited favor extended in the gospel. For Calvin, election is inseparable from the Reformation refrain of *sola gratia* because it roots salvation solely in God's grace as witnessed to in Scripture. Therefore Calvin can say, "We shall never be clearly persuaded, as we ought to be, that our salvation flows from the wellspring of God's free mercy until we come to know his eternal election."[29] If any part of election found its source in humanity, salvation would no longer be a work of grace. As Trueman summarizes, "Election is part and parcel of the Protestant polemic against any notion of merit in the Christian life."[30]

Calvin highlights the unmerited nature of salvation by founding election on the eternal good pleasure of God alone. Calvin says in his sermon on Eph. 1:4–6, "No other cause makes us God's children but only his choice of us in himself [*choisis a soy*]."[31] Calvin similarly says of our salvation that Paul "openly ascribes the whole cause [*causam totam*] to the election of God, and that gratuitous, and in no way depending on men; so that in the salvation of the godly nothing higher must be sought than the goodness of God [*Dei bonitate*]."[32] Calvin's ultimate example of the unmerited nature of election is the election of Jesus Christ's undeserving humanity into the hypostatic union in the Mediator.[33] Even responding to the call of God is not based on human work: "All who are taught by God are effectually drawn [*efficaciter trahi*] so as to come."[34] By rooting election only in God's will and purpose, Calvin affirms God's freedom in the gift of grace; nothing outside of God compels God to bestow grace. Calvin says, "For to say that 'God purposed in himself' means the same thing as to say that he considered nothing outside himself with which to be concerned in making his decree. . . . Surely the grace of

God deserves alone to be proclaimed in our election only if it is freely given [*gratuita sit*]."[35]

Along the same lines, Calvin repeatedly and vehemently rules out the possibility of God's electing on the basis of foreknowledge of future human merit or the possibility of God's planting a seed of election resulting in good works that would merit salvation.[36] The complete sinfulness of humanity precludes God's foreknowledge of any merit.[37] Thus, Calvin says that it is "impossible that God should foresee [*praevideat*] anything in man that was not worthy of destruction, until He should Himself have created him anew by His Spirit."[38] In sum, for Calvin, God's revealed electing will toward humanity is *sola gratia*, founded upon, fulfilled by, and witnessing to the unmerited grace of God.

The Call to All, Faith as Gift to Some

To whom does God extend his disclosed disposition, only to the elect or to all humanity? Here we see a paradox in which Calvin asserts that God's disclosed disposition is extended to all humanity via the call of the gospel but only received by the elect through faith, which is a gift from God according to his electing will.

First of all, God's loving desire to be reconciled to men and women is communicated to all people indiscriminately through the gracious call of the gospel. For example, Calvin expounds the words of Ezek. 18:23 that God desires all to come to life: "God wills not the death of a sinner, because he [hurriedly] meets [*occurrit*] him of his own accord, and is not only prepared to receive all who fly to his pity, but he calls them towards him with a loud voice [*alta voce*], when he sees how they are alienated from all hope of safety [*salutis*]." He goes on to explain, "We hold, then, that God wills not the death of a sinner [*nolle mortem peccatoris*], since he calls all equally to repentance, and promises himself prepared to receive them if they only seriously repent [*serio resipiscant*]."[39]

God calls all in a manner that reveals that he is ready to accept any who would come to their senses (*resipiscere*) by receiving his gift of grace. This corresponds with Calvin's typical approach to passages that seem to indicate that God desires the salvation of *all people*, as seen in his words from his commentary on 2 Pet. 3:9: "So wonderful is his love towards mankind, that he would have them all to be saved. . . . God is ready to receive all to repentance, so that none may perish."[40] He speaks similarly in his commentary on 1 Tim. 2:4[41] and in his comments on Ezek. 33:11 and 1 Tim. 2:4 in the *Institutes*.[42] Calvin is concerned with the pastoral implications of God's disclosed disposition, namely that all who look to Christ by faith would not doubt God's love for them. Along those same lines, when commenting on John 3:16, Calvin says, "For men are not easily convinced that God loves them; and so, to remove all doubt, He has expressly stated that we are so very dear to God, that on our account, he did not spare [*ne pepercerit*] even His only begotten Son."[43]

Here we also begin to see Calvin's two levels of love and election, the general and special. For Calvin, the story of Israel's election is a microcosm of the election to faith.[44] Abraham and his children were generally elected as a nation to be God's people, but within Israel, God especially elected some individuals, as in the case of God's choice of Jacob over Esau.[45] After Christ's coming, God's general election is observed in the preaching of the gospel to all people, while his special election comes to pass in those uniquely given the gift of faith by the inward call of the Spirit.[46] God's mercy is displayed in general election (God's disclosed disposition), but it is made even more clear in special election (God's revealed electing will).[47]

These two levels of election and love provide the categories for Calvin to distinguish between the universal offer of the gospel to repent and the particular gift of faith and repentance given the elect. Calvin says, "Experience teaches [*experientia . . . docet*] that God wills the repentance of those whom he invites to himself, in such a way that he does not touch the hearts of all."[48] Similarly, in his comments on John 3:16, Calvin says that God "shows He is favorable to the whole world when He calls all without exception to the faith of Christ, which is indeed an entry into life." However, God only makes the calling effective for some.[49] This calling is made effective by the enabling of the Spirit so believers know "that faith does not depend on the will of men, but that it is God who gives it."[50]

To summarize, for Calvin God's graceful, disclosed disposition toward all people is brought to fruition in the elect by the power of the Spirit according to God's revealed electing will. God's desire to rescue humans from sin in love ought to be communicated to all through the preaching of the gospel because God loves all generally and is ready to receive any who would repent and trust him. However, highlighting the sinful state of humanity, Calvin is also clear that repentance and faith are unmerited gifts given by the Spirit to those whom God has chosen from before time to be adopted as God's children in Christ.

We are left with a question: Is God's disclosed disposition one of unmerited love toward all humanity or only to the elect? For Calvin it is both, on different levels. As Muller states, "Calvin was one of the many Reformation-era inheritors of an Augustinian exegetical tradition within which those biblical passages that refer to an offer of salvation to the whole world or declare the saving power of Christ's death to all people are understood as coherent with the divine intention to save only the elect."[51]

Here it is helpful to recall Calvin's doctrine of God; Calvin is supremely confident of God's merciful, just, and judging nature as loving Father while also recognizing that human creatures cannot know God comprehensively. Thus, Calvin is content to place his confidence in God's merciful nature expressed in the legitimate offer of salvation to all people while also trusting the righteousness of God's secret counsel in his nonuniversal application of that offer of salvation. Therefore, Calvin does not speculate about God's attitude toward others but follows his own advice that "they are madmen who seek their own or others' salvation in the labyrinth [*labyrintho*] of predestination."[52] Only the gift of God's call according to God's revealed electing will can a posteriori show forth one's election. As a result, the elect embrace God's unmerited love for them and obey God's call to preach the good news of that love to all people according to God's disclosed disposition, confident that God is ready to receive any who respond in faith.[53]

With that in mind, we now note a few of the key results of God's revealed electing will toward humanity for Calvin. Although the primary result of God's revealed electing will is the adoption of individuals as sons and daughters of God by faith, this adoption includes other necessary fruit, most importantly the assurance of salvation for the believer and the believer's humble ascription of glory to God.[54] Assurance comes primarily through an awareness of Christ and his work, but it is also bolstered by the knowledge of election that reminds believers that their salvation (and their faith) is rooted in God's power and grace.[55]

In addition, God's revealed electing will results in God's glory and the believer's humility.[56] Calvin speaks of God's glory as both the revelation of his nature and the resulting, rightful praise ascribed to God.[57] In both respects, Calvin can call God's glory the "final cause" (*causa finalis*) of election.[58] As the sole originator and executor of election, God is made known and praised for his work of election. God's unmerited election also leads to proper humility as it illuminates the reality that everything good in a believer, including salvation, is from God.[59]

In sum, for Calvin, as God offers unmerited grace to all people (according to his disclosed disposition), God's revealed electing will toward humanity is exhibited as he enables a response of faith and repentance in the elect that results in assurance of adoption and humble worship of God. This revealed will corresponds directly with God's revealed nature and God's disclosed disposition and is thus known by those with faith.

Having examined God's revealed electing will, we now turn to examine the other element of God's one, righteous will, namely the veiled reprobating will of God.

GOD'S VEILED REPROBATING WILL

Recalling Calvin's comments on 2 Pet. 3:9, we now come to the portion of our study in which we shall examine the "hidden purpose of God, according to which the reprobate are doomed to their own ruin."[60] Calvin treats God's reprobating will in a variety of ways, sometimes presenting it as seemingly parallel to God's electing will (as in his introductory statements to the predestination section of the *Institutes* seen above) and other times giving it little to no attention (as in his commentary and sermons on Ephesians 1).[61] However, in an examination of texts across Calvin's project, we find that he teaches that God's veiled reprobating will is God's decision from before time according to God's secret counsel to create those whom he would leave in their sinful state to be condemned. Reprobation is caused both by God's sovereign rule over all contingent occurrences and by human rebellion against God. Calvin's key reasons for holding the doctrine of God's veiled reprobating will are the witness of Scripture, the testimony of human experience, Calvin's understanding of God's freedom, and the coherence of Calvin's broader theological project. We shall address these in turn.

The Causes of Reprobation

God's veiled reprobating will is expressed in God's decision, as determined by his secret counsel, to create those whom he would leave in their sinful state to be condemned. Calvin describes the doctrine from two different angles, either emphasizing God or human sin as the cause of reprobation.[62]

In one sense, God, as ruler of the universe, is the ultimate cause of reprobation according to his secret plan. In line with Calvin's commitment (like Augustine's) that God causes all that comes to pass,[63] Calvin links God's reprobating will with his providence, saying, "Since the disposition of all things is in God's hand, since the decision of salvation or of death rests in his power, he so ordains by his plan and will that among men some are born destined [*devoti*] for certain death from the womb, who might glorify [*glorificent*] his name by their own destruction [*suo exitio*]."[64] Calling upon Augustine, Calvin also says, "They were created [*esse . . . creatos*] by the Lord, those whom he unquestionably foreknew [*praesciebat*] would go to destruction. This has happened because he has so willed it. But why he so willed it is not for our reason to inquire, for we cannot comprehend it."[65] Calvin repeatedly asserts that there is no reason for reprobation beyond God's will (counsel, secret plan, good pleasure, etc.). For example, the only reason God chooses some and passes by others "from the foundation of the world" is "His own sheer pleasure" (*mero suo beneplacito*).[66]

In the other sense, human sin is the cause of reprobation. For Calvin, the universal and unforgivable sin of the reprobate is the denial of the gospel.[67] Since all humanity is "vitiated by sin" and "odious to God," they are thus "subject to the judgment of death" in themselves.[68] Calvin says, "For the proper and genuine [*propria genuinaque*] cause of sin is not God's hidden counsel but the evident will of man [*hominis voluntas*]."[69] In *De Aeterna*, remarking that God hates nothing that he has made except for the "degenerate nature" (*degenerem naturam*) of humanity, Calvin asserts,

> For though God for secret reasons had decreed before the defection of Adam what He would do, yet we read in Scripture that nothing is condemned by Him except sin. It remains that God had just causes [iustas . . . causas] for reprobating part of mankind, though they are hidden from us; but he hates and condemns nothing in man except what is alien to His justice [a iustitia sua alienum].[70]

While recognizing the apparent tension between them, Calvin affirms two causes of God's reprobating will. Reprobation is both God's inscrutable will from eternity and the direct result of human sin. In short, God creates some for destruction by leaving them in their state of sin and just condemnation.

Calvin's Reasons for the Doctrine

Having examined the causes of reprobation, we now turn to briefly overview Calvin's key reasons for holding the doctrine as such, particularly Scripture, experience, God's freedom and glory, and doctrinal cohesiveness. Although space does not allow extensive elaboration, an overview of Calvin's reasoning for the doctrine of reprobation enhances our understanding of why Calvin considers God's veiled reprobating will as necessary to his doctrine of predestination.[71]

Scripture's Witness

Faithful to his primary goal to be a faithful exegete of Scripture,[72] Calvin draws chiefly and extensively on Scripture to develop the doctrine of God's reprobating will. In his comments on Romans 9, Calvin highlights his intended Scriptural, nonspeculative theological methodology. After noting the human tendency to curiously enter into the dangerous "labyrinth" of predestination, Calvin wonders if the godly should altogether avoid considering predestination; he replies, "By no means [*minime*]: for as the Holy Spirit has taught us nothing but what it behooves us to know, the knowledge of this would no doubt be useful [*utilis*], provided it confined itself [*se confinebit*] to the word of God. Let this then be our sacred rule, to seek to know nothing concerning it, except what Scripture teaches us [*scriptura docet*]."[73]

Although Calvin's primary text for explicating predestination, and especially reprobation, is Romans 9–11,[74] Calvin sees the doctrine taught or implied throughout Scripture. Besides Romans 9–11, in the *Institutes* and in *De Aeterna* Calvin utilizes many other key passages, including Eph. 1:3–11, Rom. 8:28–30, Mal. 1:2–6, John 6:37 and 44, Is. 6:9, and John 17.[75] Calvin also does not limit his discussion of predestination to texts that explicitly discuss it.[76] Although it is outside our task here to examine Calvin's exegesis of these passages, his exegetical decisions are readily available in his commentaries and, to a lesser extent, in *De Aeterna* and the *Institutes*.

In short, because he sees reprobation as included in Scripture, Calvin teaches it, but he also believes that people must not elaborate beyond Scripture's clear witness in their teaching of God's reprobating will.[77]

Experience and Observation

Although Calvin perceives his explication of God's reprobating will as primarily arising from Scripture, Calvin's experience also confirms and influences his pastorally minded doctrine, in accordance with his humanist approach.[78] Calvin begins his section regarding predestination in the *Institutes* with an appeal to his observation of the generous preaching and scanty reception of the gospel.[79] Also in the *Institutes*, Calvin says, "We teach nothing not borne out by experience [*usu compertum*]: that God has always been free [*liberum*] to bestow his grace on whom he wills."[80] For Calvin, experience confirms what Scripture teaches, namely that some are chosen to eternal life and others are not.

Experience also influences Calvin's understanding of the specifics of God's reprobating will. In particular, Calvin appeals to his experience of preaching the gospel in which only twenty out of one hundred listeners would respond in faith as evidence that the number of the reprobate is clearly greater than the number of elect.[81] Similarly, Calvin observes that God apparently does not desire the salvation of the majority of the world because God allowed the Gentiles of the world to perish for thousands of years before Christ came to offer salvation to them.[82]

Calvin also appeals to God's predestination to provide pastoral support by helping his readers interpret their experience. For example, Calvin observes that although most of the world does not have faith in Christ, believers need not be nervous about or abandon their salvation, because God has only chosen a few out of the world as his.[83] Seeking to encourage pastors who are disappointed by the response to their preaching, Calvin explains that "Christ means that it is not astonishing [*nihil esse mirum*] if only a few obey His Gospel, because all whom the Spirit of God does not subdue to the obedience of faith are fierce and untamable beasts."[84] In this way, the doctrine of God's veiled reprobating will provides comfort for the elect in their life experience. In sum, experience influences and is confirmed by Calvin's teaching on reprobation.

God's Freedom and Glory

Calvin's commitment to (his specific definition of) God's freedom also supports his doctrine of God's electing and reprobating wills and accentuates the unmerited nature of election. For Calvin, God's freedom is manifest in the fact that God is not bound to offer grace to all people or reject all people but is able to offer grace to whomever he chooses.[85] Thus, "God has already shown that in his mere generosity [in the general election of Israel] he has not been bound by any laws but is free [*liberum esse*], so that equal apportionment of grace [*aequalis gratiae partitio*] is not to be required of him. The very inequality of this grace proves that it is free [*gratuitam*]."[86] For Calvin, God's freedom is here demonstrated in his only electing a portion of humanity.[87] God's freedom also highlights the merciful nature of election because the basis for choosing lies only in God's free, merciful choice and not in any human merit.[88]

For Calvin, even though "God's chief praise consists in acts of mercy,"[89] God is also glorified as his nature is made known through his reprobating work.[90] Specifically, God's reprobating work brings him glory by revealing his judgment of evil and by highlighting the contrast between the condemnation the elect deserve and the grace they receive, thus illuminating the grace of God and evoking worship and gratitude from the elect.[91]

Therefore, for Calvin, God's freedom is exercised and glory displayed in his election of some and reprobation of others.

Doctrinal Cohesiveness

Finally, let us briefly examine the way that the doctrine of God's veiled, reprobating will fits with the logic of Calvin's broader theological project. Specifically, four of Calvin's major doctrines are interdependent upon reprobation. These teachings are: (1) humanity is utterly sinful; (2) as a result of sin, humans have absolutely no merit to contribute to their salvation; (3) God actively and providentially reigns over every occurrence in the universe; and (4) not all people attain salvation.[92] Together, these elements mean that salvation, and consequently reprobation, can only be directly caused by God. If any one of these doctrinal commitments were abandoned, reprobation would not necessarily fit into the doctrinal system, but as it stands, reprobation (and election) is logically necessary alongside Calvin's other doctrinal commitments.[93]

Calvin's doctrine of God's veiled, reprobating will is to create some people whom God would allow to receive the consequences of their sin. This reprobating will is actual but epistemologically disconnected from the knowledge of God and his nature revealed in Christ, and therefore most of the divine reasons for reprobation are hidden in God's secret counsel. For Calvin, the doctrine is based on the witness of Scripture and experience, is an expression of God's freedom, results in God's glory as it reveals God's nature, and is essential for the coherence of Calvin's theological project.

THE UNITY OF GOD'S TWOFOLD ELECTING AND REPROBATING WILL

Having discussed God's revealed electing will and God's veiled reprobating will separately, we now examine how Calvin perceives these seemingly contradictory elements as unified in God's one, secret will. In Calvin's final series of lectures before his death, he describes from the book of Ezekiel the twofold picture of God's will for humanity as God's accommodation to human understanding, not an indicator of a bipolar will within God.[94] Indeed, in his Gospels commentary, Calvin says, "If it be objected, that it is absurd to suppose the existence of two wills in God [*duplicem in Deo voluntatem*], I reply, we fully believe that his will is one and simple [*unicam et simplicem*]; but as our minds do not fathom the deep abyss of secret election, on behalf of our weakness [*pro infirmatatis nostrae*], the will of God is exhibited [*proponi*] to us in two little measures [*modulo bifarium*]."[95] In short, God has one secret will that is accommodated as two wills to limited humans: God's revealed electing will that is made efficacious in the elect (as God's love is extended to all people according to God's disclosed disposition) and God's veiled reprobating will toward the reprobate.

For Calvin, to discuss God's one secret will is to press the boundaries of human understanding: "Although to our perception God's will is manifold, he does not will this and that in himself, but according to his diversely manifold wisdom, as Paul calls it [Eph. 3:10], he strikes dumb our senses until it is given to us to recognize how wonderfully he wills [*velle*] what at the moment seems to be against his will [*voluntati*]."[96] As we approach this question about the unity between the revealed and veiled elements of God's will, we approach a topic that, according to Calvin, we are not able to understand fully.

We shall first describe what can and cannot be known about God's one secret will before specifically examining the asymmetrical relationship between God's revealed electing will and God's veiled reprobating will.

An Article of Faith: Creaturely Knowledge of God's One Will

In his explicit teaching on predestination, Calvin acknowledges its mysterious character through his repeated return to Rom. 9:20, "Who are you O man to contend with God?" and Rom. 11:33, "O the depth of the riches and wisdom and knowledge of God! How unsearchable are his judgments and how inscrutable his ways."[97] In the midst of this mystery, a few important truths are revealed through Scripture and God's works, namely that creatures have no ability or authority to judge God, that God's secret will is known only to God, and that God's secret will is righteous because God is righteous.

Creatures Cannot Judge God's Secret Will

For Calvin, sinful and limited creatures have no ability or authority to judge God their Creator but must humbly submit before God's secret will. As we have already discussed, Calvin sees humanity as utterly defiled by sin in such a way that it cannot rightly perceive or interpret God's works apart from Scripture by the Spirit. Calvin thus encourages his readers to worship and adore instead of question God in light of God's secret plan: "Let us with sobriety and modesty learn to look upon those works of God which are unknown [*incognita sunt*] to us, and to concede [*deferre*] to him the praise of supreme wisdom [*perfectae sapientae*], although his counsels seem at first sight contradictory [*absurda*]."[98] Calvin concludes his discussion of predestination in *De Aeterna* by returning to this theme and condemning any who would put themselves in the place of God to judge the doctrine of predestination as it has been revealed in Scripture.[99] Therefore, regardless of the disagreeable or apparently contradictory nature of God's predestinating will, Calvin teaches that sinful and limited humans have no right or ability to judge God.

Similarly, Calvin teaches that although much of God's will has been made known in Scripture, the whole of God's will ultimately extends beyond human comprehension. Commenting on Rom. 11:34, Calvin counsels, "We must bear in mind the distinction, which I have before mentioned, between the secret counsel of God [*arcanum Dei consilium*], and his will [*voluntatem*] made known in Scripture."[100] He proceeds to explain that access to the riches of the Scriptures is opened by the Spirit to those with faith, "but the case is different with regard to his hidden counsel [*arcana consilii*], the depth and height of which cannot by any investigation be reached."[101] Calvin uses a variety of terms to describe God's hidden will, including God's "secret counsel"[102] or "secret plan"[103] (*arcano Dei consilio*), "secret good pleasure" (*arcano suo beneplacito*),[104] "secret will" (*arcano Dei arbitrio*),[105] and "secret inscrutable plan" (*arcano et inscrutabili Dei consilio*).[106] Thus, there is no space for human inquiry beyond God's one will. For example, when someone "asks why God has so done, we must reply: because he has willed it. But if you proceed further to ask why he so willed, you are seeking something greater and higher than God's will, which cannot be found."[107]

Richard Muller highlights Moïse Amyraut as an example of someone who claims more knowledge of God's will than Calvin allows. Amyraut proposes two wills in God, namely one hypothetical, universal, and conditional will alongside one effective, absolute, and unconditional will. After examining Amyraut's exegesis of Ezek. 18:23 and his use of Calvin's exegesis of the passage, Muller concludes that Amyraut misinterprets Calvin.[108] Muller asserts that for Calvin the distinction between the extent of preaching (to all) and the extent of salvation (not to all) shows the difference between God's will *ad intra* and the revelation of that will *ad extra* without implying two wills *ad intra*.[109] Calvin, consistent in his antispeculative methodology, does not think humans have adequate epistemological access to God's will *ad intra*. Instead, believers can know what God has revealed to them of his will *ad extra* and are called to trust that it somehow corresponds to God's will *ad intra*.[110] This aligns with our claims regarding God's disclosed disposition and revealed electing will made known *ad extra* and our understanding of God's one, secret will and the veiled reprobating element of that will.

In sum, God has substantially revealed his will to those with faith, particularly revealing his will of salvation toward the elect in Christ. However, God's veiled will is only partially revealed, and the unity of these two wills is known to God but is an object of faith for believers.[111] For Calvin, predestination is "a mystery which our minds do not comprehend, but which we ought to adore with reverence. . . . Let us know, therefore, that God refrains from speaking to us [to explain predestination further] for no other reason than that He sees that His boundless wisdom cannot be comprehended in our small measure [*modulo*]."[112] As much as God has revealed regarding predestination, the explanation of the totality of God's acts is hidden in his secret will. For the elect to attempt arrogantly to look into such things "is the surest way to ruin themselves and to break their necks [*se rompre le col*]."[113]

God Is Just, so God's Will Is Just

Although much cannot be said about God's one secret will, we can confidently affirm that God's inscrutable plan is just and righteous (*iustus*) because God is just and righteous.[114] As Calvin says, "Not only is God's wisdom incomprehensible, but his justice [*iustitia*] is the most perfect [*perfectissima*] rule of all justice [*iustitiae*]."[115] Remarking on Rom. 9:22, Calvin asserts, "As far as God's predestination manifests itself, it appears perfectly just [*meram iustitiam apparere*]." Therefore, Paul does not explain why some objects are made for wrath because "he indeed takes it as granted . . . that the reason is hid in the secret and inexplorable counsel of God [*inexplicabili Dei consilio absconditum*]; whose justice it behoves us rather to adore than to scrutinize [*scrutari*]."[116] Recalling that God's will is the ultimate cause of all things, Calvin remarks, "For God's will is so much the highest rule of righteousness [*summa est iustitiae regula*] that whatever he wills, by the very fact that he wills it, must be considered righteous."[117] Similarly, anyone who questions God's good pleasure as the reason for God's predestinating works "cannot allow God to reign in pure liberty so that what is pleasing to him might be received as good, just and rightful [*iuste*] without contradiction [*sans contredit*]."[118]

From these statements, one could deduce that for Calvin, God is a law to himself that transcends or redefines the human understanding of righteousness. However, Calvin clearly and repeatedly opposes the concept of a God wielding a *potentia absoluta* who could act in contradiction to his own law and nature.[119] In short, Calvin summarizes, "God's goodness is so connected with his divinity [*divinitate*] that it is no more necessary for him to be God than for him to be good [*bonum*]."[120] Calvin elsewhere explains, "We do not advocate the fiction of 'absolute might' [*absolutae potentiae*]; because this is profane, it ought rightly to be hateful to us. We fancy no lawless god who is a law unto himself . . . the will of God is not only free of all fault but is the highest rule of perfection [*summa perfectionis regula*], and even the law of all laws."[121] That God is not redefining righteousness in a manner that contradicts his law is even more clearly demonstrated in Calvin's words from *De Aeterna*, where he writes that God lives according to the law (even if we cannot see it at times) because he is the law embodied:

> Let these monstrous speculations be put far away from pious minds, that God should be able to do more than is proper to Him or to act without rule or reason [*modo et ratione*]. Nor indeed do I accept the suggestion that, because God in doing anything is free from all law, He therefore is without censure. For to make God beyond law [*exlegem*] is to rob Him of the greatest part of his glory, for it destroys His rectitude [*rectitudinem*] and His righteousness [*iustitiam*]. Not that God is subject to law, except in so far as He himself is law [*lex est*].[122]

In his *Congregation on Eternal Election* preached in response to the controversy caused by Bolsec, Calvin says that we limited humans are incapable of understanding God's reasons for doing what he does; to try would overwhelm us with his glory and throw us into an abyss. Instead, "Let us hold for a certainty that God has just cause for doing what he does—even if it is hidden from us—and that things we do not know are still reality. . . . Even if we do not see why God acts thus, we must be satisfied that he is just [*iuste*]."[123]

God's secret will is not arbitrary but corresponds to God's nature as revealed in Scripture and reflected in the law. Therefore, even though we are not able to question or to comprehend God's one secret will, we can confidently know by faith (if not by sight) that God's secret will is unified in its conformity to the merciful, righteous/just, and judging character of God. This approach clearly evinces Calvin's assumption that predestination can only be rightly examined by those with faith in Christ who already have firsthand experience and knowledge of God's nature revealed in Christ. As Calvin says, "The rule of modesty prescribed by us, on the other hand, is that, where the reason for God's works lies hidden, we none the less believe [*credamus*] Him to be just."[124]

The Final End: God's Glory

One element of God's will that has been revealed in Scripture is the ultimate purpose of God's will, which, according to Calvin, is God's glory, a common theme in Calvin's works. In his John commentary, Calvin defines the term, saying, "The glory of God is, when we know his nature [*qualis sit*]."[125] Calvin says that God's purpose, no matter how hidden, is to "declare the glory of His name.... In all His works [*factis*], the Lord has the reason of His own glory [*gloriae suae*]."[126] In short, God's glory is his acting according to his nature and thus revealing more of his nature to the world, which leads people to worship God rightly.[127] As asserted above, Calvin teaches that both God's revealed electing will and God's veiled reprobating will bring glory to God, primarily by illuminating God's mercy and secondarily showing his judgment of evil. In this way, once again, God's twofold will is unified in its telos toward God's glory.

In sum, regarding God's one, secret will, limited human creatures cannot judge God or fully grasp God's will, but they can know the character of that will, namely that it perfectly matches God's righteous nature and thus brings glory to God in the ways God's nature is revealed in its execution.

The Two Asymmetrical Elements of God's One Will

If God's revealed electing will and God's veiled reprobating will find their unity in the one, secret righteous will of God, what can we know about the relationship between these two elements of God's will toward humanity, both dogmatically and in practice? Simply put, we find that for Calvin, the two parts of God's one, secret will are asymmetrically related both dogmatically and pragmatically.[128] Here we shall see that although Calvin is committed to recognizing God as the ultimate cause of all things, Calvin appeals to nuances of causality to help parse God's will toward humanity; Calvin's intended audience in his teaching of predestination highlights the asymmetrical nature of

God's twofold will toward humanity; and finally, Calvin emphasizes election over reprobation in the practice of Christian mission.

Causality

First, in his descriptions of predestination, while affirming God's sovereign rule over all that comes to pass, Calvin (following others in the tradition before him) utilizes levels of causality that reveal the asymmetrical nature of God's electing will and God's reprobating will in relation to God's one secret will.

At times, Calvin describes election and reprobation in parallel. For example, in refuting Pighius's claim that God is gracious toward all without hating the reprobate, Calvin says, "For to the gratuitous love [*gratuito amori*] with which the elect are embraced there corresponds on an equal and common level a just severity [*iusta . . . severitas*] toward the reprobate."[129] Similarly, regarding Rom. 11:7, Calvin makes it very clear that God cannot be excused from the responsibility of reprobating: "They reason absurdly who, whenever a word is said of the proximate causes [*propinquis causis*], strive, by bringing forward these, to cover the first, which is hid from our view; as though God had not, before the fall of Adam, freely determined to do what seemed good to him with respect to the whole human race."[130] Calvin holds to the logic of his belief that God is the cause of all, including reprobation, and Calvin at times asserts that reprobation is parallel to election, particularly in regard to God's sovereign rule over all.

However, Calvin (like many others) also utilizes Aristotelian categories of causality to nuance the human understanding of God's secret will, highlighting the asymmetrical relationship of God's disclosed and veiled wills. At the center of Calvin's understanding of causality is the way he affirms multiple causes for one event.[131] Calvin attests the fall of humanity as both fully the result of God's ordination[132] and fully the result of human will, which makes the human race culpable for its sin and deserving of its just condemnation.[133] Using contemporary terminology, Calvin could be considered a type of compatibilist, allowing for real human choice *and* God's sovereign determination of all.[134] As Oliver Crisp points out, this conception is typically described as "meticulous providence."[135] God is thus sovereign over all and also not the author of sin or evil.[136] In addition, for Calvin, God's sovereign will does not rob humans of their active will. For example, the fall of Judas was ordained by God but was also Judas's choice and responsibility,[137] and believers are exhorted to "act passively" (*passive . . . agere*) in the working out of their salvation which is completely a gift.[138] For Calvin, one event can have multiple causes as perceived from different perspectives.

Although God is the ultimate cause of all aspects of predestination, Calvin's causal descriptions of reprobation and election are not parallel.[139] In *De Aeterna,* Calvin differentiates between the proximate cause (*causa propinqua*) of reprobation as the fall of humanity, and the remote (*remota*) cause as God's election of some and reprobation of others.[140] Later, he terms the foremost cause of reprobation as "unbelief [*increduli*] in the gospel."[141] Remarking on John 3:19, Calvin points out that the blame for condemnation falls not on Christ but on the those who reject the gospel: "It is their own wickedness [*pravitatem incredulis*] which hinders unbelievers from approaching to Christ."[142] Thus, while God is the ultimate cause of reprobation, human sin and unbelief are the proximate and epistemically accessible causes of reprobation and its corresponding condemnation.

In stark contrast to the mixed causality of reprobation, Calvin's causes for election are solely rooted in God and his freely given mercy. Explicitly utilizing Aristotelian categories in his comments on Eph. 1:5–8, Calvin says of election, "The efficient cause [*causa efficiens*] is the good pleasure of the will of God; the material cause [*causa materialis*] is Christ; and the final cause [*causa finalis*] is the praise of His grace." A few verses later, he adds that the formal cause (*causa formalis*) of election is the preaching of the gospel.[143] In the *Institutes,* Calvin grounds the salvation of the elect in trinitarian causality: "The efficient cause [*effectum*] of our salvation consists in God the Father's love; the material cause [*materiam*] in God the Son's obedience; the instrumental cause [*instrumentum*] in the Spirit's illumination, that is faith; the final cause [*finem*], in the glory of God's great generosity."[144] In short, election is made known as the work of God from first to last. Thus, in distinction with reprobation that mysteriously finds its remote cause in God and its proximate cause in sin, election's terms of causality are directly related to the trinitarian God in accordance with God's revealed nature.[145]

Thus, election and reprobation are united in God's one, secret will, but the nearby causes (*causae propinquae*) are very different between the two.[146] At the divine level of causality, election and reprobation are somewhat parallel; in contrast, from the human perspective, the *causae propinquae* which are perceptible to humanity are not parallel. The *causae propinquae* of reprobation are rooted fully in humanity and the *causae propinquae* of election are rooted fully in God, highlighting the asymmetry of election and reprobation.[147] Election is comprehended to be rooted in God from first to last whereas reprobation is mysteriously caused by God and openly caused by fallen humanity.

Along the same lines, without surrendering his commitment that God is the cause of all things, Calvin at times emphasizes God's passive role in reprobation, highlighting God's saving action for the elect alongside his *lack* of saving movement for the reprobate.[148] In his sermon on Eph. 1:4–6, Calvin says, "Now some are accounted reprobates: and why is that but because God looking upon them in themselves passes them by [*les dedaigne*]. But he chooses us in our Lord Jesus Christ and looks upon us there, as in a mirror [*en un miroir*] that is pleasing to him. And so you see how the difference comes about."[149] Again, even though Calvin believes it would be "highly absurd" (*plus . . . insulse*) to simply attribute election to God and reprobation to humanity, God's saving action in election is not directly paralleled with God's passivity toward the reprobate in their sinful state.[150]

Therefore, utilizing the nuances of causality, Calvin highlights the asymmetrical relation between the electing and reprobating wills of God; God's electing will takes primacy in its visible connection with human knowledge of God and his work in the world. Although Calvin teaches that God is the active cause of election and reprobation in one sense, he also teaches that salvation is directly caused by God and connected with God's revealed nature whereas condemnation is proximately caused by human sin and only caused by God in a way that is not humanly comprehensible. Further, God's mercy toward the elect is displayed in his active election as a result of his gracious mercy in contrast with his passive allowing the reprobate to remain in their state of sin and deserved condemnation (according to his veiled reprobating will).

God's Glory

The asymmetrical nature of election and reprobation is further underlined in the manner that God is glorified in the two different actions. As mentioned above,[151] besides showing forth God's righteous condemnation of evil, reprobation brings God glory primarily because it highlights the merciful nature of election. For example, regarding Rom. 9:22, Calvin explains that when Paul speaks of the reprobate making known "the riches of [God's] glory," Paul is actually employing metonymy with the word "glory" to refer to the mercy of God toward the elect that is highlighted in the display of their just deserts in the condemnation of the reprobate, for "God's chief praise is in acts of kindness [*benefactis*]." He proceeds to say, "The elect are instruments or organs, through whom God exercises His mercy, that through them he may glorify his name."[152] Therefore, because the expression of God's mercy brings him the most praise, reprobation subordinately glorifies God by highlighting God's mercy. Once again, election and reprobation are asymmetrically related.

Calvin's Audience: the Elect

Similar to the way that the true knowledge of God is only available to those with faith, predestination can only be rightly understood by the elect who have come to know God's revealed nature through trust in Christ. As a result, the Christian audience of Calvin's lectures and writings also evinces the asymmetrical relationship between the electing and reprobating elements of God's will in Calvin's teaching. In short, Calvin teaches predestination to those with faith for the edification of the elect.

The bulk of Calvin's theological teaching is explicitly directed toward Christians. Calvin's stated purpose for the *Institutes* from 1539 onward is to "prepare and instruct candidates in sacred theology for the reading of the divine Word."[153] In his dedicatory letter for his first commentary, on Romans, Calvin explains his decision to write the commentary as follows, "I could not prevent myself from trying to see what good my efforts in this regard might achieve for the Church of God."[154] Many of Calvin's occasional writings, such as *De Aeterna,* are intended to defend the Church against blasphemous teachings, again assuming that the audience is Christians who are in danger of being led astray. Throughout Calvin's dogmatic teaching,[155] his intended audience is the elect, the only ones who can receive the truth of God by the Spirit.

For Calvin, like all biblical doctrine, what God has revealed about predestination is for the edification of the elect. Throughout Calvin's teaching on predestination, he focuses on how the doctrine benefits the elect by affirming the unmerited grace of God in election, by highlighting the depth out of which God has rescued the elect, by explaining the experiences of the elect in regard to the preaching of the gospel, and by engendering love for, obedience to, and worship of God by the elect.

Even Calvin's teaching on reprobation is for the good of the elect. Since election is fully the work of God by the Spirit, Calvin has no need to preach condemnation to the reprobate as if he could scare them out of their status as reprobate. On the contrary, even in Calvin's very brief teaching about the eternal destiny of the reprobate in the *Institutes*, he says the purpose of the teaching on reprobation is so "we [the elect] ought especially to fix our thoughts upon this: how wretched is it to be cut off from all fellowship with God." Instead of appealing to God's justice and glory in God's condemnation of the reprobate, Calvin uses the Bible's teaching on hell to encourage people to persevere in worshipping God "until he himself is 'all in all.'"[156]

Thus, Calvin's teaching on predestination is for the benefit of the elect and assumes that the recipients are the elect who already know by faith God's nature as witnessed to in election. Once again, God's electing will is primary while God's reprobating will is secondary.

God's Revealed Will and Veiled Will in Christian Mission

Having seen Calvin's dogmatic elevation of God's revealed electing will and work over and above his veiled reprobating will and work, we now turn to examine Calvin's practical teaching on Christian mission in light of the revealed electing and veiled reprobating elements of God's will. We find that for Calvin, God's disclosed disposition that corresponds directly to God's revealed electing will guides the attitude and actions of the elect toward all humanity in preaching to all, hoping for the salvation of all and praying for all, while God's veiled reprobating will reminds believers of God's sovereign rule over all things.[157]

First, Calvin teaches that Christians are to proclaim the good news of God's fatherly love and mercy (God's disclosed disposition) to all people. As Calvin says, "Until the day of revelation comes, we are to do what our Lord commands and exhort [*hortemur*] all without exception to faith and penitence."[158] Not everyone receives this grace, but we should teach that "God's loving-kindness [*benignitatem*] is set forth to all who seek it, without exception," because those "on whom heavenly grace has breathed" will seek after it.[159] The logic from the 1 Tim. 2:4 commentary follows these lines: preaching gives life; Scripture commands that we preach to all; therefore from our perspective, God regards all people as worthy to share in salvation; however, as far as results are concerned, God calls only the elect through the preaching.[160] Therefore, for Calvin, the responsibility and call of Christians is to proclaim to all people indiscriminately the good news of God's redeeming love in Christ, recognizing that any response of repentance and faith will be engendered by the Spirit in the elect.[161] Even though this proclamation may seem disingenuous in light of God's reprobating will toward some people, for Calvin it is an expression of God's nature proclaimed to all in obedience to God's command and in accord with God's mercy that is offered to all. It is God's disclosed disposition toward humanity.

It is open to question whether this is a disingenuous manner of acting. One might say that this is similar to a person offering a pile of money to someone who is chained up and unable to receive the gift and then proceeding to blame the potential recipient for rejecting the gift. However, from Calvin's perspective, this illustration would fall short in the fact that it assumes too much knowledge of God's reprobating will and subjects God to finite human judgment and perspective. We are also ignorant of who is able (by God's empowering) to stand up and receive the gift. According to Calvin's logic, in the day of judgment, it will be clear that some people did not receive the gift, but by trusting in God's merciful and just character, believers trust that the events that transpired were somehow merciful and just.

Reprobation is included in Christian teaching, but only to the end of edifying the faithful. As we have seen, Calvin requires that the doctrine of reprobation be taught according to God's accommodation in Scripture because it witnesses to grace, explains experience, engenders humility, and results in praise to God.[162] Although Calvin does assign reprobation to exceptionally rebellious biblical figures like Pharaoh,[163] he rejects any teaching that tells people that they are reprobate or that they "will not believe because they have been condemned." These approaches are cursing, not teaching, and result in sloth and evil.[164] Thus, even in teaching about reprobation, God's revealed electing will takes priority.

Second, Calvin teaches that Christians should hope that God's disclosed disposition would be extended to and received by all. Calvin's hope for the salvation of all is not solely founded upon ignorance of who is reprobate and who is elect but also upon God's gracious work in people's lives that goes beyond our knowledge. Quoting Augustine, Calvin says, "For as we know not who belongs to the number of the predestined or who does not belong, we ought to be so minded as to wish that all men be saved [*omnes velimus salvos fieri*]."[165] He even says regarding Achan's detestable theft of the devoted things and his and his household's subsequent death penalty that their execution may have provided a possible chance for repentance.[166] John Thompson points out that for Calvin, since "*no one* can know the reprobation of another," believers are not to curse their enemies but to pray for them while trusting God's ultimate condemnation of injustice and evil.[167] It is worth noting that at times (e.g., John 6:64), Calvin hints at the fact that the reprobate can be known by their fruit, but even then he points out that only God (and the divine Christ) knows people's hearts, so conclusions must not be drawn too quickly.[168]

Calvin also applies this hope in God's unseen work in his doctrine of church discipline.[169] Besides protecting God's name from dishonor and the church from corruption, church discipline exists to bring about the repentance of a sinner. Calvin specifically teaches that excommunication does not determine that one is reprobate. Instead, it is "not our task to erase from the number of the elect those who have been expelled from the church, or to despair as if they were already lost." Instead the church is to hope for them and pray for them, allowing God to judge them and hopefully restore them.[170] Even when commenting upon Heb. 6:4 that says that "it is impossible to restore again to repentance" those who have tasted of God's grace and turned away, Calvin retains hope that they might return to God. He says that those who rush forth to destruction do show their reprobation, "but when anyone rises up again after falling, we may hence conclude that he had not been guilty of defection [*defectione*]."[171] For Calvin, Christians are meant to live in such a way as to hope that God's disclosed disposition of mercy and love will be realized and received by all, while at the same time recognizing that the gift of faith will only be given to some.

God's disclosed disposition that corresponds with God's revealed electing will has directive power, whereas God's veiled, reprobating will only has explanatory power. In this way, God's disclosed disposition and electing will again has priority over God's veiled reprobating will.

Third, Calvin shows the priority of God's disclosed disposition and electing will in the Christian responsibility to pray for all, regardless of their status as elect or reprobate. For example, Calvin's conclusion in his commentary on 1 Tim. 2:4 is that we are not to differentiate what type of people might hear the gospel, and we are "to be solicitous and to do our endeavor for the salvation of all whom God includes in his calling, and to testify this by godly prayers."[172] Calvin personally practiced this exhortation to pray for all. For example, it was his custom to end his Sunday afternoon (and weekday) sermons with a variation on the phrase, "And may it please him to grant this grace not only to us, but also to all peoples and nations [*aussi à tous peuples et nations*]."[173] For Calvin, the Christian responsibility is to pray for all people, regardless of their perceived status as elect or reprobate, again giving priority to God's disclosed disposition of love toward all.

It is worth remembering that for Calvin, prayer for all people is guided by God's disclosed disposition from our perspective but still humbly offered to God in submission to his one secret will which includes his veiled reprobating will. Commenting on Jesus' prayer for the elect in John 17:9, Calvin says:

> The prayers which we offer for all are still limited to the elect of God. We ought to pray that this man, and that man, and every man, may be saved and thus include the whole human race, because we cannot yet distinguish [*nondum distinguere*] the elect from the reprobate; and yet by desiring the coming of God's kingdom we likewise pray that God may destroy all His enemies [*hostes suos perdat*] . . . we pray for the salvation of all whom we know to have been created after the image of God and who have the same nature with ourselves; and we leave to the judgment [*iudicio*] of God those whom he knows to be reprobate [*interitum*].[174]

For Calvin, since the reprobate are ones who remain in sin and are thus ultimately God's enemies, our prayers cannot actually be extended to them because that would be rebellion against God's will. Prayer is therefore a microcosm of the preaching of the gospel: we pray for all who are made in God's image as an expression of his love; we pray for all because we are ignorant of whom God has chosen as his; we submit to God's judgment in making our prayers efficacious for whomever God has secretly chosen to redeem; we trust in the God of mercy, justice, and judgment to rightly condemn his true enemies as only God has authority to do.[175]

As we have seen here, Calvin retains the tension of God's twofold will toward humanity in Christian practice. Regardless of how perceived pastoral needs would incite one to silence regarding God's veiled reprobating will,

Calvin does not allow such a step.[176] As Link observes, "It speaks well of Calvin that he resisted the temptation to find a solution or an understandable intellectual, rational means to diffuse this dilemma."[177] Instead, Calvin calls us to look upon the mirror of Christ to contemplate our own election. Link concludes, "This mirror indeed becomes the manifestation of God's faithfulness. And is that not a basis with which those who have recognized the certainty of their election can share the promise of God's faithfulness with those who have yet to do so?"[178] In other words, Calvin's admonition to the elect is to witness to the God they have come to know in Christ and leave the results of that witness in the hands of that loving, powerful, and righteous God.

In sum, God's disclosed disposition in correspondence with God's revealed will has prescriptive power as it guides Christian practice as believers preach the gospel to all, hope for the salvation of all, and pray for all. In contrast, God's veiled will only has descriptive power, explaining why some people seemingly do not come to a place of saving faith. Once again, the two wills are asymmetrically related within God's one secret will.

Throughout this subsection we have been asking the question of the relationship between the revealed electing and veiled reprobating elements of God's will. Although Calvin is clear and consistent on the unity of God's will, we have found that Calvin gives priority to God's revealed electing will, both dogmatically and practically. God's revealed electing will that is reflected in God's disclosed disposition of love for all correlates directly with, and explicitly emerges from, God's merciful, just, and judging nature revealed most clearly in Christ. This revealed will directly glorifies God, edifies the elect, and provides the grounds and direction for Christian mission. On the other hand, God's veiled reprobating will provides only partial knowledge of God, partial witness to God's glory, partial edification for the elect, and explanations for unsuccessful Christian witness. Therefore, although united in God's one will, God's revealed electing will and God's veiled reprobating will are asymmetrical causally, epistemologically, doctrinally, and practically.

GOD'S TWOFOLD WILL AND THE KNOWLEDGE OF GOD

In light of our findings, how does God's twofold and asymmetrically related will revealed in predestination make God known? In short, God's revealed electing will, as it has been accommodated to the elect, provides direct knowledge of God in accordance with God's revealed nature, and God's veiled reprobating will flows from that same God in a mysterious manner, beyond human knowledge. Thus, Calvin teaches *that* God causes reprobation without explaining *how* or *why* God causes reprobation.[179] As Jacobs argues,

Calvin finds ground for substantial teaching about election in the fact that election is mediated by Christ, and thus is only known in and through Christ. However, all knowledge of reprobation occurs outside of Christ and God's nature revealed in Christ; for Calvin, reprobation is a Christ-less doctrine. According to Calvin's theological commitments, any teaching on reprobation can only have boundary-significance (*Grenzbedeutung*), providing "boundary lines [*Grenzlinie*] and not comprehensively describing the realm of reprobation."[180] Accordingly, Calvin repeatedly refers his readers to God's secret counsel as the reason for reprobation. This veiled reprobating will is made known insofar as we recognize it is a fact, but it only corresponds with God's revealed nature in part, namely confirming God as judge of evil and magnifying God's grace extended to the elect.[181]

Steve Holmes similarly asserts,

> The weakness in Calvin's account of predestination, I suggest, is that the doctrine of reprobation is detached, Christless and hidden in the unsearchable purposes of God. As such it bears no comparison with the doctrine of election, but remains something less than a Christian doctrine. There is, in Calvin's account, a fundamental difference between election and reprobation. Contra Barth, Calvin's failure is not that he teaches a symmetrical double decree . . . but that he has almost no room for the doctrine of reprobation in his account.[182]

Reprobation Is an Epistemologically Christ-less Doctrine.

In sum, for Calvin, the God who is revealed in his works, including Scripture and the incarnate Christ, is the God of both election and reprobation. However, those with faith only gain direct and accurate knowledge of God and his will through his electing actions, while his reprobating actions provide veiled and unsure insight into God and his will. In short, the known God of election inscrutably causes reprobation.

QUESTIONS FOR CALVIN: ASSURANCE, BEZA, AND METHODOLOGY

Having seen the way Calvin holds together the electing and reprobating elements of God's one will, we now begin a critical examination of Calvin's doctrine of predestination and its relation to God's disposition toward humanity that will continue in dialogue with other theologians (including Barth's claim of a *Deus nudus absconditus* in Calvin's doctrine) in chapter 7. Here we address the question of assurance of faith in Calvin's teaching on predestination before examining the relationship between Calvin's and Beza's teaching on predestination and providing a few brief critical questions regarding Calvin's methodology.

Assurance: Christ as Mirror

The question of assurance of salvation that has been posed since the earliest days of the Church (e.g., Romans 8:31–39) was present in Calvin's time as it is today,[183] particularly in light of the teaching of God's twofold will expressed in predestination. In short, if God chooses some for salvation and passes over others, how is one to know that he or she is chosen? Calvin was aware of the desire for assurance regarding one's salvation in light of his teaching about God's secret counsel.[184] Although Calvin replied to this concern in a variety of ways, we shall highlight his three most important assurances of salvation, namely the gracious nature of election, the experience of election via calling, and most of all, the person and work of Christ who assures us of God's favorable disposition.[185]

First, as we have already observed, Calvin's teaching on predestination reveals the utterly gratuitous nature of salvation. The elect come to faith based on no merit of their own. Consequently, the security of their salvation rests not in their power but in God and his power.

Second, recognizing that speculation about one's election in the labyrinth of predestination would not provide assurance, Calvin teaches that the elect can be assured of their salvation through their experience of the calling of faith and its accompanying sanctification.[186] Instead of such speculation about "God's eternal plan [*concilium*] apart from his Word," Calvin advises his readers to find the unimaginable comfort of looking for certainty in God's Word via God's call (*vocatio*), through which God gives peace.[187] This assurance is founded on the truth of God's Word but experienced via one's personal call to faith, which Calvin explains elsewhere as embracing God's merciful promises in a manner "that renders the conscience calm and peaceful [*sedat et serenat*] before God's judgment."[188]

The fact Calvin teaches that God is ready to receive any who would respond to the call of the gospel in faith explains why Calvin asserts calling as providing assurance. He says regarding Ezek. 18:23, "The Prophet only shows here, that when we have been converted [*conversi fuerint*] we need not doubt that God immediately [*statim*] meets us and shows himself propitious."[189] For Calvin, election precedes faith, and faith attests to one's calling as a gift from the Spirit. Therefore, simply to have faith assures the believer that he or she is one of the elect and included in God's electing will according to God's merciful, fatherly love.[190]

However, Calvin's desire to be faithful to Scripture and interpret human experience led him to include some elements in his doctrine of calling that could undermine the assurance of God's call,[191] namely the teaching of God's temporary illumination, which can be seen as a subset of Calvin's teaching on God's reprobating will.[192] Addressing the description of the apostates in Hebrews 6, Calvin says that God at times provides a temporary faith to the reprobate which lacks the roots to endure.[193] Similarly, those who seem to fall away from Christ are unknowingly like Judas "who never cleaved to Christ with the heartfelt trust in which the certainty of election has, I say, been established for us." This false faith is even accompanied by "signs of a call that are similar [*similia*] to those of the elect."[194]

Instead of perceiving such teaching as a pastoral pitfall, Calvin says that these warnings should keep us "in fear and humility" as we recognize the weakness of our human nature while trusting God to strengthen our faith and "have us to remain and rest tranquil as in a safe haven [*in tutu porto*]."[195] Similarly, Calvin says that such instances of temporary faith should not disrupt the peace of our call because God does not allow any to fall away who have "true faith [*vera fide*]."[196] For Calvin, the doctrine of temporary faith urges believers on to faith and piety while finding assurance in God's powerful, merciful, righteous nature. In sum: from Scripture and experience, we recognize that some seem to have temporary faith; the sovereign God who causes all that comes to pass is the cause of this temporary faith; be careful not to fall away; and do not be anxious because the merciful and powerful God of Jesus Christ holds and sustains you in your faith.

Although Calvin perceives this call of faith as sufficient grounds for assurance of one's inclusion in God's electing will, he offers the most substantial assurance in the *speculum electionis*, Jesus Christ, the mirror of our election.[197] In *De Aeterna*, Calvin says:

> For whoever does not walk in the plain path of faith can make nothing of the election of God but a labyrinth of destruction [*exitialis*]. Therefore, that the remission of sins may be a certainty [*certa*] to us, our consciences rest in confidence of eternal life, and we call upon God as Father without fear, the beginning [*exordium*] is not to be made here. We must begin with what is revealed [*patefactum*] in Christ concerning the love of the Father for us and what Christ Himself daily preaches to us through the Gospel. Nothing higher is demanded of us than that we be the sons of God. But of the gratuitous election [*atqui gratuitae*] by which alone we may attain this highest good, the mirror of adoption [*adoptionis speculum*], earnest and pledge is the Son, who came forth for us from the bosom of the Father to make us heirs of the heavenly kingdom by ingrafting us into His body.[198]

For Calvin, God's fatherly love is finally and ultimately known by looking to Christ.[199] Calvin specifically teaches that one cannot inquire into the secret counsel of God to find assurance of salvation: "Since the certainty of salvation [*salutis certitudo*] is set forth to us in Christ, it is wrong and injurious to Christ to pass over this proffered fountain of life from which supplies are available, and to toil to draw life out of the hidden recesses of God [*ex reconditis Dei abyssis*]."[200]

Christ as the mirror provides sufficient assurance of God's will to answer any number of questions, including the mystery of God's veiled reprobating will and Calvin's doctrine of temporary faith. "If Pighius asks how I know I am elect, I answer that Christ is more than a thousand testimonies [*mille testimoniis*] to me. For when we find ourselves in His body, our salvation rests in a secure and tranquil place [*in secura tranquillaque statione*], as though already located in heaven."[201]

In sum, Calvin perceives his doctrine of predestination as providing assurance of faith because it grounds the work of salvation solely in God's grace that is attested to by one's call to faith by the Spirit, which is only experienced by grace and is attested to by God's gift of sanctification. Beyond his or her call to faith, the believer finds ultimate security by looking to Christ, the mirror of election, who reveals God's nature, God's disposition, and God's electing will in his salvific person and work.

In light of this abundant assurance in Christ, for Calvin, neither the doctrine of temporary faith nor God's reprobating will undermine one's assurance of salvation. Instead, since neither doctrine provides clear insight into God's nature, they must be interpreted in light of God's revealed nature, God's disclosed disposition, and God's electing will as directly displayed in the preaching of the gospel and most clearly in Christ. In its correct subordinate place, and from the vantage point of faith, God's veiled reprobating will (including God's choosing to provide temporary faith to some) is not a threat to one's assurance of salvation but a fact that explains common experience and highlights the depths out of which the elect have been rescued.

Therefore, beyond the *desire to believe* that witnesses to one's calling, by looking to Christ, those with faith know God's merciful nature revealed in accord with God's disclosed disposition and electing will. For Calvin, to look to Christ is to find assurance of salvation. We shall return to this argument in chapters 7 and 8 in light of the fact that what seemed so persuasive to Calvin has not proven universally assuring to others.

Beza and Calvin on Predestination

It has been often claimed in recent theological discourse that Theodore Beza, Calvin's successor in Geneva, corrupted Calvin's "christocentric" teaching by moving predestination into the center of Reformed theology.[202] Beginning in Calvin scholarship with Muller's *Christ and the Decree* in 1986, the "Beza thesis" (along with the Calvin vs. the Calvinist claim) has been thoroughly refuted, primarily through the demonstration that the Reformed tradition developed from Medieval theology through a range of theologians over a number of years.[203] Specifically regarding Beza, the argument for continuity is especially convincing because Calvin unmistakably knew about and seemingly accepted Beza's teaching on predestination.[204]

However, a cursory glance at Beza's *Tabula Praedestinationis* diagram[205] reveals statements that contrast with this chapter's conclusions regarding Calvin's teaching on predestination. For example, at the top of the chart, Beza depicts in a parallel manner God's decrees to "elect in Christ those to be saved" and "to reject those to be damned by their own fault" to the end of God's glory. Further down, Beza depicts a symmetrical relationship between the eternal life given to the elect and the just punishment of sinners, which he explains happen "in accordance with His eternal decree" as the glory of God is manifest through God, "the supremely merciful and the supremely severe." The inherent limits of any diagram aside, Beza's depiction seems to indicate two distinct symmetrical dispositions and wills of God toward humanity, an elevation of a certain definition of God's glory as equally the *telos* of election and reprobation, and an order of logic that begins with God's decree, all of which contrast with Calvin's account. How are these differences to be accounted for?

Space here does not permit a full comparison of Beza's and Calvin's teaching on predestination. Instead, drawing on Muller's careful discussion,[206] we find that Beza's account of predestination, particularly in his *Tabula*, reveals general, material continuity with Calvin's teaching while also displaying discontinuity in specific emphases.[207] We shall note the context of the document, highlight three important areas of continuity and three elements of discontinuity before providing a brief summary.

First, regarding its context, Beza's *Tabula* was written in response to the Bolsec controversy of 1551 in order to provide an orderly and scripturally supported account of the doctrine of predestination.[208] Correspondence suggests that Beza began writing the document during the Bolsec affair in Geneva, likely at Calvin's bidding, and completed it in 1555. Contrary to what the complete title, *Summa Totius Christianismi*, may suggest, Beza does not seek to provide a summary of Christian theology in the *Tabula*.[209] Instead, Beza felt that Calvin's *Concerning the Eternal Predestination of God* was insufficient because it primarily responded to Pighius's arguments instead of expositing the doctrine of predestination in proper order. Therefore, in Muller's words, Beza provides an orderly account of "the relationship of the various elements of the *ordo salutis* to the divine decree, with an emphasis on Christ and the graciously given faith that receives Christ."[210] To understand the diagram aright, one must also examine the accompanying text that includes eight chapters of explanation with over six hundred Scripture citations.[211]

Second, Beza's *Tabula* demonstrates general continuity with Calvin's teaching on predestination.[212] All of Beza's claims can be substantiated in Calvin's teaching, even the statements that seem at odds with Calvin's overall understanding. We note three examples here that relate to our study of God's disposition toward humanity. First, Beza claims that the final end of God's counsel (*ultimus est consiliorum Dei finis*) is "neither the salvation of the elect nor the damnation of the reprobate, but the setting forth of his own glory [*ipsius gloriae*] in saving the one by his mercy [*per misericordiam*] and condemning the other by his just judgement [*iusto iudicio*]."[213] In Calvin's polemic against Pighius, Calvin similarly claims regarding predestination, "In all His works, the Lord has the reason of His own glory [*suae gloriae*]."[214] This aligns with Calvin's teaching of God's one, secret, righteous, twofold will that corresponds to and illuminates his nature, thus resulting in glory ascribed to God.

Second, Beza teaches that God created people "in two thoroughly different ways" (*duobus modis penitus diversis*) in order to set forth his glory in mercy to one and condemnation to the other.[215] Along the same lines, as we noted above in Calvin's starkest statements about predestination, he teaches that "all are not created [*creantur*] in equal condition; rather, eternal life is foreordained for some, eternal damnation for others."[216] At the same time, in continuity with Calvin, Beza describes a drastic asymmetry between election and reprobation in many respects. For example, election is caused only by God in his mercy, whereas "the whole fault [*tota . . . culpa*] of the Reprobates' damnation lies in themselves [*in ipsis haereat*]."[217] Thus, as Holmes points out, Beza's table of predestination manifests the way that reprobation was not considered Christological for him. Like Calvin's account, for Beza, election is directly connected to Christ while reprobation happens outside of Christ.[218] Again, the elect are certain of their own election as it is revealed by the Spirit, but no one (including the reprobate) knows who the reprobate are.[219] We are called to preach the gospel to all, even the most heinous sinners, in hopes they will respond in faith through God's mercy, even in the last hour of their lives.[220]

Finally, even though the diagram suggests the opposite, Beza is clear that teaching about the decrees comes only *after* one knows God's disclosed disposition, electing will, and nature by faith, demonstrated in the fact that gospel proclamation does not begin with the heights of God's incomprehensible majesty as displayed in God's decree but instead moves from "the bottom" [*imum*] of sin, law, and grace.[221] As demonstrated here, Beza's account largely agrees with Calvin's teaching on predestination.

However, Beza's teaching also displays discontinuity with Calvin in his specific emphases. For example, as seen above, and often drawing upon Paul's teaching in Rom. 9:20–23 about the potter and the clay, Beza implies that God is *equally glorified* in his merciful rescue of the elect and in his just condemnation of the reprobate. Along with Rom. 9:20, Beza's published diagram has Prov. 16:4 ("The LORD has made all things for himself, yea even the wicked for the day of evil.") at the top, further witnessing to this conviction.[222] In contrast, although Calvin states that God is glorified in all his works, Calvin describes an asymmetrical relationship between God's glory and God's expression of mercy and wrath. To reiterate, in his commentary on Rom. 9:20–23, Calvin says that God's glory is displayed in the condemnation of the reprobate "because the greatness of divine mercy towards the elect is hereby more clearly made known."[223] Although Beza makes a similar point at times, Calvin goes even further by saying that God's "glory" mentioned in this verse "has been used [as a metonymy] for God's mercy . . . for his chief praise is in acts of kindness."[224] For Calvin, God's glory is not equally manifest in expressing condemnation and mercy.[225] There is an asymmetrical relationship between the two, as God's nature is plainly displayed in election but only partially revealed in reprobation.

As another example of discontinuity, even though Calvin abides by the logic of his doctrines of predestination and providence to teach that God creates some people to save and others to condemn, Calvin's teaching on creation (and his infralapsarian approach elsewhere) reveals that God's primary purpose in creation was not to create humanity for condemnation.[226] This stands in contrast with Beza's supralapsarian diagram and indication that God created "in two thoroughly different ways." Thus, Muller says that Beza's teaching provides a "point of transition between supralapsarian aspects of Calvin's thought and a more strictly defined doctrinal model."[227]

As a final example, this time of a wrongly perceived discontinuity between Calvin and Beza, Beza's diagram works from the order of being (*ordo essendi*), whereas (as we have seen) Calvin consistently works from the order of knowing (*ordo cognoscendi*), allowing knowledge of God's decree only after one has come to know Christ by faith. However, a reading of the text alongside the diagram shows that, as noted above, Beza does not believe Christian preaching should begin with God's incomprehensible decrees. He only allows for that type of reasoning for those whose eyes have become accustomed to God's light.[228] As Muller summarizes, Beza teaches that "believers *do not* learn of their election by following the arrangement of the chart from top [God's decree] to bottom [salvation]!"[229] Thus, upon closer examination, we find that this perceived discontinuity disappears; both Calvin and Beza teach that people can only learn anything about predestination a posteriori, after they have placed their faith in Christ. Perhaps the biggest obstacle to the proper understanding of Beza's teaching was his decision to try to encapsulate Scripture's complex and nuanced teaching on predestination in a simple diagram!

In conclusion, we have seen that Beza's teaching on predestination has general material continuity with Calvin's teaching but also includes discontinuities in emphasis, particularly regarding the relationship between God's glory and mercy and regarding God's creation of people for condemnation. Thus, Beza's teaching regarding God's disposition toward humanity as seen in predestination does differ from Calvin's. Calvin teaches that in predestination, God's one, righteous will is expressed in a twofold, asymmetrical manner that highlights God's mercy and affirms God's merciful disposition toward humanity, whereas Beza teaches that God's one, righteous will is expressed in a secret, double will toward humanity that results in God's glory. Beza does not significantly depart from Calvin's teaching of God's wholly gratuitous election in Christ but seeks to appropriate it into a doctrinal model. As Muller states, Beza's approach in the *Tabula* shows "a desire for terminological clarity and careful distinction between ideas that look past the style of Calvin's *Institutes* towards the scholastic approaches of Reformed orthodoxy."[230] Apparently, Calvin did not see those divergences as significant enough to ask Beza to change the document when he was given the opportunity in 1555. Perhaps Calvin saw room for his interpretation and emphases within Beza's broader doctrinal framework. As another possibility, as Beeke suggests, maybe Beza's departure from Calvin was not as apparent in his preaching and pastoral work as it is in the bare facts of the occasional and polemic *Tabula*.[231]

Having examined Calvin's and Beza's teaching on predestination, we now consider a few critical questions arising from Calvin's account.

Critical Questions for Further Consideration

We have observed that Calvin teaches that in predestination God accommodates to those with faith his one, secret, and righteous will in a twofold but asymmetrical manner: (a) God's revealed electing will for the elect that corresponds to God's revealed nature and to his disclosed merciful disposition toward all people; and (b) God's veiled reprobating will for the reprobate. With that in mind, we shall here briefly point out six critical questions regarding Calvin's methodology and doctrine that have arisen in the course of this chapter:

1. Does Calvin let experience play a disproportionately large role in his theology? Although Scripture forms the foundation of his teaching on predestination, we have also observed how experience informs his teaching on God's reprobating will—for example, providing confirmation that God does indeed choose people to reprobate and in whom to instill temporary faith. However, when Calvin goes beyond the simple confirmation of Scripture's teaching by attributing relative numbers to the elect (1 percent or 20 percent depending on the day) because of his experience in preaching the gospel, he violates his nonspeculative methodology. Granted that his purpose in providing numbers is clearly to prevent preachers from being discouraged and granted that there is some biblical warrant for assuming a small number of the elect (e.g., Matt. 7:13–14), he still should have avoided speculation and left the quantity of the elect or reprobate rightly in God's secret counsel, allowing space for God's continued, mysterious pursuit of people to their last breath.
2. Why is it that when Calvin deduces God's nature from his works that he does not include reprobation as one of the works that informs God's nature? The fact that Calvin does not include reprobation as providing substantial insight into who God is separates him from the many others, like Barth, who conclude that Calvin's doctrine undermines one's ability to know and trust God. Why didn't Calvin see that possibility?
3. In his detailed teaching on reprobation as part of God's plan, does Calvin violate his nonspeculative, scriptural methodology? As noted above, Jacobs thinks that, because of his polemic debates with opponents of his doctrine of predestination, Calvin provides material teaching on what should have remained simply a boundary marker. Does Scripture even clearly assert a doctrine of reprobation? If so, was Calvin scripturally justified in laying out specifics of *how* and *why* God brings about reprobation? Does Scripture justify such significant talk about God's *secret* will? Should reprobation have remained as the unknown, skeletal shadow of God's election by grace? In that case, reprobation could be spoken of as a bare fact that eludes explanation or justification in God, reminiscent of the existence of evil in the world. Would not this latter approach have been more faithful to the holistic biblical account and also helped Calvin avoid some statements that tend to undermine the assurance of salvation in Calvin's teaching on predestination?
4. Why does Calvin overlook the inherent missional nature of election? Scripture is clear that Israel is meant to be "a light to the nations" (Is. 42:7,

49:6). The disciples are chosen to be sent (John 20:21). The Spirit fills the faithful for the explicit purpose of witnessing to the ends of the earth (Acts 1:8). Instead of being chosen at the expense of the lost, in the Bible, the elect are chosen for the sake of the lost. Could it be that if Calvin had recognized the missional nature of election that he would have never faced accusations that his teaching presented a tyrant God or a *Deus nudus absconditus* because God's love for all people would have been intrinsically present to any teaching on election? Recent work in Biblical scholarship has found this theme as central to a proper understanding of election.[232]

5. Where is the empathy for the reprobate? Would it not be more consistent with Calvin's doctrine of God that God would be grieved over the state of the reprobate instead of coldly condemning them as his enemies, especially in light of Calvin's teaching of the inherent dignity and value of all humans as image bearers? Or does Calvin's account of predestination rule out the possibility of God's being empathetic at all? Particularly, if the law is summarized in love of God and love for neighbor, how can it be that God (who is the embodiment of the law) seemingly does not love the reprobate "neighbor" (even in their state as enemies of God and ones deserving condemnation)? Similarly, in his descriptions of reprobation, does Calvin show adequate empathy for the human beings who remain forever alienated from God? By assuming God's righteousness in his condemnation of the reprobate, Calvin can tend toward dehumanizing them.

6. Finally, does Calvin go too far in his dismissal of logic regarding reprobation alongside the preaching of the gospel and hope for the salvation of all? Although the lawyer Calvin clearly values logical thinking in other discussions (e.g., God's causality of all things), he is content to say that God both desires the salvation of all and chooses to pass over some for salvation. He similarly teaches that we should preach to all and hope for the salvation of all while affirming our hatred of God's enemies, which includes the reprobate who remain clothed in their rebellious sinful nature. These seeming contradictions do not make sense logically. Is Calvin so convinced of God's nature and disposition that he can somehow overlook such logical contradictions? If so, how?

Although other questions could be raised, these six touch on key concerns that, if addressed, could significantly strengthen the consistency and scriptural faithfulness of Calvin's account of predestination. We shall address these further in chapter 8.

CONCLUSION: ONE SECRET WILL DISCLOSED AS MERCY, VEILED AS CONDEMNATION

In conclusion, for Calvin, God's one, righteous, and secret will is accommodated to the elect in a twofold but drastically asymmetrical manner in the doctrine of predestination, namely as God's revealed electing will for the elect and God's veiled reprobating will for the reprobate. God's merciful disclosed disposition toward humanity, the inclination of God that corresponds with God's electing will, is extended to all humanity and effected in the elect. For Calvin, God's electing will takes dogmatic and practical priority over the skeletal fact of God's reprobating will. Thus, election corresponds with God's revealed nature and spurs the proclamation of God's disclosed disposition to the world while reprobation remains a bare fact for which God is responsible but, from the human perspective, largely does not correspond with God's revealed nature or provide significant knowledge of God. In Holmes's words, for Calvin, reprobation is a "Christless doctrine,"[233] one that connects with the God revealed in Jesus Christ primarily through God's hidden counsel.

Finally, as we have seen, Calvin did not see his doctrine of predestination as undermining the assurance of salvation for any who look to Christ in faith; Calvin's teaching reveals primarily continuity along with small but significant discontinuity with Beza's doctrine of predestination; and Calvin's approach leaves a number of critical questions that have plagued the doctrine for the past five hundred years.

From the perspective of faith, Calvin joyfully and confidently ascribes to the doctrine of predestination as an expression of the grace that is offered to all by the merciful, righteous, and judging Father who, from before time in his powerful governance of the universe, enables some to receive the offered grace while mysteriously leaving others to the just deserts of their sin.

Having examined Calvin's teaching on the doctrine of God and predestination, we now turn to a brief integration of our findings up to this point.

NOTES

1. *Inst.* 3.21.1, p. 921; *CO* 2:679. According to Battles's notes, this paragraph was new in the 1559 edition.

2. *Comm. Ezek.* 18:23; *CO* 40:445–446.

3. By "predestination," I (following Calvin's typical practice) refer to the doctrine that includes both (positive) election (to life and eternal communion with God) and (negative) reprobation (to death and damnation).

4. Cf. Wilhelm Niesel, *The Theology of Calvin,* trans. Harold Knight (London: Lutterworth Press, 1956), 159. Cf. Charles Partee, *The Theology of John Calvin* (Louisville: Westminster John Knox Press, 2008), 244–48.

5. van der Kooi, *As in a Mirror*, 159.

6. Muller, *Calvin and the Reformed Tradition*, 43–44. Cf. I. John Hesselink, "Calvin's Theology," in *The Cambridge Companion to John Calvin*, ed. Donald K. McKim (Cambridge: Cambridge University Press, 2004), 77–80.

7. In light of the fact that Calvin was only one contributor to the diverse Reformed tradition that developed over hundreds of years, we avoid using the term "Calvinist." Cf. Muller, *Calvin and the Reformed Tradition*, 277.

8. *CO* 8:249–366. Cf. de Greef, *The Writings of John Calvin*, 158–59.

9. See chapter 7 below for further discussion. Cf. Bullinger to Calvin, 1 December 1551, *CO* 14:215. Cf. Richard Muller, *Christ and the Decree: Christology and Predestination in Reformed Theology from Calvin to Perkins* (Durham, NC: Labyrinth Press, 1986), 45. Cf. Cornelis P. Venema, *Heinrich Bullinger and the Doctrine of Predestination: Author of "the Other Reformed Tradition"?* (Grand Rapids: Baker Academic, 2002).

10. Christian Link, "Election and Predestination," in *John Calvin's Impact on Church and Society: 1509–2009*, ed. Martin E. Hirzel and Martin Sallmann (Grand Rapids: Eerdmans, 2009), 107. Cf. Eberhard Busch, *Gotteserkenntnis Und Menschlichkeit* (Zürich: Theologisher Verlag Zürich, 2005), 67. Cf. Augustine, "On the Predestination of the Saints," in *Saint Augustine: Four Anti-Pelagian Writings* (Washington, DC: Catholic University of America Press, 1992). Cf. Martin Luther, "On the Bondage of the Will," in *Discourse on Free Will* (New York: Ungar, 1961).

11. Gibson, *Reading the Decree*, 76. Cf. *Comm. John* 13:18; *CO* 47:310–311. Cf. *Harmony of the Gospels*, Matt. 11:27; *CO* 45:319.

12. *Comm. Rom.* 9:14, *CO* 49:181.

13. Gibson, *Reading the Decree*, 35–36. Although Calvin emphasizes the *electio Patris*, he also understands Christ as subject (*autorem*) of election as the divine Son (*Comm. John* 13:18; *CO* 47:311) and as executor of election as Mediator (Gibson, *Reading the Decree*, 76. Cf. Muller, *Christ and the Decree*, 18).

14. *Inst.* 3.21.5, p. 926; *CO* 2:683.

15. *Comm. John* 3:16; *CO* 47:63–64.

16. *Comm. Is.* 42:6; *CO* 37:65.

17. As van der Kooi says, "Calvin desired to be a Biblical theologian first and foremost, and with regard to the discussion of election sought to respect the Biblical-theological connections which he had discerned" (*As in a Mirror*, 161).

18. Many claims have been made asserting the significance of the placement of Calvin's teaching on predestination at the end of Book 3 in the *Institutes* and its movement from the doctrine of providence in the 1539 edition to soteriology in the 1559 edition. Although it seems foolish to ascribe no significance to the placement of the doctrine, the specific meaning remains unclear. Hesselink believes that the placement may have theological significance, "for [predestination] is not discussed theoretically in connection with the doctrine of God or creation but is simply a discussion of the experiential fact in reference to the attitudes of believers and unbelievers" (*Calvin's First Catechism*, 42–43). Muller has compellingly argued that Calvin was likely following a *loci* approach to the ordering of the *Institutes* which does not indicate priority of significance based on order (*The Unaccommodated Calvin*, 118–39). Carl Trueman ("Election: Calvin's Theology and Its Early Reception," in *Calvin's*

Theology and Its Reception: Disputes, Developments, and New Possibilities, ed. J. Todd Billings and I. John Hesselink [Louisville, KY: Westminster John Knox Press, 2012], 98), Randall Zachman (*John Calvin as Teacher, Pastor, and Theologian: The Shape of His Writings and Thought* [Grand Rapids: Baker Academic, 2006], 101), van der Kooi (*As in a Mirror*, 161), and Gibson (*Reading the Decree*, 170) all, with various emphases, also assert that Calvin's order serves his rhetorical aims for rightly communicating the story of salvation.

19. This corresponds in Calvin and the Reformed tradition's terms as God's preceptive, signified, or revealed will.

20. In Calvin and the Reformed tradition, God's secret or decretive will.

21. Cf. *Inst.* 1.6.3, p. 73; *CO* 2:55; *Inst.* 1.18.3, p. 234; *CO* 2:171; *Inst.* 3.2.1, p. 543; *CO* 2:398. Cf. *Comm. 1 Tim.* 6:16; *CO* 52:332.

22. *Comm Matt* 6:10; *CO* 45:198. Cf. *Comm Matt* 22:37; *CO* 45:644.

23. Calvin passionately opposes the idea of a God of *potentia absoluta* who could act in a way that does not correspond to his nature. See "God Is Just, So God's Will Is Just" below.

24. *Comm. 2 Pet.* 3:9; *CO* 55:475–476. Cf. *Comm. Rom.* 11:34; *CO* 49:231.

25. *De Aeterna*, p. 113; *CO* 8:307.

26. *Inst.* 3.23.1, p. 948. Cf. *Comm. Rom.* 9:14; *CO* 49:181.

27. *Comm. Rom.* 11:2; *CO* 49:212.

28. *Comm. Eph.* "Argument"; *CO* 51:141.

29. *Inst.* 3.21.1, p. 921; *CO* 2:679. Cf. *Comm. Rom.* 9:11; *CO* 49:177. Cf. *Comm. Rom.* 11:6; *CO* 49:215.

30. Trueman, "Election," 100.

31. *Sermons on Ephesians*, 1:4–6, p. 39; *CO* 51:274.

32. *Comm. Rom.* 9:11; *CO* 49:177.

33. *Inst.* 2.17.1, p. 529; *CO* 2:386.

34. *Comm. John* 6:45; *CO* 47:150. Cf. *Inst.* 3.24.1, p. 966; *CO* 2:712.

35. *Inst.* 3.22.3, p. 935; *CO* 2:689.

36. For example, *Inst.* 3.22.3, p. 935; *CO* 2:689.

37. Cf. *De Aeterna*, pp. 155–56; *CO* 8:341–342.

38. *De Aeterna*, p. 115; *CO* 8:308.

39. *Comm. Ezek.* 18:23; *CO* 40:445.

40. *Comm.* 2 Peter 3:9; *CO* 55:475.

41. *Comm. 1 Tim.* 2:4; *CO* 52:268.

42. *Inst.* 3.24.16, p. 984; *CO* 2:726. Here, specifically drawing on the context of the 1 Timothy passage, Calvin says that Paul's words mean that God desires that there would be no discrimination in the preaching and hearing of the gospel based on social class.

43. *Comm. John* 3:16; *CO* 47:65.

44. *Comm. Rom.* 11:2; *CO* 49:212.

45. We shall see below that Calvin here misses the missional element of Israel's (and Abraham's) election for the sake of the world and God's blessing of the world.

46. *Inst.* 3.21.5–7, pp. 926–31; *CO* 2:682–687.

47. *Comm. Rom.* 9:6; *CO* 49:174–175. Cf. *Sermons on Ephesians,* 1:3–4, p. 23; *CO* 51:260.

48. *Inst.* 3.24.15, p. 983; *CO* 2:725. Note how experience informs Calvin's exposition. We shall return to this concept below.

49. *Comm. John* 3:16; *CO* 47:65. Cf. J. Mark Beach, "Calvin's Treatment of the Offer of the Gospel and Divine Grace," *Mid-America Journal of Theology* 22 (2011).

50. *Comm. John* 6:44; *CO* 47:149. Cf. *Comm. Heb.* 6:4–5; *CO* 55:72. Cf. *Comm. Rom.* 10:16; *CO* 49:206.

51. Muller, *Calvin and the Reformed Tradition*, 78.

52. *Comm. John* 6:40; *CO* 47:147.

53. As we shall see below ("Causality"), Calvin did not see a problem in saying that one event has two distinct causes; here human faith and God's electing will are both real (compatibilist) causes of salvation.

Calvin also sees God's extension of his mercy to all as a further witness to the guilt of the reprobate (*Inst.* 3.24.15, p. 983; *CO* 2:725).

54. Cf. van der Kooi, *As in a Mirror*, 170–71.

55. *Comm. Eph.* 1:3; *CO* 51:146. Cf. *Inst.* 3.24.5, 970; *CO* 2:715. Cf. *Sermons on Ephesians,* 1:7–10, p. 60; *CO* 51:292.

56. *Inst.* 3.21.1, pp. 921–22; *CO* 2:679.

57. "God will have the whole praise [*toute la louange*] of our salvation be attributed to him" (*Sermons on Election and Reprobation,* no. 2, p. 37; *CO* 58:38). Cf. *Comm. Mal.* 1:2–6; *CO* 44:409.

58. *Comm. Eph.* 1:5; *CO* 51:148.

59. *Inst.* 2.2.11, p. 269; *CO* 2:195. Cf. *Inst.* 3.23.13, p. 962; *CO* 2:709.

60. *Comm. 2 Pet.* 3:9; *CO* 55:475.

61. Cf. Paul Jacobs, *Prädestination Und Verantwortlichkeit Bei Calvin* (Darmstadt: Wissenschaftliche Buchgesellschaft, 1968).

62. For more on Calvin's compatibilist view, in which there could be more than one cause for the same event, see "Causality" section below.

63. *Inst.* 3.23.2, p. 949; *CO* 2:700.

64. *Inst.* 3.23.6, p. 954; *CO* 2:703. My translation in part.

65. Quoting from Augustine, *Letters* clxxxxvi. 7.23, in *Inst.* 3.23.5, p. 952; *CO* 2:702. Cf. Augustine, *Letters, Vol. 4 (165–203)* (Washington, DC: Catholic University of America Press, 1955).

66. *Comm. Rom.* 11:6; *CO* 49:215. Cf. *Inst.* 3.23.1, p. 948; *CO* 2:699. Cf. 3.22.11, p. 947; *CO* 2:698.

An obvious question here relates to Calvin's anthropology. Do human beings inherently have value to God? We know from Calvin's account of creation that his answer is yes. Nevertheless, Calvin's commitment to the greatness of God's majesty vis-à-vis human comprehension allows this type of contradiction. In short, for Calvin, God's posture does not make sense, but the most high God knows what he is doing.

67. *Inst.* 3.3.23, p. 619; *CO* 2:454.

68. *Inst.* 3.23.3, p. 950; *CO* 2:700.

69. *De Aeterna*, p. 122; *CO* 8:314.

70. *De Aeterna*, pp. 99–100; *CO* 8:295–296.

71. In this section, it is particularly important to remember that for Calvin "predestination" always refers to double predestination, including both election and reprobation.

72. Muller, *The Unaccommodated Calvin*, 5.

73. *Comm. Rom.* 9:14; *CO* 49:181. My translation.

74. For example, *Inst.* 3.22.4–6, pp. 936–40; *CO* 2:690–693. For a detailed examination of Calvin's exegesis of Romans 9–11, see Gibson, *Reading the Decree*.

75. All except the Malachi text are explicitly mentioned in *De Aeterna*.

76. For example, *Sermons on Election and Reprobation* from Genesis 25–27. Cf., for example, *Comm. John* 3:16; *CO* 47:63–66.

77. It is an open question whether Calvin abides by this rule, particularly in his estimation of numbers of the elect and reprobate. Jacobs says that Calvin violates this principle in his fleshing out of the doctrine of reprobation—for example, identifying false signs of faith seen in some of the reprobate for those who fall away from faith (*Prädestination*, 144).

78. Cf. *Inst.* 1.1.1, p. 35; *CO* 2:31. Cf. Huijgen, *Accommodation*, 305.

79. *Inst.* 3.21.1, pp. 920–21; *CO* 2:678–679.

80. *Inst.* 3.22.1, pp. 932–33; *CO* 2:687.

81. *Inst.* 3.24.12, p. 979. In his comments on John 17:20, the number of recipients is scarcely 1 percent (*vix centesimus*) (*Comm. John* 17:20; *CO* 47:386).

82. *De Aeterna*, p. 108; *CO* 8:302–303. For Calvin, any who were not of the people of Israel or any who did not directly respond to the preaching of Christ were assumed to be condemned in their sin. Cf. Gibson, *Reading the Decree*, 81. Calvin apparently does not perceive this elevation of experience as a violation of his non-speculative, Scripture-based methodological commitments. More on that at the close of this chapter.

83. *Comm. John* 6:44; *CO* 47:149. Cf. *Comm. John* 6:65; *CO* 47:161.

84. *Comm. John* 10:26; *CO* 47:249. My translation.

85. Paul Helm, "John Calvin and the Hiddenness of God," in *Engaging the Doctrine of God: Contemporary Evangelical Perspectives*, ed. Bruce L McCormack (Grand Rapids: Baker Academic, 2008), 72. Cf. Gibson, *Reading the Decree*, 171.

86. *Inst.* 3.21.6, p. 929; *CO* 2:685.

87. Another (not necessarily contradictory) approach to divine freedom is Barth's depiction that God's freedom is to be himself and to act accordingly in "divine life and love" (*CD* II/1, p. 301; *KD*, p. 339).

88. *Inst.* 3.23.10, p. 959; *CO* 2:707.

89. *Comm. Rom.* 9:23; *CO* 49:188.

90. *Inst.* 1.1.2, p. 43; *CO* 2:33. Cf. *Inst.* 3.22.11, p. 947; *CO* 2:698.

91. *Comm. Rom.* 9:23; *CO* 49:188. Zachman asserts that Calvin's assumption is that "the love of God is best revealed against the horizon of God's wrath" (*Reconsidering John Calvin*, 4). Cf. *Harmony of the Gospels*, Matt. 11:25; *CO* 45:317.

92. Trueman, "Election," 100. Trueman asserts the first three, but I add the fourth to clarify against Augustinian universalism that logically provides the possibility of only one reprobate being (Oliver Crisp, *Deviant Calvinism: Broadening Reformed Theology* [Minneapolis: Fortress Press, 2014)], 97–124).

93. According to Jacobs, Calvin includes his teaching on the doctrine of reprobation for the purpose of doctrinal cohesiveness, but Calvin wrongly extends the teaching in his defenses of the doctrinal system and God's free grace against attacks. He says, "The extension of the teaching of reprobation is understandable theologically-historically, but theologically-systematically it is not to be justified" (*Prädestination*, 147; my translation).

94. *Comm. Ezek.* 18:32; *CO* 40:459. Cf. *Comm. Ezek.* 18:23; *CO* 40:445–446, quoted in part above.

95. *Harmony of the Gospels*, Matt. 23:37; *CO* 45:317. My translation.

96. *Inst.* 3.24.17, p. 986; *CO* 2:728. Cf. *De Aeterna*, p. 184; *CO* 8:366.

97. These verses commonly occur throughout the four predestination chapters of the *Institutes* (3.21–24) and throughout *De Aeterna*. For an example of Calvin's appeal to both verses in one place, see *Inst.* 3.23.5, pp. 952–53; *CO* 2:702. Cf. *Comm. Rom.* 9:20; *CO* 49:186.

98. *Comm. Ezek.* 18:25; *CO* 40:450. Cf. *Comm. Rom.* 9:19; *CO* 49:185.

99. *De Aeterna*, p. 161; *CO* 8:346–347. Cf. *Comm. Rom.* 9:20; *CO* 49:186. Cf. *De Aeterna*, p. 64–66; *CO* 8:266–269.

100. For us, the first is God's one, secret, righteous will and the latter is God's disposition toward humanity.

101. *Comm. Rom.* 11:34; *CO* 49:231.

102. *Comm. Rom.* 9:22; *CO* 49:187.

103. *Inst.* 3.23.4, p. 952; *CO* 2:702.

104. *Inst.* 3.22.7, p. 941; *CO* 2:694.

105. *Comm. Rom.* 9:14; *CO* 49:181.

106. *Inst.* 3.24.12, p. 978; *CO* 2:722.

107. *Inst.* 3.23.2, p. 949; *CO* 2:700. Cf. *Comm. Rom.* 9:15; *CO* 49:181–182. Cf. *Comm. Rom.* 11:34; *CO* 49:231.

108. Muller, *Calvin and the Reformed Tradition*, 107–25. "What Calvin in no way countenanced was a notion of a double will in God, one hypothetical to save all, the other absolute to save only the elect" (p. 122).

109. Muller, *Calvin and the Reformed Tradition*, 119. The *ad intra-ad extra* terminology is Muller's, not Calvin's.

110. Regarding Calvin's connection between soteriology and the partial but reliable revelation of God *ad intra*, see Gibson, *Reading the Decree*, 84.

111. Like the knowledge of God, we have skeletal knowledge *that* God has one secret will without understanding *how* exactly that will is expressed in what appears to be two wills.

112. *Comm. Rom.* 9:20; *CO* 49:186. Regarding a reason for choosing the elect and not the reprobate, Calvin says, "God does indeed have a definite, real reason for what he does, but it is too secret, sublime, and concealed [*recondita*] for it to be grasped by the measure of our mind, which is so narrow and mean" (*BLW*, p. 191; *CO* 6:365). Cf. *Comm. Rom.* 9:18; *CO* 49:184.

113. *Sermons on Ephesians*, 1:7–10, p. 59; *CO* 51:291.

114. Latin *iusititia* can be translated into English as "justice" or "righteousness."

115. *Comm. Ezek.* 18:25; *CO* 40:450.

116. *Comm. Rom.* 9:22; *CO* 49:187.

117. *Inst.* 3.23.2, p. 949; *CO* 2:700.

118. *Sermons on Ephesians,* 1:4–6, p. 42; *CO* 51:277.

119. For an excellent summary of recent Calvin scholarship regarding *potentia absoluta*, see Huijgen, *Accommodation*, 262–63. Cf. van der Kooi, *As in a Mirror*, 136. Cf. Steinmetz, *Context*, 40–50.

120. *Inst.* 2.3.5, p. 295; *CO* 2:213. This matches Barth's definition of freedom noted above.

121. *Inst.* 3.23.2, p. 950; *CO* 2:700. Calvin also asserts that unlike creatures, God's attributes match up exactly with his will: "For since God's goodness, wisdom, power, righteousness, and will are united together by a kind of, so to speak, circular connection, it is the work of a wicked, devilish imagination to break this bond apart" (*BLW*, p. 148; *CO* 6:334). Cf. *1538 Catechism*, p. 17, s. 13; *CO* 5:333.

122. *De Aeterna*, p. 179; *CO* 8:361. Cf. "Nor must we, therefore, deem his power to be limited, when he is a necessity to himself [*dum sibi ipse est necessitas*]; or that anything of his liberty and authority is diminished, when he willingly and freely binds himself. And let us especially remember that his power is connected by a sacred restraint [*sacro nexu*] with his grace and with faith in his promise. Hence it may be truly and properly said, that he can do nothing but what he wills and promises" (*Comm. Gen.* 19:22; *CO* 23:277; my translation).

123. *Congrégation, CO* 8:105–106; Trans. from Philip C. Holtrop, *The Bolsec Controversy on Predestination, From 1551 to 1555* (Lewiston: Edwin Mellen Press, 1993), 709–10. Cf. "Yet we should be always sustained by this bridle—he is just [*ipse esse iustum*]" (*Comm. Ezek.* 18:25; *CO* 40:451). Cf. *1538 Catechism*, p. 17; *CO* 5:333. Cf. van der Kooi, *As in a Mirror*, 177. Cf. Niesel, *Theology of Calvin*, 167.

124. *De Aeterna*, p. 88; *CO* 8:286.

125. *Comm. John* 17:4; *CO* 47:378. My translation.

126. *De Aeterna*, p. 119; *CO* 8:312. Cf. *Comm. Rom.* 11:36; *CO* 49:232. Cf. *Comm. Col.* 1:14; *CO* 52:84.

127. Cf. Billy Kristanto, *Sola Dei Gloria: The Glory of God in the Thought of John Calvin* (Frankfurt: Peter Lang, 2011), 149–55. Cf. Parker, *Knowledge of God*, 54.

128. Hesselink contends that although Calvin teaches double predestination, "Calvin does not, however, teach that there is a symmetry or parallel between election and reprobation" ("Calvin's Theology," 84). Although Beza is often accused of teaching a symmetry between election and reprobation, we see below that this would also be a misrepresentation and oversimplification of Beza's stance.

129. *De Aeterna*, p. 90; *CO* 8:287. Cf. *Inst.* 3.21.5, p. 926; *CO* 2:683. *Comm. Rom.* 9:11; *CO* 49:177.

130. *Comm. Rom.* 11:7; *CO* 49:216. In conformity with his nonspeculative and pastoral methodology, Calvin generally teaches an infralapsarian perspective in which he sees Christ's redeeming work as logically proceeding from the fall of humanity (e.g., *Comm.* 1 Pet. 1:20; *CO* 55:225; *Comm. Gen.* 1:26–3:23; *CO* 23:25–80). However, particularly when reflecting upon God's sovereignty, Calvin can make supralapsarian statements, as seen here. Cf. *Inst.* 3.23.1, p. 947–48; *CO* 2:699.

Note also here Calvin's reasoning: single predestination is not only nonbiblical but also illogical.

131. van der Kooi, *As in a Mirror*, 168–69. Cf. Trueman, "Election," 101.

132. God's "dreadful" (*horribile*) decree of the fall of humanity (*Inst.* 3.23.7, p. 955; *CO* 2:704).

133. *De Aeterna*, pp. 98, 101; *CO* 8:295, 297. Calvin also contends that since God is the remote cause of sinful actions caused proximately by humans, God is not the author of sin (*De Aeterna*, p. 181; *CO* 8:363).

134. Michael McKenna, "Compatibilism," *The Stanford Encyclopedia of Philosophy* (2009), http://plato.stanford.edu/archives/win2009/entries/compatibilism/. Paul Helm proposes that Calvin is influenced by various streams of thinking, most notably Stoicism and determinism, that influence Calvin's specific type of compatibilism, which Helm calls "partly compatibilistic" (*Calvin at the Centre* [Oxford: Oxford University Press, 2010], 227–72).

Muller concludes, "Calvin's approach to human freedom is untechnical and, consequently, somewhat vague, perhaps even imprecise. He certainly did assume both an overarching divine determination of all things and a human freedom from necessity or coaction" (*Divine Will and Human Choice: Freedom, Contingency, and Necessity in Early Modern Reformed Thought* [Grand Rapids: Baker Academic, 2017], 192).

The compatibilist discussion was significantly shaped by P. F. Strawson's recovery of focus on moral responsibility and free will in the 1960s. Recently, Peter van Inwagen, an incompatibilist, has asserted that the concept of the free will is incoherent on both compatibilist and incompatibilist terms, which he proposes leads to the "problem of free will" of how to explain what humans experience and identify as free will ("How to Think about the Problem of Free Will," *The Journal of Ethics* 12, no. 3–4 [2008]).

135. "The idea that God orders all things that come to pass, such that no event occurs without his concurrently bringing it about in conjunction with mundane creaturely causes, is usually referred to as *meticulous providence*, in order to distinguish it from those accounts of divine providence where God does not decree or otherwise bring about all that comes to pass" (Crisp, "Calvin on Creation and Providence," 53). In a positive sense, Jacobs describes this view as the "willing necessity" of the elect in their sanctification by choosing according to God's will for their sanctification (*Prädestination*, 136).

136. Busch affirms that Calvin teaches us to hold both the cause of humanity and the cause of God. We cannot understand how these are held together because God's counsel is simply beyond human understanding (*Gotteserkenntnis Und Meschlichkeit*, 78).

137. *Comm. John* 17:12; *CO* 47:382.

138. Commenting on Phil. 2:12–13 in *Inst.* 2.5.11, p. 330; *CO* 2:239.

139. *Inst.* 3.24.14, p. 981; *CO* 2:724. Jacobs concludes that God's causality in reprobation is more mechanistic (*mechanischen*) than coercive (*Prädestination*, 157).

140. *De Aeterna*, p. 100; *CO* 8:296. Cf. *Comm. Mal.* 1:2–6; *CO* 44:407.

141. *De Aeterna*, p. 160; *CO* 8:346.

142. *Comm. John* 3:19; *CO* 47:67. Cf. *Comm. John* 3:17; *CO* 47:66. Cf. *Inst.* 3.23.8, p. 957; *CO* 2:705. Cf. *Comm Is.* 6:10; *CO* 36:137–138.

143. *Comm. Eph.* 1:5, 8; *CO* 51:148, 150.

144. *Inst.* 3.14.21, p. 787; *CO* 2:578. Cf. *Comm. Rom.* 3:22; *CO* 49:60.

145. Jacobs similarly points out that whereas God is the *fundamentum* of election, he is not the *fundamentum* of reprobation. Similarly, regarding sanctification and responsibility, there is a logically analytic (*analytisches*) relationship between Christ-election-sanctification, whereas the relationship between reprobation and sin is solely logically synthetic (*synthetisches*) and has no personal grounding in Satan in the manner that election is grounded in Christ (*Prädestination*, 155–56).

146. van der Kooi, *As in a Mirror*, 169.

147. Cf. *Congrégation*, *CO* 8:111, trans. from Holtrop, *The Bolsec Controversy*, 714.

148. As Link says, "There is thus no symmetrical balance between election and condemnation. This 'condemnation' is the passive manner in which God passes over certain people in his election" ("Election and Predestination," 118). Cf. *Congrégation*, *CO* 8:113–114; trans. from Holtrop, *The Bolsec Controversy*, 716.

149. *Sermons on Ephesians*, 1:4–6, p. 41; *CO* 51:275–276.

150. *Inst.* 3.23.1, p. 947; *CO* 2:698. Cf. *De Aeterna*, p. 109, n. 3.

151. See "God's Freedom and Glory" above.

152. *Comm. Rom.* 9:22; *CO* 49:188.

153. *Inst.* "John Calvin to the Reader," p. 4; *CO* 2:1–2.

154. *Comm. John*, "The Epistle Dedicatory to Simon Grynaeus," *CO* 10:403.

155. We shall further examine the audience in Calvin's preaching in chapter 5.

156. *Inst.* 3.25.12, pp. 1007–8.

157. For an interesting proposal regarding Calvin's logic here, see Helm, "Calvin, Indefinite Language, and Definite Atonement."

158. *De Aeterna*, p. 158; *CO* 8:344.

159. *Inst.* 2.3.10, p. 304; *CO* 2:220. Cf. *Comm. Rom.* 11:2; *CO* 49:212.

160. *Comm. 1 Tim.* 2:4; *CO* 52:268.

161. Cf. *Comm. John* 6:65; *CO* 47:161.

162. Cf. *Inst.* 3.23.13, pp. 961–63; *CO* 2:708–710. Cf. *Sermons on Ephesians*, 1:3–4, pp. 22–34; *CO* 51:259–270.

163. *Harmony of Moses*, Ex. 9:16; *CO* 24:112–113.

164. *Inst.* 3.23.14, p. 963; *CO* 2:710. Cf. *De Aeterna*, p. 137–38; *CO* 8:327–328.

165. *Inst.* 3.23.14, p. 964; *CO* 2:711. Quoted also in *De Aeterna*, p. 138; *CO* 8:328. Augustine, *On Rebuke and Grace*, trans. Philip Schaff (New York: Christian Literature Publishing, 1886), XV.46.

166. "It may be that death proved to them a medicine" (*Comm. Josh.* 7:24; *CO* 25:480).

167. John L Thompson, *Reading the Bible with the Dead: What You Can Learn from the History of Exegesis That You Can't Learn from Exegesis Alone* (Grand Rapids: Eerdmans, 2007), 65–66. Cf. Dowey, *Knowledge of God*, 214.

168. *Comm. John* 6:64; *CO* 47:160. Rhetorically, Calvin seems periodically to violate this conviction, calling his opponents such titles as "dead dog," "worthless," and

"monsters" (*De Aeterna*, p. 54; *CO* 8:258–259). However, even with these enemies of the faith, Calvin typically avoids labeling them as reprobate. For example, Michael Servetus, who was infamously executed by the Genevan council while Calvin was the chief minister; Calvin sought his return to the true faith right up to his execution (Gordon, *Calvin*, 223). Cf. Herman Selderhuis, *John Calvin: A Pilgrim's Life* (Grand Rapids: InterVarsity Press, 2009), 203–6.

169. *Inst.* 4.11–12, pp. 1211–54; *CO* 2:891–924.

170. *Inst.* 4.12.9, p. 1237; *CO* 2:911.

171. *Comm. Heb.* 6:6; *CO* 55:72.

172. *Comm. 1 Tim.* 2:4; *CO* 52:269.

173. *Sermons on Ephesians*, pp. 21, 49, 65, and so forth; *CO* 51:258. *CO* typically does not include the prayers. McKee has observed that this set prayer was used by Calvin on Sunday afternoons and every weekday except Wednesday, on which day Calvin used a different set prayer (*The Pastoral Ministry and Worship in Calvin's Geneva* [Geneva: Librairie Droz S.A., 2016], 507).

174. *Comm. John* 17:9; *CO* 47:380. The objection could here be raised regarding how Jesus' command to love our enemies and pray for them aligns with hoping for the destruction of all of God's enemies. I think Calvin would say that this type of question arrogantly puts us in the place of judging God. God always acts according to his merciful, righteous, and judging nature, even when we cannot perceive how.

175. This is an example of Calvin's (and God's) lack of visible empathy for these human beings who are sentenced to condemnation. See "Methodological Questions for Further Consideration" below.

176. *Inst.* 3.23.1, pp. 947–49; *CO* 2:698–699. Calvin also rejects the differentiation between God's will and permission that was later approved at the Synod of Dordt. For Calvin, such a distinction is meaningless because "the will of God is the necessity of all things." However, Calvin's rejection of God's permission does not impede him from designating the evident cause of condemnation (*evidentem damnationis causam*) as the sinful nature of humanity (*Inst.* 3.23.8, pp. 956–57; *CO* 2:705).

177. Link, "Election and Predestination," 121. As Busch says, the attempt to have that solution is to try, like Adam and Eve, to "be like God" (*Gotteserkenntnis Und Meschlichkeit*, 78). Cf. van der Kooi, *As in a Mirror*, 160 n130.

178. Link, "Election and Predestination," 121.

179. Using our previous terminology, God's veiled will provides only skeletal knowledge, while God's disclosed will provides material knowledge of God's electing work.

Muller asserts that there is no way to contemplate reprobation in God because our sins are the source of our reprobation, not God (Muller, *Christ and the Decree*, 80).

180. Jacobs, *Prädestination*, 144. My translation.

181. Cf. Muller, *Christ and the Decree*, 25.

182. Stephen R. Holmes, *Listening to the Past: The Place of Tradition in Theology* (Grand Rapids: Baker Academic, 2002), 129–30. Holmes also suggests that Barth's uniqueness in the Reformed tradition is that he has a doctrine of reprobation whereas the tradition does not (p. 122).

183. Cf. Zachman's study on the quest for assurance in Luther's and Calvin's theologies (*The Assurance of Faith: Conscience in the Theology of Martin Luther and John Calvin* [Minneapolis: Fortress Press, 1993]).

184. For example, *De Aeterna*, p. 126; *CO* 8:318.

185. Huijgen's demonstration that Calvin taught assurance based upon sound soteriology, showing what is necessary for salvation instead of certainty that is grounded in the doctrine of God, confirms this approach (*Accommodation*, 270).

186. Zachman, *Assurance of Faith*, 219. Cf. *Inst.* 3.24.8, p. 974; *CO* 2:719.

187. *Inst.* 3.24.4, pp. 968–69; *CO* 2:714–715.

188. *Inst.* 3.2.16, p. 561; *CO* 2:411.

189. *Comm. Ezek.* 18:23; *CO* 40:446.

190. We are assured "by believing in Jesus Christ" (*Sermons on Ephesians*, 1:4–6, p. 47; *CO* 51:281).

191. Cf. Zachman, *Assurance of Faith*, 246.

192. Cf. *Inst.* 3.2.10–13, pp. 554–59; *CO* 2:405–410.

193. *Comm. Heb.* 6:4–5; *CO* 55:72. Cf. *Inst.* 3.2.12, p. 556; *CO* 2:407.

194. *Inst.* 3.24.7, p. 973; *CO* 2:718. Cf. *De Aeterna*, pp. 151–52; *CO* 8:338–339.

195. *Comm. Heb.* 6:4–5; *CO* 55:72.

196. *Inst.* 3.24.7, p. 973; *CO* 2:718.

197. Cf. Zachman, *Assurance of Faith*, 218.

198. *De Aeterna*, p. 113; *CO* 8:307.

199. *Comm. John* 15:9; *CO* 47:342. Cf. *Harmony of the Gospels*, Matt. 11:27; *CO* 45:320.

Zachman suggests the best solution to the problem of assurance for Calvin lies "in his understanding of Christ as the image of the Father." However, Zachman says that the loving Father revealed in and through Christ provides everything in Christ except election, making election *and* Christ as the source of all good things, and thus undermining assurance once again (*Assurance of Faith*, 246).

This suggestion holds significant contemporary appeal, especially considering Calvin's frequent references to God as loving Father, but for Calvin it would not fit with his broader doctrine of predestination that must include an understanding of God as righteous Judge. For Calvin, any true assurance must take into account God's mercy, righteousness, and judgment, which are all displayed in Christ, the mirror of election. It is confidence in Christ's saving work and grace that provides assurance, not a doctrine of God that eliminates the fear of judgment. For Calvin, simple as it may sound, the only certainty comes by looking at Christ; if one is looking to Christ, he or she has no need to fear.

200. *De Aeterna*, p. 126; *CO* 8:318. Cf. *Sermons on Ephesians*, 1:4–6, p. 47; *CO* 51:281–282. Cf. *De Aeterna*, p. 127; *CO* 8:318. Cf. Gibson, *Reading the Decree*, 65.

201. *De Aeterna*, p. 130; *CO* 8:321.

202. For example, R. T. Kendall, *Calvin and English Calvinism to 1649* (Oxford: Oxford University Press, 1979). Cf. Brian A. Armstrong, *Calvinism and the Amyraut Heresy: Protestant Scholasticism and Humanism in Seventeenth-Century France* (Madison, WI: University of Wisconsin Press, 1969). Cf. Holmes Rolston, III, *John Calvin versus the Westminster Confession* (Richmond, VA: John Knox Press, 1972).

Cf. Alister E. McGrath, *Reformation Thought: An Introduction* (Malden, MA: Blackwell Publishers, 1999), 140–43.

203. Cf. Muller, *Christ and the Decree*. For a concise summary of the developments in Calvin scholarship on this topic, see Raymond A. Blacketer, "The Man in the Black Hat: Theodore Beza and the Reorientation of Early Reformed Historiography," in *Church and School in Early Modern Protestantism*, ed. Jordan J. Ballor, David S. Sytsma, and Jason Zuidema (Leiden: Brill, 2013). Cf. Raymond A. Blacketer, "Blaming Beza: The Development of Definite Atonement in the Reformed Tradition," in *From Heaven He Came and Sought Her: Definite Atonement in Historical, Biblical, Theological, and Pastoral Perspective*, ed. David Gibson and Jonathan Gibson (Wheaton, IL: Crossway Books, 2013). Cf. Muller, *Calvin and the Reformed Tradition*.

In light of this helpful updated understanding, Calvin can now be appropriately appreciated for both his continuity *and* discontinuity with the Christian tradition before, during, and after his time, as exhibited in this comparison with Beza.

204. For example, Beza's letter to Calvin requesting feedback on the document, July 29, 1555 (*CO* 15:701–705).

205. See Heinrich Heppe, *Reformed Dogmatics*, trans. G. T. Thompson (Eugene, OR: Wipf & Stock, 2007), 147–48.

206. Richard Muller, "The Use and Abuse of a Document: Beza's *Tabula Praedestinationis*, the Bolsec Controversy, and the Origins of Reformed Orthodoxy," in *Protestant Scholasticism: Essays in Reassessment* (Eugene, OR: Wipf & Stock, 2005).

207. Cf. David C. Steinmetz, *Reformers in the Wings: From Geiler Von Kayersberg to Theogore Beza* (Oxford: Oxford University Press, 2001), 114–20.

208. Muller, "Use and Abuse," 35.

209. As Blacketer points out, it provides "the 'sum total' of Christianity in the same way that John 3:16 might be said to be the sum total of the faith" ("The Development of Definite Atonement," 132).

When Beza wrote his own summary of Christian doctrine, *Confessio christianae religionis*, in 1558, predestination was not the central dogma, organizing principle, or even a specific locus ("Use and Abuse," 74). Cf. Joel R. Beeke, "Theodore Beza's Supralapsarian Predestination," *Reformation and Revival Journal* 12, no. 2 (2003), 75.

210. Muller, "Use and Abuse," 34.

211. In the original Latin version, the text is broken up into short "aphorisms" of one to five sentences followed by extensive Scripture proof texts (*probationes*) printed in full.

212. Cf. Muller, "Use and Abuse."

213. *Tabula*, 3; 1:179.

214. *De Aeterna*, p. 119; *CO* 8:312.

215. *Tabula*, 2; 1:173. My translation.

216. *Inst.* 3.21.5, p. 926; *CO* 2:683.

217. *Tabula*, 3; 1:178. Both Calvin and Beza teach that the fall and reprobation still occur according to God's ordination, even though sin emerges from humanity, not from God.

218. Holmes, *Listening to the Past*, 131.

219. *Tabula*, 8; 1.204.

220. *Tabula*, 8; 1.204.

221. *Tabula*, 7; 1.197. Cf Muller, "Use and Abuse," 53.

222. Romans 9 is a central text across Beza's predestination teaching (*Tabula*; 1.170).

223. *Comm. Rom.* 9:23; *CO* 49:188. Calvin's translation decision there also highlights this exegetical choice.

224. *Comm. Rom.* 9:23; *CO* 49:188.

225. This corresponds with Calvin's teaching that God's mercy is at the center of his nature. Cf. chapter 2.

226. Cf. Oliver Crisp asserts that Calvin is supralapsarian in regard to the incarnation but infralapsarian in regard to Christ's priestly mediation (*Revisioning Christology: Theology in the Reformed Tradition* [Burlington, VT: Ashgate, 2011], 38). Cf. Joseph Tylenda, "Controversy on Christ the Mediator: Calvin's Second Reply to Stancaro," *Calvin Theological Journal* 8, no. 2 (1973), 147. Cf. Herman Bavinck's claim that "in Calvin's works the supralapsarian approach alternates with the infralapsarian" (*Reformed Dogmatics,* trans. John Vriend [Grand Rapids: Baker Academic, 2004], 364–65). Cf. Muller, *Divine Will and Human Choice*, 191.

227. Muller, "Use and Abuse," 58. Muller helpfully points out that Beza's supralapsarian tendency is not speculative but focused on the "temporal execution of the divine purpose," p. 59.

228. *Tabula*, 7; 1.197. Cf. Muller, "Use and Abuse," 51–53.

229. Muller, "Use and Abuse," 53.

230. Muller, "Use and Abuse," 54. It is important to remember that humanism and scholasticism are not mutually exclusive. Calvin uses many scholastic methods while opposing the abuses of theological schools that utilize scholastic methods toward speculative and useless ends. Cf. Muller, *The Unaccommodated Calvin*, 39–61. Cf. David C. Steinmetz, "The Scholastic Calvin," in *Protestant Scholasticism: Essays in Reassessment* (Eugene, OR: Wipf & Stock, 2005).

231. Beeke notes that "supralapsarian tendencies are wholly absent in [Beza's] eighty-seven extant sermons" ("Beza's Predestination," 77).

232. Cf. Richard Bauckham, *Bible and Mission: Christian Witness in a Postmodern World* (Grand Rapids: Baker Academic, 2003). Cf. Christopher R. Seitz, *Figured Out: Typology and Providence in Christian Scripture* (Louisville: Westminster John Knox, 2001). Cf. N. T. Wright, *Paul: In Fresh Perspective* (Minneapolis: Fortress, 2005).

In his commentary on Is. 42:7, Calvin applies the passage directly to Christ, thus ignoring Israel's role as a light to the nations themselves (*Comm. Is.* 42:7; CO 37:65).

233. Holmes, *Listening to the Past*, 129–30.

Chapter Four

Integration

One Disposition and a Twofold Will

Having carefully examined Calvin's teaching on God's disposition toward humanity in his doctrines of the knowledge of God and predestination, we now seek to follow Calvin's example by describing the doctrine with "lucid brevity" to provide the reader with a simple and unambiguous picture of our findings regarding God's disposition toward and will for humanity.

THE LINEAR DESCRIPTION: CONCLUSIONS CATALOGUED

Unsurprisingly, based on the complexity of this topic in the Bible and in human comprehension, the answer to the question of God's disposition toward humanity for Calvin the biblical scholar is also slightly complex.[1] In sum, we have found that according to Calvin's teaching, God does have *one* disposition toward humanity, and God has one, secret, righteous will for humanity that is expressed in a decidedly asymmetrical, twofold manner.

Here I shall provide a series of statements summarizing Calvin's teaching. These statements are not necessarily in order of development, but they emerge in a synthetic fashion from his reading, teaching, and preaching of Scripture. They are listed in one potentially logical order. Calvin teaches that:

1. God can only be known by those with faith.
2. God's nature is revealed through his works, particularly his works of creation and providence, his works recorded in Scripture, and most of all in the life, death, resurrection, and ascension of the incarnate Word, Jesus Christ.

3. God's unchanging nature is one of love (mercy), righteousness, wisdom, goodness, power, judgment (of evil), holiness, and so forth. This nature can be confidently known by those with faith in Christ.
4. God has one, secret, righteous will that corresponds with God's unchanging nature but is not comprehensively known by any persons.
5. God's gracious actions (a) in creation, (b) in Christ's multifaceted and complete reconciling work that is sufficient for the redemption of all people, and (c) in election to salvation as witnessed to by Scripture and experience all directly correspond with God's revealed nature and exhibit God's one disclosed disposition toward humanity that is effected in the elect via God's electing will.
6. From our human perspective, the limited efficiency of Christ's reconciling work along with God's sovereign rule over the fall and reprobation (creating some people whom he would allow to remain in their sin) as detailed in Scripture and witnessed to by experience only correspond in part with God's revealed nature. These actions occur in accordance with God's veiled reprobating will.
7. Both elements of God's twofold will (electing and reprobating) are included in God's one, righteous will, even though humans cannot understand how.
8. Because God has made himself known to those with faith, they are to abide in God's revealed nature, disclosed disposition, and electing will, thereby trusting by faith that all of God's actions align with his nature and righteous will. Believers submit to God's secret counsel and hidden wisdom but not by detaching God and his acts from his righteous character and will. Instead, they recognize God's transcendence along with their epistemic limits and thus humbly submit to the limits of their knowledge of God while trusting the priority of what they do know about God.[2]
9. Therefore, those with faith proclaim God's disclosed disposition of love to all humanity because it accords with God's nature and provides an accurate depiction of God's inclination toward humanity that is appropriated to any who receive it. They trust and proclaim the only God that can be known, the God who has made himself known to those with faith.
10. Finally, believers also submit to God's inscrutable wisdom and rule in the fact that some people seemingly do not come to a place of trusting in Christ and have therefore been passed over by God. This fact is inexplicable but true. It provides no unique information about God's nature, nor does it explicitly inform us of God's disposition toward humanity.[3]

THE NARRATIVE DESCRIPTION: CONCLUSIONS CHRONICLED

To explain this synthesis in a more descriptive manner, God has one disposition toward humanity along with one righteous will that is expressed in a decidedly asymmetrical, twofold manner. For Calvin, the only disposition of God that can be known and proclaimed is one of mercy, righteousness, and judgment (of evil) that has been most clearly revealed in Jesus Christ and is experienced via God's gracious election to salvation. However, God's one righteous will has two parts which are distinctly asymmetrical in regard to their connection to God's nature, human epistemic access, and proclamation, upon which I shall expand here.

First, regarding God's nature, God's revealed electing will and God's disclosed disposition correspond directly with God's loving, wise, righteous, good, powerful, judging nature. In contrast, humanity can only perceive a few connections between God's veiled reprobating will and God's nature, namely his judgment of evil, his freedom (as Calvin understands it), his sovereign rule, and the magnification of his love for the elect (via the contrast). Beyond this, it is not clear how God's reprobative actions toward people correspond with his loving, wise, powerful, good, righteous nature.

Second, these two components of God's one will are markedly asymmetrical in regard to human epistemic access. On the one hand, only God's electing will (and God's corresponding disclosed disposition) can be known positively and substantially, and then solely by those with faith. Believers can know God's nature through God's works, especially Christ's redeeming life, death, resurrection, ascension, and ongoing priestly intercession that restores the elect to communion with God without regard for human merit. Thus, throughout his teaching and preaching, Calvin consistently returns to his description of God as loving Father in accordance with God's nature.[4] On the other hand, God's veiled reprobating will is only known in part, as a shadow of God's electing will.

Metaphorically, God's revealed electing will and corresponding disclosed disposition have been set out in the light of day for all to see while his veiled reprobating will is locked in a black box with no way of opening it. By peaking in through the cracks, silhouettes can be deciphered that roughly correspond with what is seen in broad daylight, but the resultant quality and quantity of information is minute compared with what is on display in broad daylight.

Third, the two components of God's one will are drastically asymmetrical in terms of proclamation. In the gospel, Christians proclaim the good news of God's gracious love revealed in Christ's multifaceted and complete work of redemption that provides the content of and grounds for God's revealed disposition toward humanity. Although God's judgment of evil and sin is unquestionably part of the good news of the gospel, it is proclaimed in the context of God's revealed nature and merciful, disclosed disposition toward humanity in the hope that all who hear will repent and receive the free grace of God in Christ. Calvin is clear that proclamation of judgment is not an end in itself. Rightly used, it can only help humble people enough to receive God's grace in Christ.[5] Humans, including the leaders of the church, never assign any person to reprobation but long for each person's redemption until his or her last breath. The church's task is to proclaim God's disclosed loving disposition to all people and trust that the results will somehow cohere within God's one righteous will. Therefore, as informed by God's electing will, God's disclosed disposition provides the content of the preaching of the gospel, which we shall examine in Calvin's preaching ministry in chapter 5.

To summarize, in Calvin's exposition of the breadth of Scripture, God has one disclosed disposition toward humanity along with one, secret, righteous will that is expressed in a decidedly asymmetrical, twofold manner. God's disclosed disposition of love, righteousness, wisdom, power, goodness, and judgment (of evil) concurs with God's unchanging nature and God's works in election, is known by those with faith, and is proclaimed to all. God's veiled, sovereign, and reprobating will is known as a fact but (from the human perspective) does not comprehensively emerge from or reflect God's nature.

For Calvin, this understanding of God's disposition toward humanity and God's twofold will does not lead to insecurity regarding the knowledge of God because of the clear revelation of God's loving disposition toward humanity in Christ and because of the drastic asymmetry between the revealed electing and veiled reprobating parts of his will. Calvin wholeheartedly espouses trust in and proclamation of the only God that can be known, the God revealed in creation and redemption, according to the witness of Scripture.

We now turn to examine Calvin's own preaching to test our findings in his preaching of Scripture and the gospel of Jesus Christ.

NOTES

1. The plenitude of distinct approaches to this topic throughout the history of the church witnesses to its complexity. We shall observe a few other approaches in chapter 7.

2. Obviously, not every person will be comfortable theologically or logically with this step. For Calvin, this is what made the most sense of the biblical witness and his experience, but other Christian theologians have provided different accounts through the ages. See chapter 7.

3. Again, this step is potentially controversial, but this was Calvin's approach. We shall address it more fully in chapter 7.

4. For an excellent recent essay on God's fatherhood and our adoption in Calvin's theology, see Canlis, "The Fatherhood of God and Union With Christ in Calvin."

5. Calvin also sees the preaching of the gospel as revealing and amassing the guilt of those who reject Christ, but this is a side effect, not the primary goal, of the gospel proclamation.

Chapter Five

Calvin's Preaching

Testing Our Findings

As we turn to Calvin's preaching regarding God's disposition and will, we begin with three relevant statements from his 1554 sermon on 1 Tim. 2:3–5:

> The will of God is opened to us, as often as we hear His Word preached, whereby He calleth and exhorteth us all to repentance. . . . In that which God exhorteth all men [*en general les hommes*], we may judge that it is His will [*volunté*] that all men should be saved [*tous soyent sauvez*].[1]

> Experience demonstrates, and so does Holy Scripture, that he giveth not conversion [*la conversion*] to all men.[2]

> It is true that God changeth not; neither hath He two wills; nor doth He use any counterfeit dealing: and yet the Scripture speaketh unto us in two ways concerning His will. And how can that be? How cometh it to pass that His will is spoken of in two different ways? It is because of our grossness [*rudesse*] that it is necessary for God to transfigure and condescend to us . . . because we cannot comprehend him [*ne le comprenous*] in His incomprehensible majesty.[3]

Having summarized our findings regarding God's disposition toward humanity in Calvin's theological project, we now aim to test our conclusions by examining Calvin's preaching. If it is true that Calvin believes Scripture teaches that God has one disposition toward humanity alongside his one righteous will that is enacted in a twofold, decidedly asymmetrical manner, then his preaching of Scripture will also display this conviction. Specifically, based on our findings, we would expect his preaching to witness primarily to God's disclosed disposition toward humanity as he proclaims the God who has made himself known in creation, election, and redemption and who relates to his people according to his fatherly love and revealed nature. Calvin's preaching would clearly extend to all his listeners an invitation to respond to the good news of God's gracious electing love displayed in the person and work of Jesus Christ, a response enabled by God's revealed electing will. Calvin's preaching would also include a call to share the gospel of God's love with all people. We would also expect Calvin's preaching to acknowledge God's veiled reprobating will that is enacted toward some people, whereby God leaves them in their rebellious state, but we would expect to see an emphasis on God's electing will as Calvin holds together the unity of God's one, righteous will in the midst of its asymmetrically understood twofold administration.

As we shall see, and as the sermon on 1 Tim. 2:3–5[4] quoted at the head of this chapter displays, Calvin's preaching directly fulfills these hypotheses. The 1 Timothy sermon provides a striking demonstration of our findings, particularly notable in how well it corresponds to our proposal.[5] In interpreting the text that says, "God wills for all people to be saved," Calvin explicates his understanding of God's one disposition toward humanity alongside God's single, righteous, twofold, and decidedly asymmetrical will for humanity.

For Calvin, God's will that all would be saved is an indicator that salvation is no longer limited to the people of Israel but is now extended to all peoples and nations who would receive God's grace, as evinced in the call to share the gospel to the ends of the earth.[6] Calvin is quite clear that God wills all people to be saved, but he is also convinced that God does not save everyone. Therefore he is compelled to parse the details of how it is that God's one will looks like two wills.

As seen above, Calvin's response is that God does not have two wills but has accommodated his one will to our limited human understanding "because we cannot comprehend him in His incomprehensible majesty." God has not revealed his eternal counsel or election, "which was before the beginning of the world: but only showeth what His will is as far as it can be known by us [*peut estre congu de nous*]."[7] God has revealed his merciful disposition and electing will in order to assure his listeners of their salvation[8] and empower them to proclaim the good news of Jesus to the world.[9] Calvin ends the sermon with the exhortation, "We must labor as much as possible to draw those to salvation who seem to be afar off. And above all things, let us pray to God for them, waiting patiently till it please Him to show His good will [*bon vouloir*] toward them, as He hath declared [*declaré*] it to us."[10]

This example from 1 Timothy displays Calvin's affirmation of the ability of believers to know, trust, and proclaim God's one disclosed disposition of mercy revealed in Jesus Christ. At the same time, Calvin acknowledges the reality of God's veiled reprobating will in his passing over some people for salvation. This sermon also demonstrates the fact that Calvin saw these two wills toward humanity accommodated to limited human understanding as two parts of God's one righteous will.

In this chapter, after providing a brief introduction to Calvin's preaching ministry, we shall test our findings in Calvin's preaching itself. We first utilize three sermon series as case studies: fifty-two sermons on Acts 1–7 that Calvin preached in 1550–1551, thirteen sermons on Genesis 25–27 that Calvin preached in 1560, and a special collection of nine sermons on Matthew from Holy Week of 1558. Then, to broaden the range of the data, we survey a variety of sermons from 1549 to 1560, each of which addresses a text or topic that relates to God's disposition toward humanity. As we shall see, these sermons demonstrate that Calvin's understanding and proclamation of God's disposition toward humanity align with our previous conclusions.

CALVIN AS PREACHER

Before examining Calvin's preaching itself in regard to God's disposition toward humanity, we shall provide a brief overview of Calvin's understanding of preaching and survey his preaching career to set the context for our examination. In short, Calvin sees preaching as a calling from God to speak God's word to a congregation in a lively manner that witnesses to the comprehensive message of Scripture fulfilled in Jesus Christ. As we shall see, Calvin devoted immense time and effort to preaching throughout his ministry career.[11]

Drawing primarily upon T. H. L. Parker's *Calvin's Preaching* and Elsie McKee's monumental *The Pastoral Ministry and Worship in Calvin's Geneva*, we shall examine Calvin's understanding of the authority, purpose, and message of the preached word, Calvin's methods of preaching, and Calvin's preaching ministry itself.

The Authority, Purpose, and Message of Preaching

Calvin believes preaching receives its authority from Scripture and is intended to build up the church according to the essential message of the whole of Scripture. We shall examine each of these in turn.

For Calvin, preaching derives its authority from Scripture, which is the word of God. Calvin is clear that the whole of the Scriptures, Old and New Testaments, have authority because "there the living words of God were heard."[12] Even though the humanist Calvin clearly acknowledges the human elements of Scripture,[13] he sees Scripture as not ultimately "delivered according to the will and pleasure of men, but dictated [*dictatum*] by the Holy Spirit."[14] The bridge between Calvin's view of the authority of Scripture and the authority of preaching lies in Calvin's commitment that, as T. H. L. Parker says, "the preacher is to invent nothing of his own but declares only what has been revealed and recorded in Holy Scripture."[15]

Parker highlights two images that Calvin often uses to describe the authority of preaching, namely the sermon as the "school of God" and preachers as ambassadors of God. For Calvin, sermons are the school of God, in which God in Jesus Christ is the ultimate teacher. The preacher delivers what he or she has been taught in the Scriptures, and the message of the sermon (in correct correspondence with Scripture) is not solely a pointer but is as powerful and effective as Scripture itself.[16] Similarly, Calvin describes the preacher's role as an ambassador of God (2 Cor. 5:20), sent by God with God's message. Instead of the preacher simply being a messenger who repeats instructions, Calvin is clear that God empowers preaching by the Spirit to be God's living and powerful word.[17] Therefore, preaching that is rightly derived from, subordinate to, and conformed to the message of Scripture is God's word, enlivened and empowered by the same Spirit who enlivens and empowers Scripture itself.[18]

Along with his understanding of preaching as God's word, Calvin believes that the purpose of preaching aligns with the central purpose of Scripture, namely building up the people of God for salvation according to the message of the Bible. In his sermon on 2 Tim. 3:16–17, Calvin says that Scripture is meant "not only to show us what is the majesty of God but to edify us unto salvation. . . . When I expound Holy Scripture, I must always make this my rule: that those who hear me may receive profit from the teaching I put forward and be edified unto salvation [*edifiez à salut*]."[19]

Because the sermon derives its message and authority from Scripture, the message of each sermon is to align with, flow from, and witness to the essential message of the whole of Scripture. Parker points out that for Calvin (and most Christian theologians before him), the entire Bible declares one unified message.[20] In other words, because of the unity and truthfulness of Scripture, "That which is true of the whole is true of the parts. Therefore the parts are to be understood according to the whole."[21]

Calvin offers many simple summaries of the teaching of Scripture in his writing and sermons.[22] As one brief example, in his sermon on 2 Tim. 3:16–17, Calvin says,

> Here, then, is the summary [*somme*] of the teaching of Holy Scripture: That we know that God has wished us to put our trust completely in him, and that we may have our refuge in him; and then that we know how and by what means he declares himself our Father and Saviour—that is, in the person of our Lord Jesus Christ, whom he has given over to death for us. For this is how we are reconciled to him, this is how we are cleansed from all our stains and pollutions,

this is how we are accounted righteous [*reputez iustes*]. And from this proceeds the trust [*fiance*] we have to call upon God, knowing that he does not reject us when we come to him in the name of him whom he has made our Advocate."[23]

For Calvin, the message of each sermon should somehow correspond to the central teaching of the Bible that God has made himself known and adopted those with faith as his children through the reconciling work of Jesus Christ.[24]

Therefore, like all of his preaching, we expect Calvin's preaching regarding God's disposition toward humanity to be specifically founded in Scripture, seek the edification of the church, and be presented in correlation with the broader message of Scripture.

Calvin's Preaching Methods

Having surveyed Calvin's understanding of the authority, purpose, and message of preaching, we now examine Calvin's methods of proclamation, namely "lively" expository preaching in which the text is explained and applied to the congregation.[25]

Consistent with his firm belief in the inspiration and authority of the whole of Scripture, Calvin practiced verse-by-verse preaching through complete books of the Bible.[26] Distinct from other Reformed churches of his time, Calvin's Genevan churches almost exclusively utilized this *lectio continua* method,[27] and he expounded most of the books of the Bible in thousands of sermons over his pastoral career.[28] Calvin also expected that preaching be "lively." In a letter to the Duke of Somerset regarding preaching in England, Calvin states, "[The] preaching ought not to be lifeless but lively [*vive*], to teach, to exhort, to reprove."[29] Calvin diligently prepared for his sermons, but he never used a manuscript or even notes. Instead, he would enter the pulpit with nothing more than the original language Bible text and proceed to preach for nearly an hour with life and passion.

Following the model of God's accommodation of himself and his truth to humanity, Calvin also sought to explain and apply his sermons to his listeners.[30] To do this, he employed nonacademic language and familiar illustrations to communicate effectively with the people, regardless of their level of education.[31] At the same time, he engaged the learned (often refugees) by acknowledging and referencing more complicated theological topics, albeit without exploring the details.[32] Even though he was preaching out of the original language text, he almost never quoted the Greek or Hebrew or even mentioned the Greek or Hebrew languages.[33] It is clear that the depth of his learning informed his teaching (as he had often written commentaries on the text from which he was preaching), but he did not parade his scholarly acumen. Similarly, Calvin, the lawyer, skilled writer, and rhetorician did not believe that preachers should make a show of their presentation. For example, in his letter to Somerset, he critiques preachers who go about "sowing their silly fancies" and make a "parade of rhetoric, only to gain esteem for themselves."[34]

In summary, Calvin sought to communicate the truth of Scripture to the congregation in an understandable manner so they could receive the truth and respond to it. As he comes to texts that address God's disposition toward humanity, we would expect him to engage those texts faithfully and explicate them in a manner that the congregation could readily understand and apply.

Calvin's Preaching Ministry

We know little about Calvin's preaching ministry before 1549. Calvin preached at least some before his arrival in Geneva in 1536, where he was to teach theology but quickly took up preaching as well. We know of no preaching in Strasbourg from 1538 to 1541, but when he returned to Geneva in 1541, he immediately resumed preaching on the same verse at which he had stopped in the sermon series three years earlier.[35] Through thorough investigation, McKee has provided a well-informed hypothesis regarding which books of the Bible Calvin likely preached through from 1541 to 1549, notably finding likely occasions for the preaching of Romans (1536–1538) and the Gospel of John (1542–1546), two of Calvin's favorite New Testament books from which we lack any extant sermons.[36]

Calvin devoted substantial time and energy to preaching. It is not known how much Calvin preached from 1541 through 1549 in Geneva, but from 1549 until his death, Calvin preached two different sermons on each Sunday along with a sermon on each of the six weekdays every other week. He typically preached hour-long sermons from the New Testament on Sundays and the Old Testament on weekdays.[37] On the off weeks, he lectured in theology three times during the week. He also often preached at the *Congrégation* meetings on Fridays. He did all this alongside his commentary work, occasional writings, and personal correspondence.

Excellent records[38] of Calvin's preaching begin in September 1549, when French refugee Denis Raguenier was hired by *La compagnie des étrangers* (the committee of foreigners/refugees) to record the sermons. Well ahead of his time, Raguenier had developed a method of shorthand that allowed him to make transcripts of Calvin's sermons, recording about six thousand words per hour in shorthand before dictating the text to scribes who completed them in script. Although it took Raguenier approximately a year to develop his skills sufficiently to keep pace with Calvin, Parker has demonstrated the excellent quality of Raguenier's stenography work in the consistency of the manuscripts over the years.[39] According to Raguenier's count, he recorded 2,042 of Calvin's sermons from 29 September 1549 to late 1560, only interrupted by two sicknesses that made him miss a segment of sermons.[40] Calvin did not edit or see the sermons[41] before they were published,[42] and the proceeds from eighteen volumes of selected sermons that were published (all in French) directly supported the many refugees in Geneva.

From this brief examination of Calvin's preaching ministry, we see that Calvin believed that preaching was a calling from God to explain and apply a Scripture text to a congregation in accordance with the message of the gospel as witnessed to in the Old and New Testaments. Calvin worked tirelessly at this task. As we now examine specific sermons relating to our question of God's disposition toward humanity, we know that he considered them an expression of the word of God proclaimed in accord with God's redemptive purposes fulfilled in Jesus Christ.

SERMONS ON ACTS 1–7 (1549–1550)

On Sunday mornings from August 25, 1549, to January 11, 1551, Calvin preached fifty-eight sermons at St. Pierre parish on chapters 1–7 of the Acts of the Apostles.[43] Although six of those sermons and the remaining sermons on Acts 8–28 have been lost, the collection of fifty-two sermons[44] is Calvin's earliest extant sermon series.[45] The series on Acts is also an example of Calvin's extended preaching of a text that is not primarily addressing election or reprobation, thus providing helpful data in the evaluation of our findings. In short, in a sermon series and Scripture text that is not primarily focused on election and reprobation, does Calvin's preaching reflect our previous conclusions?

In the course of this study of these sermons on Acts, we shall see that Calvin indeed primarily proclaims God's disclosed disposition and electing will to his hearers while acknowledging the reality and drastic relative incongruity of God's veiled will toward humanity, thus demonstrating the validity of our previous findings.

Our conclusions are demonstrated in Calvin's sermons on Acts 1–7 in three overlapping ways. First, in his sermons, Calvin calls for and models the preaching of the good news of God's love revealed in Jesus to all people and hopes for the salvation of all. Second, Calvin describes God's twofold will toward humanity in the way that humans use their agency to accept (by God's enabling grace) or reject the gospel. Finally, Calvin reminds his hearers to trust ultimately in God's love revealed in Jesus Christ when considering their salvation. We shall expand on each of these observations below.

God's Merciful Call to All

In Calvin's sermons on Acts 1–7, Calvin calls for and models the preaching of the good news of God's love revealed in Jesus to all people in hope for the salvation of all.

First, Calvin exhorts the Christian community in Geneva to proclaim the good news of God's love revealed in Jesus to all people and hope for the salvation of all people, thus demonstrating Calvin's commitment to proclaiming God's disclosed disposition to all. Calvin teaches that God wants his kingdom to grow, which happens as people come to salvation through the preaching of the Word to all. Calvin says, "Now there is nothing in this world to be desired more than to see the church grow and have an infinite number of believers [*que le nombre des fideles soit inifini*]." Therefore, the people are to "work to win [*travaillons à gaigner*] the whole world to God and bring it to obedience unto him . . . desir[ing] especially that the gospel be extended and increased throughout the whole world [*par toute le monde*]."[46] In other words, Calvin admonishes the Genevan community to preach to all like Peter did, in hope "that they would be converted to God."[47]

In a sermon on Acts 7, Calvin provides another clear example of his call to the Christian community to preach the gospel to all people in hopes that they would turn to God, on this occasion basing his logic on God's work of creation and redemption. There, describing Stephen's speech to the Council, Calvin says,

> "So we see how we are to proceed when announcing God's word to men. If possible, we are to try to lead [*admener*] men to God and his truth . . . we must make every effort to draw everybody to the knowledge of the gospel. For when we see people going to hell who have been created in the image of God and redeemed by the blood of our Lord Jesus Christ [*rachaptez par le sang de nostre Seigneur Jesus Christ*], that must indeed stir us to do our duty and instruct them and treat them with all gentleness and kindness as we try to bear fruit in this way."[48]

In this and other similar statements,[49] Calvin repeatedly points out that all people have been created in God's image and redeemed by the blood of Jesus. These statements do not indicate that Calvin is a universalist, but they do affirm the fact that Calvin sees the work of Christ as sufficient for the redemption of all, efficient for some.[50] Calvin calls the community to preach so that the sufficiency of the cross of Christ will become efficient for more people, as God opens up their hearts by the power of the Spirit. As a result, believers must seek (with gentleness and goodwill) to draw them into faith "in every way available."[51] For Calvin, because of God's boundless generosity in creation and redemption, the people of God are meant to extend the message of God's boundless love to all people in hopes that they would respond in faith.

Calvin also teaches the Genevan community to work and hope for the redemption of all people through a few of his closing prayers in the Acts series. For example, in a prayer that echoes his set weekday and Sunday afternoon prayer, Calvin spontaneously leads the St. Pierre congregation in prayer three times in the extant series, "May he grant that grace not only to us but to all the peoples and nations of the earth [à *tous peuples et nations de la terre*]."[52] He also prays that as a result of their repentance, the community would "live in this world in such harmony and friendship with one another that unbelievers will themselves see our good works and be constrained to praise him [*constrainctz de louer*]."[53] Although he does not pray in this way every week, these prayers demonstrate Calvin's manner of inviting the congregation to hope for God's grace to be extended to all peoples.

Second, Calvin not only calls the Genevan community to preach the gospel to all in hopes that they would respond in faith, but he models that approach in his own preaching. As observed earlier, Calvin does not believe that anyone can know whether someone else is numbered among the elect.[54] Therefore, when he preaches to the Genevan community, he is not preaching to a group of individuals who he has concluded sincerely trust in Jesus Christ, nor does he claim to have received special insight into God's eternal election. Instead, he simply proclaims God's disclosed disposition to them, preaching that God loves them, and he calls them to repent and be forgiven. For example,

> "So let us each examine ourselves. And while God favors us by inviting us with fatherly gentleness [*doulceur paternelle*], he asks only that we come to him [*venions à luy*], and he helps us so we can sense the gracious comforting of our Lord Jesus Christ. . . . Therefore, when our Lord Jesus Christ calls us, let us not be so wayward that we completely oppose him, but let us acknowledge that we must find all our consolation in his word."[55]

In short, he calls *all* of his listeners to respond in trust to God's loving call in Jesus Christ.

Calvin's proclamation of God's disclosed disposition to all is also demonstrated in his consistent use of the first person plural pronouns in all of his sermons.[56] One of a myriad of potential examples is Calvin's call to his listeners from Acts 7:37–38. There he asserts, "We have the Son of God, who is life eternal. He speaks to *us* [through his word] . . . Let *us* be very careful then not to reject this God-given blessing for fear of being totally deprived [*privez*] of it in the end."[57] As we have seen, Calvin does not assume that every hearer is an heir to eternal life, but by speaking of "us," Calvin calls the whole community to have hearts that are open to the word of God. Similarly, in his sermon on Acts 7:45–50, Calvin says, "Since God favors us by showing us the way of salvation, let us take care to follow where he calls us [*nous appelle*]."⁵⁸ Finally, Calvin uses "us" in his admonitions to the people of God to be assured of their salvation in Jesus: "When he calls us to the hope of eternal life, we are to consider his desire to save us as completely assured."⁵⁹ In short, without assuming that all his listeners are elect, Calvin models the proclamation of God's disclosed disposition to all people in his preaching.

In his preaching ministry, Calvin teaches and models the proclamation of God's disclosed disposition of love to all people in hope for each person's salvation. Calvin's message paraphrased is: "In love God has made the world, sustained the world, and redeemed the fallen world in Jesus Christ; repent and believe this good news." What we notably do not observe is any reserve about proclaiming God's love and the redemption of Jesus Christ; Calvin preaches God's loving disclosed disposition to all who would hear.

God's Twofold Will: Enabling Grace and Human Rejection of Grace

In his sermons on Acts 1–7, while appealing to all through the gospel of Jesus Christ according to God's disclosed disposition, Calvin also acknowledges God's veiled will toward humanity in the fact that some people are not enabled by God's regenerative grace to trust in Jesus Christ. They act according to the influence of evil and their sinful nature in choosing to reject the gospel. In short, the call goes to all, but God mysteriously enables an affirmative response in only some according to his revealed electing will. This aligns directly with our previous findings.

In his sermon on Acts 5:30–32, Calvin teaches that although the gracious call of the gospel of Christ goes out to all, "we do not have the free choice to turn to him, but it is his office to provide what we lack [*default*]" as he "strips us of everything that belongs to our human nature and regenerates us by his Holy Spirit."⁶⁰ Likewise, in his sermon on Acts 5:13–16, Calvin asserts that in our human sickness, none of us can move to God of our own accord.⁶¹ Humans cannot respond affirmatively to the gospel of Jesus "until he changes their wicked hearts [*changé leurs maulvais courages*] and gives them a new affection to bring them to his will [*à sa volunté*]."⁶²

While people can only receive the gospel by faith through God's enabling, Calvin also teaches that humans have real agency to accept or reject the gospel of Jesus. This corresponds with our previous observations, namely that as a proponent of meticulous providence (a type of compatibilism), Calvin allows for real human choice alongside God's sovereign determination of all.⁶³

For example, Calvin affirms human agency by repeatedly calling the congregation to place their faith in Christ. Commenting on Peter's preaching in Acts, he calls the Genevan community to choose to listen to God:

> When we hear the word of God we must listen [*nous escoutions*] in all reverence to what it says, for, no matter the level of our ignorance, we will be without excuse before God when we refuse to hear his teaching, but we will be convicted of ingratitude for having scorned the grace he has offered to us.[64]

In other words, "Since our God so gently invites us, what will happen to us if we do not listen to him?"[65]

Sadly, some do not come to God because they "are so dull of hearing" that nothing can get through to them. In their decision, they choose to see God as their judge (*juge*).[66] In this choice, they display their hardness of heart. Although all things occur under God's sovereign rule, this hardness of heart is caused not directly by God but by sin and evil. For example, in a sermon on Acts 5, Calvin teaches that in light of God's fatherly love revealed in Jesus Christ, "a person has to be in the full possession of the devil if he does not accept that honor and that grace given to us only for our salvation."[67] In another passage, Calvin puts the weight of rejection on humans, teaching that rebellion against God's word is from humanity, not God. That rejection does not "proceed from [God's] nature. The fact is that we are ill-disposed to pay attention when God speaks to us. For his part, he asks only to instruct us in all gentleness and kindness," but we reject his teaching and push away more and more.[68] Calvin also says that when people reject God, God *then* hardens their hearts and they become spiritually blind, overpowered by evil.[69]

Calvin's comments from his sermon on Acts 7:42–43 clearly display this interplay between human agency and God's sovereignty:

> Let us also learn to glorify God when he punishes men in this way. Although he ought to do us ill, we must, when we see poor souls going to hell that way, try to draw them back to the path of salvation. Yet, let us not attribute that judgment to God's cruelty and blame him [*l'accuser*] as if his punishments were excessive. Let us acknowledge, rather, that men are rightly blinded in that way, rebuked, and thoroughly confounded.[70]

For reasons known to God alone, he only opens the hearts of some to receive the good news of Jesus, but the primary cause of people's rejection of Christ and their subsequent judgment is human rebellion and evil, not God.

In sum, Calvin teaches that as the gospel of God's love is rightly proclaimed to all, God enables some persons to put their faith in Jesus Christ while mysteriously leaving others in their sinful rejection of the gospel. Just as we would expect, Calvin highlights the multiple layers of causality that helps his listeners trust in God's goodness in light of the sad reality of reprobation. In this, God's twofold, asymmetrical will toward humanity is on display along with the paradox of God's sovereign reign and real human agency.

Trusting in God's Love Revealed in Christ

In alignment with our findings regarding Calvin's teaching on God's disposition toward humanity, in his sermons on Acts, Calvin reminds his hearers to trust confidently in the God who is revealed in Jesus Christ when considering their salvation. For example, "Jesus Christ reveals the heart [*le coeur*] of God his Father, not in part, but in its fullness, in such a way that we cannot fail to be aware of what constitutes our salvation [*apartenir pour nostre salut*]."[71] Calvin warns the community to never look elsewhere than the word of God that has been spoken in the law and the prophets and ultimately fulfilled in Jesus Christ to understand redemption.[72] In short, "[God's] word gives a true picture of him [*sa vraye ymage*]."[73] Because of how God has revealed himself in Jesus, believers can be assured of their salvation because "[God] is leading us to heaven, and the door is always open to us in the person of our Lord Jesus Christ [*la porte nous est ouverte en la personne de nostre Seigneur Jesus Christ*]."[74] In other words, Calvin says that through the gospel we receive testimony to all of God's gifts to us.[75]

Thus we see that Calvin clearly teaches that the Genevan community can steadfastly trust God's character as it has been revealed in Scripture and most of all in Jesus Christ. In short, he admonishes trust in God's revealed nature, disclosed disposition, and corresponding electing will.

Conclusion

Calvin's preaching of Acts 1–7 from 1550 to 1551 clearly demonstrates his commitment to proclaiming God's revealed nature and disclosed disposition to all people while acknowledging the reality of God's veiled will toward some people. It is noteworthy that Calvin does not explicitly direct certain elements of his preaching to the elect, nor does he add disclaimers to his proclamation of God's grace to the congregation. Instead, he confidently proclaims the God who has revealed himself in creation and redemption, thus hoping for the salvation of all, calling for repentance and faith, and admonishing people to turn away from their sins and turn to God. While acknowledging that some will harden their hearts to the message of the gospel and while affirming the necessity of God's activity for a person to receive the gospel, Calvin proclaims God's disclosed disposition of love and admonishes others to do the same.

SERMONS ON GENESIS 25–27 (1560)

From September 4, 1559, to approximately August 7, 1561, Calvin preached ca. 262 weekday sermons on the book of Genesis.[76] Following his custom in preaching the Old Testament, he typically preached one sermon each weekday (including Saturday) every other week. In 1560, while Calvin was continuing his preaching on Genesis, thirteen sermons from the series were published in a separate volume entitled, "Thirteen Sermons of Master John Calvin Concerning the Free Election of God in Jacob and the Rejection in Esau."[77] We examine those sermons here.

These thirteen sermons provide another excellent case study as we test our conclusions regarding Calvin's proclamation of God's disposition toward humanity. The sermons were preached ca. July 22–August 10, 1560,[78] after the final edition of the *Institutes* was published. Thus, in contrast to the sermon series on Acts ten years earlier, these sermons provide a glimpse into Calvin's later years of preaching, near the end of his life and pastoral ministry. Secondly, they are an example of Calvin's weekday Old Testament preaching. Finally, these sermons are a particularly appropriate test case for this study because they were specifically identified by the Genevan community during Calvin's lifetime as sermons that addressed and clarified the topic of election and reprobation, thus directly illuminating Calvin's preaching on God's disposition toward humanity. If Calvin's mature preaching does indeed conform to what we have discovered over the course of this study, these sermons should display that fact.

In these thirteen sermons, we shall see that Calvin proclaims God's loving disposition to all his listeners, affirms God's twofold will enacted in the paradox of human agency along with the necessity of God's enabling grace regarding salvation, and calls his listeners to repose wholly and confidently in God's revealed nature.

The Gospel Extended to All

First, in Calvin's sermons on Gen. 25:12–27:38, he again proclaims the love of God revealed in Jesus Christ to all his listeners and prays for the salvation of all peoples and nations. In these sermons, Calvin once more specifically denies epistemological access to another person's status as elect (or not). Even if people appear to be chosen by their ways of life, God may not enable perseverance of their faith to the end.[79] Calvin also considers it possible that his listeners could turn away from the faith.[80] These examples confirm that Calvin is not assuming that every listener is included in the elect; the identities of the elect are known only by God. The fact that Calvin does not assume special insight into the eternal election of his listeners makes his proclamation of God's love revealed in the gospel more striking.

For instance, Calvin repeatedly rhetorically includes his listeners as those who are elect and adopted in Christ and whom God approaches with fatherly love. Examples in these sermons are far too many to recount here, but I shall provide a sampling. To begin, in his first sermon on Gen. 25:21–22, a sermon that specifically explicates the doctrine of election and reprobation, Calvin calls his listeners to confirm their election. Using his customary first person plural pronouns, he explains that not all of "us" are guaranteed "our" eternal inheritance, but Calvin invites his listeners to walk in their election. He thus proclaims God's disclosed disposition to the congregation, implying that God loves them and has chosen them, so they are to walk in and confirm that truth.[81] Later in the sermon, while acknowledging that God does not enlighten all who hear the gospel proclaimed, Calvin calls his listeners to "speak of the inestimable blessing [*bien inestimable*] that God hath bestowed upon us," that God allowed "us" to receive his word by his mercy.[82] Calvin extends God's loving invitation in Jesus Christ to the entire congregation.

In his second sermon (of two) on Gen. 25:21–22, Calvin addresses many of the common objections to the doctrine of predestination. In the midst of his arguments, he periodically returns to speak of the elect, always using the first person plural pronouns. For example, "The Scripture . . . pronounceth clearly and manifestly, that God hath chosen us in Jesus Christ before the creation of the world, according to his good pleasure, the which he hath purposed in himself;" this is not based on human merit, but "our election is founded [*est fondee*] in Jesus Christ."[83] Calvin also says that his listeners can be certain of their salvation because they have tasted various signs of election like the knowledge of God's goodness, the hope of salvation, and the way that they have renounced the evil of the world.[84] In both cases, Calvin preaches to the congregation as if they are all elect even though he does not claim such knowledge. In other words, Calvin proclaims God's disclosed disposition to them and invites them to find assurance in God's love for them in Jesus Christ.[85]

In addition, throughout the thirteen sermons, Calvin exhorts all his listeners to trust in Jesus Christ as he is made known in the gospel. For example, Calvin preaches that the congregation is "blessed in Jesus Christ through faith. For altogether like as he is presented unto us by the gospel, so likewise we must accept him: and if we remain unbelievers, this is because we shut the door as it were, against all his graces."[86] God has opened the door through the gospel that "we might have familiar access [*acces privé*] to call upon him."[87] Calvin also hopes for the salvation of each person, proclaiming that the sacrifice of Jesus was made "for the reconciliation of the world [*la reconciliation du monde*]."[88] For Calvin, through the preaching of the good news of Jesus Christ, God opens the door of faith to all who would hear and respond to him in faith.

In sum, Calvin proclaims God's disclosed disposition and revealed nature to all his listeners without claiming special knowledge that they are all elect.

In my own paraphrase, Calvin admonishes all who would hear, "God loves you and has opened the door to your adoption in Jesus Christ; now receive that gift by faith and walk in your election to the end of your life."

Along with Calvin's preaching of the gospel to all, Calvin also displays the primacy of God's disclosed disposition in his prayers at the close of his sermons. His typical closing for weekday sermons (except Wednesdays),[89] "that not only [God] will show this favor unto us, but to all peoples and nations of the earth [*mais aussi à tous peuples et nations de la terra*],"[90] is significant particularly in light of what precedes this line, for example, that God would "support us in our weaknesses, that we never leave to be his Children, albeit we honor him not as our father, as were meet. And that he will not only show us this favor."[91] He also prays that "we" would submit to God in times of oppression,[92] that "we be partakers of the glory [*participans de la gloire*] which he hath purchased unto us through our Lord Jesus Christ,"[93] and that "we" would be armed with God's power to fight all temptations,[94] just before asking God to extend that favor to all peoples and nations. Calvin prays according to God's disclosed disposition and according to God's merciful and just nature, asking God to bless all peoples with what he has petitioned for the church.

In sum, Calvin's preaching here clearly exhibits his approach of declaring God's disclosed disposition of lovingkindness revealed in Jesus Christ to all his listeners. He also displays the primacy of God's disclosed disposition in his prayers in the sermons for all peoples. This affirms our findings regarding the precedence of God's disclosed disposition in Calvin's proclamation ministry.

God's Twofold Will: God's Sovereignty and Human Agency

Second, in his sermons on Gen. 25:12–27:38, Calvin again teaches that both God and human persons are active in the salvation of the elect and the condemnation of the reprobate, albeit in different ways.

First, in salvation, according to his electing will, God provides what is necessary for persons to choose to appropriate that salvation. As an expression of his merciful, faithful, and righteous nature, God provides everything the elect need for salvation, including calling them to faith by the Holy Spirit and empowering them to persevere in the faith intentionally and volitionally.[95] At the same time, believers are to choose to receive the gospel,[96] fight for their salvation,[97] pray for their deliverance from worldly passions that would pull them away from God,[98] and, when they find God calling them out of sin, to listen, repent, and return to God.[99]

Although Calvin calls his listeners to preach the gospel (of God's gracious, disclosed disposition) to all and hope for every person who hears it to respond with faith in Christ, he acknowledges God's veiled, reprobating will as well.

Calvin explains that in order for persons to put their faith in Christ, they need the preaching of the word of the gospel along with the witness of the Holy Spirit.[100] In other words, in those who reject the gospel, God has for an inscrutable reason not accompanied the preaching of the word to them with the inner witness of the Holy Spirit; God has passed them over, leaving them in their sin, as their choice to reject the gospel indicates.

Similarly, even though Calvin proclaims that Christ's sacrifice was for the reconciliation of the world, Calvin recognizes that not all will choose to receive it: "The Gospel is preached to the end we might find God merciful to us all: but there are many that through their contempt and ingratitude heap upon themselves their own damnation. . . . [God has] declared unto us that his word is the open way to the heavenly life," so "we" preach it and let God work through it, knowing that he will bless all who "receive this word by faith [*par foy*]."[101] Christians are to seek to bring others to repentance, hoping for their salvation, but "when we shall have labored to bring those to repentance that have offended, if we see them obstinate [*obstinez*], we can no further press or urge them."[102] When the elect hear the message of the gospel, they receive its benefits as God speaks not only outwardly but also inwardly, but "when God generally setteth salvation before us in Jesus Christ his only Son, it is to make the reprobate so much the more inexcusable [*plus inexcusables*] for their unthankfulness, inasmuch as they have disposed [*mesprisé*] so great a benefit."[103]

Just as we observed in Calvin's sermons on Acts, God is the ultimate cause of reprobation, but human beings are the proximate cause. Thus Calvin teaches that the reprobate choose to reject God *and* God allows them to make that choice. They are disobedient because they do not have God's Spirit helping them. In other words, in the mystery of God, he passes them over, leaving them to be subject to their own sinful desires and "beastliness."[104]

This paradox of human agency and God's regenerative grace or lack thereof highlights the way that Calvin in his preaching depicts God's twofold, asymmetrical will toward humanity. God's loving disposition is preached to all; God actively enables salvation for some people in clear congruence with his revealed nature while passively and inexplicably leaving others in bondage to their sinful nature. In short, Calvin's preaching here further supports our findings that Calvin proclaims God's disclosed disposition to all while acknowledging God's twofold, drastically asymmetrical will toward humanity.

Trusting in God's Loving and Just Nature

Third, in his sermons on Gen. 25:12–27:38, Calvin calls his listeners to trust in God's disclosed merciful, righteous, loving, powerful, and just nature, finding comfort and security in God's fatherly love, even when life's circumstances or desires for doctrinal explanations tempt them otherwise.

Without using the technical terms that he uses in the commentaries and the *Institutes* (e.g., *qualis sit Deus*), Calvin describes how God has made his nature known throughout Scripture and most clearly in Jesus Christ. He says that his listeners are able to trust God wholeheartedly because he has revealed himself even more clearly than he did to the patriarchs and prophets "and in a more familiar sort in the person of his only begotten Son."[105]

Although Calvin acknowledged God's fatherly love in his Acts preaching, he highlights God's fatherly loving nature much more commonly in his Genesis sermons. As one example out of many, in his sermon on Gen. 26:23–35 (God's extension of the Abrahamic blessing to Isaac), Calvin emphasizes God's fatherhood toward the congregation, admonishing his listeners to know God as their loving Father, recognizing that the best word that any human being can receive is the word that God loves them because it provides them an assurance of God's loving and powerful care regardless of what comes in life or death.[106] Elsewhere, Calvin points out that Jesus tells us that,

> we have one God together with him, inasmuch as he is man and in that he is our brother: that we have the same God who is his God, and the same father who is his father [*que nous avons un Dieu que est son Dieu, et que nous avons un Pere qui est son Pere*]. When we hear these things, is there any farther cause for us to doubt [*doute*] or to be shaken [*branle*]?[107]

In sum, because God has revealed his loving nature in Jesus Christ, those with faith can confidently trust God.

Without setting aside the primacy of God's fatherly love revealed in Jesus Christ, Calvin also highlights other elements of God's nature as the text dictates (e.g., as a judge in Gen. 26:6–10),[108] consistently preaching God's revealed nature to encourage his listeners in their faithful trust in and obedience to God.[109]

Similarly, Calvin's sermons echo our previous findings in that he counsels his listeners not to seek beyond what God has revealed of himself, trusting God particularly when inexplicable doctrinal questions arise. This is especially applicable in relation to the discussion around the doctrine of election and reprobation because Calvin's preaching demonstrates his belief that humans cannot fully understand how reprobation corresponds with God's revealed nature. Therefore, when describing the way that God chose Jacob and rejected Esau before either was born, Calvin acknowledges the inscrutability of this act, admonishing his listeners not to seek to stretch their limited minds around the God who is "comprehended [*comprins*] neither in heaven nor in earth," who holds the whole world as a grain of dust, and who has "an infinite power, and infinite justice and wisdom, and hath incomprehensible counsels."[110] Beyond innate creaturely limitations, humanity's sinful state makes people even less qualified to judge God's actions. Calvin thus calls his listeners to be content with what God has revealed and not seek to go beyond that, lest they get wrapped "in a Labyrinth."[111]

Calvin also reminds the congregation that God and his ways are righteous, even if they do not appear righteous. Regarding God's choice to show mercy to whoever pleases him, Calvin asserts that God has reasons, "but it followeth not therefore that we can comprehend it. . . . We must therefore know that in respect of us, there is no reason: but the counsel of God ought to be unto us in all respects the rule of righteousness, wisdom and equity."[112] In other words, even though his listeners do not know the reasons for God's reprobation, Calvin admonishes them to assume that God's secret counsel corresponds to his righteous, wise, and equitable character and one righteous will, precisely as we found in our study.

In sum, in Calvin's preaching, he calls his listeners to accept the reality of God's veiled, reprobating will toward some persons while assuming by faith that God's reprobating actions somehow correspond to God's revealed nature and fatherly love proclaimed in God's disclosed disposition, exhibited in election, and most clearly displayed in Jesus Christ.

Conclusion

Calvin's so-called "Sermons on Election and Reprobation" provide an excellent case study for testing our findings in regard to Calvin's preaching. In these thirteen sermons expounding Gen. 25–27, Calvin preaches God's two asymmetrical dispositions toward humanity precisely the way we would have expected. He extends the offer of the gospel of Jesus Christ to all his listeners, hoping and praying for the salvation of all, thus proclaiming and elevating God's disclosed, loving disposition toward humanity as the primary content and grounds of his proclamation. Calvin also acknowledges God's veiled reprobating will, noting that God does not enable faith in every person while still admonishing all of his listeners to trust in God's loving, righteous, and judging nature that has been most clearly revealed in Jesus Christ. Even if his listeners are unable to understand how God's disclosed disposition, revealed nature, and electing will correspond with God's veiled, reprobating will, Calvin asserts that they all cohere in God and in his one righteous will.

SERMONS ON THE PASSION AND RESURRECTION OF CHRIST (1558)

From April 3 to April 10, 1558, Calvin paused his sermon series on the book of Galatians to preach a series of nine sermons on Matt. 26:36—28:10.[113] Calvin preached the morning and afternoon sermons on Sunday, April 3, and then preached one sermon a day until Easter Sunday morning, April 10. As was his custom, Calvin then resumed his preaching in the Galatians series with the appropriate text on the afternoon of Easter Sunday.

In these nine Holy Week sermons, Calvin's preaching again aligns with what we have found in our study. Calvin's general approach throughout the sermons is to proclaim God's loving disposition toward all his listeners, assuring them of God's love for them revealed in Jesus Christ, even in the midst of their deserved wrath. While primarily proclaiming God's disclosed disposition, Calvin acknowledges God's veiled will in the fact that God does not bring all people to faith in Christ. At times, Calvin also directly exhorts his listeners to trust in God's one, righteous will even when they cannot understand how what looks like two wills cohere in God. We shall briefly elucidate each these observations.

God's Loving Disposition toward All

First of all, Calvin proclaims God's loving disposition to his listeners, describing to them God's loving, just, and powerful nature most clearly revealed in Jesus Christ. Again, Calvin affirms the fact that, like Judas, there will "always be domestic enemies" *in the church* who are "full of betrayal and disloyalty."[114] Nonetheless, as in all of his sermons, Calvin almost exclusively uses the first person plural pronouns, with which he proclaims God's love for his listeners (and himself). For example, in the Good Friday sermon, Calvin says regarding Jesus' experience of forsakenness on the cross, "When our Lord Jesus was put into such an extremity, as if God his Father had cut off from him all hope of life, it is inasmuch as he was there in our person [*en nostre personne*], sustaining the curse of our sins, which separated us from God."[115] Similarly, he says, that our assurance of salvation comes from knowing that no matter how many sins we have committed, they will be buried because "our Lord Jesus by his obedience has justified us [*nous a iustifiez*] and rendered us acceptable [*nous a rendus agreables*] to God his Father."[116] Calvin is clear: without any disclaimers or modifiers, he explains to his listeners that because of Jesus' suffering and death in their place, they can be assured of God's forgiveness and love for them.

In the Saturday service, Calvin similarly encourages all his listeners to trust God's paternal love for them in their trials, saying that even though God's people provoke God's wrath daily with their sin, they need "not doubt that he is always Father to us."[117] Affirming God's merciful and judging nature, Calvin even considers God's wrath on sin as part of the good news of God's love. He says that his listeners will only be properly grateful for their salvation when "we examine our condition, and see that we are as sunk in hell, and know what it is to have provoked the wrath [*l'ire*] of God."[118] Calvin preaches to all his listeners God's judgment in God's condemnation of sin and God's mercy in God's provision of the way of forgiveness and reconciliation in Jesus Christ. Calvin preaches God's revealed nature and disclosed disposition to his listeners.

Calvin not only extends God's love revealed in Jesus Christ to all his listeners, he teaches them that God loves the whole world and invites them to proclaim that love. In creation, in which God placed the "germ [*semence*] of religion"[119] in every human being, and more clearly in the mission of Jesus Christ, God has revealed his love for the world. For example, Calvin says in the first Sunday morning sermon that Jesus did not only die for "us . . . but He willed in full measure to appear before the judgment seat of God His Father in the same and in the person of all sinners [*en la personne de tous pecheurs*], being then ready to be condemned, inasmuch as He bore our burden."[120] In his arrest, Jesus wants the disciples to see "how he does not spare himself for their sakes, nor for the sake of the human race [*toute le genre human*]."[121] At the Friday service, Calvin describes the death of Jesus as "the reconciliation of the world [*monde*],"[122] and on Easter Sunday he reminds his listeners that "the Son of God has so manifested himself [after his resurrection], and that he wished the fruit of it to be communicated to all the world."[123] Those who are united with Christ (as evidenced at the Lord's Supper) are to seek "to draw [their] companions" to the same.[124] Calvin proclaims God's love for the world and exhorts his listeners to proclaim it as well.

God's Veiled Reprobating Will toward Some

Secondly, even as Calvin primarily proclaims God's disclosed disposition of love toward the world, he still acknowledges the reality of God's judgment and the fact that God does not bring all people to the saving knowledge of Jesus Christ, thus recognizing God's veiled will toward some. Although it is a rare occurrence in this series, on the first Sunday morning sermon, Calvin reminds his listeners that the incredible benefits of Christ are only appropriated by those with faith. He says that his listeners should never doubt that God in his goodness is always ready to receive them and that "we shall feel that it is not in vain that our Lord Jesus fought to win such a victory for all those [*pour tous ceux*] who have come to him by faith."[125] Similarly, Calvin points out that people have the choice to reject God's offer of salvation in Christ, just as the people of Israel rejected Jesus and brought God's wrath upon themselves.[126]

Calvin also teaches that God deals with the reprobate and the elect differently, although rarely using those terms. God differentiates between the elect and the reprobate in the grace exerted upon each. Calvin says, "The death and passion of our Lord Jesus does not bear fruit in all men, because it is a special grace [*une grace speciale*] that God gives to his elect when he touches them by his Holy Spirit."[127] Describing that special grace, Calvin says that by the cleansing blood of Jesus and by the Holy Spirit, "we are purified and God accepts us for his people, and we are assured; although his wrath and his vengeance is upon all the world [*sur tout le monde*], yet he regards us in pity and he owns us as his children [*ses enfans*]."[128] God is wrathful toward the sin of the world, but that sin has been removed from his children by his grace. Likewise, the majesty of God is terrifying to all who glimpse it; "when God has thus terrified unbelievers, he leaves them there as reprobate men [*gens reprouvez*], because they are not worthy of experiencing His goodness in any way. Therefore, also, they flee his presence. . . . The faithful, after having been frightened, rise up and take courage, because God consoles them and gives them joy."[129] Even though God does not extend that special grace to the reprobate, Calvin is still clear that God is not the primary cause of reprobation. Instead, he asserts that the reprobate have been blinded by Satan, are insane, and "are depraved of sense and of reason."[130]

In sum, in his preaching, Calvin acknowledges and preaches the reality of God's veiled reprobating will toward some people in the fact that God passes them by without rescuing them from their sin. Although this teaching is present in the sermons, it is rare and typically used to highlight the grandeur of God's loving disposition and electing will made known in Jesus Christ. These observations once again concur with our previous findings.

God's One Righteous Will

Third, Calvin affirms human limitations in the comprehension of God's one, righteous will. For example, Calvin declares regarding God's will: "Since he willed that [Jesus] be the sacrifice to wipe out the sins of the world [*effacer les pechez du monde*], Scripture had to be fulfilled."[131] This is precisely what we found in our study. For Calvin, the only will of God that people can comprehend and proclaim is God's revealed electing will expressed in God's disclosed disposition of love for the world. However, as we have seen above,

Calvin also teaches that God does not wipe away the sins in every person in the world. In this case, Calvin admonishes his listeners to submit themselves to God's wisdom and one righteous will, even when they cannot understand: "Now we see in the first place that the will of God ought to stop us and hold us in check so that, when things seem to us savage and against all reason, we may value more what God has ordained than what our brain [*cerveau*] can comprehend."[132] He goes on to say that what we argue with God about arises from our "rudeness" because our "three drops of sense" do not compare with God's infinite wisdom. Instead of questioning God's wisdom, we are called to adore humbly and reverently that which is concealed, "confessing that everything God does is just and upright [*iuste e droict*], though as yet we may not perceive how."[133] God's judgments and will are always righteous. Therefore, Calvin exhorts his listeners to submit to God, trust him, and rest in his revealed nature, even when they cannot understand.

As another example of Calvin's preaching regarding God's one righteous will, in a discussion of why Jesus had to suffer and die, Calvin says that "God has only a single and simple will [*une seule volonte et simple*], but it is admirable to us, and he has such strange ways of proceeding [*façons de proceder si estranges*] that we must lower our eyes and yet recognize that our Lord Jesus suffered" to reveal the infinite love of God in the costliness of salvation to God.[134] God has one will, a will that dramatically and vibrantly demonstrates the unfathomable depths of God's love, but that will is sometimes expressed in ways that are incomprehensible for humanity.

In sum, God has one righteous will that is known by humanity in his disclosed disposition and electing will. This one will includes God's veiled will that appears to human ears and hearts inconsistent with God's disclosed, loving disposition and electing will. This is exactly what we found in our study.

Conclusion

In Calvin's 1558 Holy Week sermons, Calvin's preaching again aligns with our previous findings as he primarily proclaims God's loving, disclosed disposition extended to all humanity that corresponds with God's electing will while also acknowledging God's veiled, reprobating will toward some people. He sees God's loving disposition and asymmetrical twofold will held together in the one, righteous will of the God who has made himself known in creation and redemption.

We now turn to a survey of various other sermons for further examination of Calvin's proclamation of God's disposition toward humanity.

SERMON SURVEY

Although an analysis of Calvin's two thousand plus recorded sermons is clearly beyond the scope of this project, we turn now to a brief survey of sermons from Calvin's Genevan preaching career to continue the test of our findings regarding Calvin's understanding of God's disposition toward humanity in Calvin's preaching. Having already examined an extended series of Sunday morning sermons from 1549 to 1551 (Acts), a series of weekday sermons from 1560 (Genesis), and a Holy Week series from 1558, we shall now look at a number of sermons that fill in between those three series chronologically and biblically. This survey incorporates sermons from across the biblical canon and includes Sunday morning and evening sermons and weekday sermons. By surveying the spectrum of Calvin's preaching over ten years in the midst of varying sociopolitical seasons in Geneva,[135] we receive trustworthy indications regarding Calvin's preaching of God's disposition toward humanity.

Throughout this survey, we find that Calvin is remarkably consistent in proclaiming God's disclosed, loving disposition and revealed nature to all his hearers while still acknowledging the reality of God's veiled, reprobating will and affirming the unity of God's righteous will. We shall briefly review relevant selected sermons from Calvin's series on Micah (1550–1551), Psalm 119 (1553), Job (1554), Deuteronomy (1555), 2 Timothy (1555), and Galatians (1557–1558).[136]

For the purposes of this survey, we shall highlight from each sermon or set of sermons the ways that Calvin proclaims God's disclosed disposition of love and electing will, God's veiled reprobating will, and God's one righteous will. As we shall see, for a variety of contextual and biblical reasons, Calvin does not always address all three foci in every sermon or every sermon series. Although much more could be said about each one of these sermons and the sermon series from which they are drawn, this broad survey provides a valuable wide-ranging assessment of our findings from this study of God's disposition toward humanity in the theology of John Calvin.

Micah (1550–1551)

Calvin's sermons on the book of Micah occurred in late 1550 and early 1551 in Calvin's normal weekday preaching. For this survey, we examine his sermons on Mic. 6:6–8[137] and Mic. 7:10–12[138] because of the ways these biblical texts respectively address walking in justice and mercy (6:6–8) and facing enemies (7:10–12).

In the sermons, Calvin clearly proclaims God's disclosed, merciful disposition and revealed nature to his listeners. In the Micah 6 sermon, Calvin preaches that Mic. 6:8 reveals sin, ridding his listeners of any excuses of ignorance. God has made it clear, "You are to act with justice and equity [*droict et equité*] toward your neighbors, to be merciful and kind, and to walk humbly with your God."[139] Calvin then connects that call to God's disclosed nature and disposition. He says the text exhorts them to serve God by being "humble, gentle, and merciful, for in doing so we resemble [*ressemblerons*] God and witness that we are his children, in whom he has engraved his image."[140] Calvin proclaims the God who is humble, gentle, and merciful.

Mic. 7:10–12 is a text that addresses God's judgment on evil and the suffering of the faithful at the hands of their enemies. In his sermon on the text, Calvin again points out that no human being can discern whether another person is elect of God based on outward appearance or circumstances. He says, "For it is not upon to us to determine whether God favors or hates a person, simply on the basis of our eyes. Only fools make such judgments."[141] This again emphasizes the fact that Calvin does not assume to know the eternal standing of every one of his listeners, even as he consistently affirms God's love for and call to them.

In this sermon, Calvin also addresses the significant and confusing question of what a Christian's attitude should be toward those whom God condemns. Since Christians are called to love their enemies and pray for them, "Ought we not demand the salvation of the world [*le salut de tout le monde*]?"[142] In Calvin's extended answer, he explains that believers' perspectives change when they fix their eyes on God's judgment instead of theirs. In that case, they can rejoice at the damnation of the wicked because they see that God is glorified and his kingdom is advanced through the condemnation of God's enemies. However, Calvin hastens to qualify that statement in light of the nearly inescapable human (sinful) tendency toward hatred and vengeance. He thus concludes that the call is to

> strive to procure the salvation of all as best we can, and let us implore God to have mercy on those whom he has redeemed by the blood of his Son. That is what we must do. And that is why the Scripture admonishes us not to judge anyone hastily. Although we may deem a person wicked, we do not know whether God may rescue them [*le reduyra*] in the end, thus making him subject to his obedience.[143]

In these sermons on Micah, Calvin exhorts his listeners to reflect God's heart of love for all people by proclaiming God's loving disposition to all and hoping for the salvation of all while also recognizing that God's condemnation of evil (including those who reject redemption in Christ) will ultimately serve

God's righteous purposes and is thus to be celebrated. In other words, believers are to proclaim God's disclosed disposition while trusting that God's veiled reprobating will enacted toward some people flows from God's one, good, righteous will.[144]

Psalm 119 (1553)

Calvin's twenty-two sermons[145] on Psalm 119 were preached on Sunday afternoons from January to July 1553.[146] As one might expect in sermons on Psalm 119, the most common theme that runs through the sermons is Calvin's exhortation to trust in God's promises as he has graciously revealed them in Scripture. For this study, we examine his sermons on verses 41–48, 81–88, and 121–128 because of the manner in which these texts address God's love and judgment.

As we have seen in all of his preaching, Calvin again consistently and nearly exclusively uses the first person plural pronouns, calling his listeners to trust God and God's promises to them. Calvin makes statements like, "For God never ceaseth to do us good, and will daily give us new matter to trust [*fier*] in him, to love and serve him."[147] Similarly, Calvin admonishes those who are suffering, "I say, let us always be firm and constant, trusting that God will be our savior [*nostre Sauveur*], since he hath so promised us."[148] Many similar examples abound as Calvin calls all his listeners to trust God's disclosed disposition of love toward them as revealed in Scripture and in Jesus Christ.

At the same time, Calvin also recognizes the fact that some will not receive and trust God's promises revealed in Christ. In other words, Calvin recognizes God's veiled will that is manifest in the way that some people remain in their ungodly opposition to God. Calvin primarily uses these examples when he is admonishing his listeners to trust God and avoid following these improper examples.[149]

In the sermon on Ps. 119:121–128, Calvin preaches about the believer's proper attitude toward unbelievers. Following David's example, Calvin admonishes his listeners to have loving compassion toward those who seem rebellious and even opposed to them. Like David, they are to desire "the conversion of all men . . . to use the effect of charity towards all, and pray unto God that he would save them [*devons requerir à Dieu qu'il les suave*]." However, Calvin also affirms that some will not repent and thus follows David's example by praying that God would act in his office of judge toward them, laying "forth his justice in punishing the offenses, and the horrible wickednesses committed here below . . . punishing those which had been so obstinate, and hard-hearted against him."[150] In this case, Calvin again trusts in

God's loving disposition toward all and hopes for the conversion of all while also welcoming the reality that God will judge all who do not turn to God. Calvin proclaims God's disclosed disposition of love extended toward all while embracing the reality and goodness of God's veiled will that is enacted according to God's revealed nature.

Finally, as we have seen is his custom on Sunday afternoons, he ends all of these sermons with a prayer that extends the desire for God's way and grace to be known "unto all peoples and nations of the earth."[151]

Calvin's sermons on Psalm 119 also confirm our findings regarding his understanding of and proclamation of God's disposition toward humanity, particularly affirming God's loving disposition toward all people while acknowledging God's veiled will that corresponds, at least in part, with God's just and judging nature.

Job (1554)

On February 26, 1554, Calvin began his weekday series on the book of Job that would last until March 6, 1555, 158 sermons later.[152] We briefly examine here his opening sermon on Job 1:1, in which Calvin introduces many of the key themes of the book of Job, including God's sovereignty over all. Although this sermon does not directly address the question of God's disposition toward humanity, a few notes are appropriate.

Regarding God's sovereignty, Calvin admonishes his listeners to trust in God's just nature, even when circumstances would tempt them otherwise. Calvin says,

> God has such dominion over his creatures that he can dispose of them at his pleasure [à son *plaisir*], and when he shows a strictness [*rigeuer*] that we at first find strange, yet that we should keep our mouths closed in order not to murmur; but rather, that we should confess that he is just [*iuste*], expecting that he may declare to us why he chastises us.[153]

This affirms our findings as another way of describing Calvin's understanding of the single, righteous will of God that is at times enacted in ways that do not appear righteous to human eyes.

In this sermon, Calvin also points out that the devil seeks to make the faithful think that God is their enemy and no longer is merciful toward them.[154] This affirms Calvin's understanding of God's merciful disclosed disposition toward humanity and highlights a pastoral emphasis for Calvin, namely that his listeners would confidently know and embrace God's loving disposition toward them.

In this introduction to Job, we see Calvin's affirmation of God's sovereign, just, and righteous rule that may not appear just from the human perspective, and we see Calvin's concern that his listeners always know and embrace God's mercy toward them.

Ten Commandments—Deuteronomy 4–6 (1555)

As a part of his two hundred weekday sermons on Deuteronomy,[155] Calvin preached sixteen sermons on the Ten Commandments from June 7 to July 19, 1555.[156] Because these sermons are focused on God's commands to honor God and seek the best for neighbor, these sermons do not contain significant doctrinal preaching regarding God's disposition toward humanity. Instead, in these sixteen sermons, Calvin's understanding of God's disposition toward humanity is displayed through his overall approach and tone. Even as he preaches what it means to follow God's law, Calvin does not address some people as elect and others as reprobate. Calvin proclaims the God of love and majesty who has revealed himself and his will in Scripture. Calvin invites his listeners to draw near to that God in reverent fear, active obedience, and deep gratitude at God's unmerited mercy and kindness toward them. For example, Calvin says, "God wills to draw [*veut attirer*] us to himself, but we must not infer that men can merit [*meriter*] anything by serving God.[157]

At times, Calvin acknowledges the fact that God does not draw all people to him, but that type of comment is rare. When this occurs, he offers it as an answer to an hypothetical question to prevent his hearers from questioning God's goodness and wisdom based on their observations of people's rejection of the gospel. For example, in sermon 15, Calvin acknowledges that people only come to know God as a loving Father in Jesus Christ through faith as a gift of God's grace. Anticipating the question in his listeners' minds, Calvin admonishes them not to step into the "labyrinth" of God's counsel regarding why God "reforms some by his Holy Spirit and leaves others to go astray [*errer*]."[158] Without exploring the question extensively, Calvin briefly mentions that God has revealed his desire for the salvation of all people and the offer of salvation to all in order to further reveal the guilt of those who reject God's word. In other words, Calvin proclaims God's loving disposition to all while affirming his doctrine that not all people come to faith in Jesus Christ and while affirming the fact that somehow this turn of events corresponds to God's one, righteous will.[159]

Calvin's sermons on the Ten Commandments again support our findings regarding Calvin's preaching, especially broadly affirming God's loving disposition revealed in election extended to all and occasionally acknowledging God's veiled reprobating will toward some.

2 Timothy (1555)

On Sunday mornings and afternoons from September 16, 1554 to August 11, 1555, Calvin preached through 1 and 2 Timothy, offering fifty-four sermons on 1 Timothy and thirty sermons on 2 Timothy.[160] Calvin thought very highly of the second letter to Timothy,[161] and these sermons (like the Deuteronomy sermons) were preached during tumultuous and contentious times in Geneva.[162] Having already discussed the 1 Tim. 2:3–5 sermon,[163] for our survey, we have selected two more sermons from a text that directly addresses God's disposition toward humanity, namely 2 Tim. 1:8–10. This text asserts God's unmerited calling "before the world began." In these two sermons, Calvin clearly highlights God's disclosed disposition and revealed nature made known in Jesus Christ and briefly mentions God's veiled reprobating will.

First, in these sermons, Calvin directly and repeatedly describes God's disclosed disposition and revealed nature that have been made known in Jesus Christ. In the first of the two sermons, Calvin confidently proclaims, "For he hath already saved us [*nous a desia suavez*], in that he hath called us to the gospel, and redeemed us from sin. He hath called us [*nous a appelez*] with an holy calling; that is to say, he hath chosen us to himself, out of the general confusion of mankind."[164] Responding to the rhetorical question of why it is that God chose us since it is exceedingly clear that no human being merits God's election, Calvin responds that it is not our place to seek a reason. Instead, "[God's] bare will [*simple vounté*] may suffice us for all reason," but we are able to know that God "was moved only by his just will, which is a rule of all justice [*la regle de toute iustice*]."[165] God's revealed, electing will is part of God's one, secret, and righteous will and corresponds with God's revealed nature.

According to Calvin's sermon on 2 Tim. 1:9–10, believers find assurance of their salvation in their hearing the truth of the gospel and in the accompanying call of the Spirit who "is an undoubted witness of our salvation, if we receive it by faith."[166] Unlike human inability to know if anyone is reprobate, people are able to know their own election as the Spirit reveals it to them, opening up to them "the wonderful secrets of God [*secrets admirable de Dieu*]."[167] The call of the gospel also reveals God's gracious disclosed disposition toward his listeners from before the world began.[168] Calvin goes on to say, "We must note these two things: that in the person of our Lord Jesus Christ we have all that we can desire; that we have full and perfect trust in the goodness of God and the love He beareth us."[169] According to Calvin, in the gospel of Jesus Christ (and its accompanying call by the Holy Spirit), God has revealed and confirmed his loving disposition toward his listeners.

Second, Calvin also mentions God's veiled reprobating will, although comparatively rarely. Calvin points out that the gospel is rejected by some who "cast away [*repoussent*] the grace that is offered them" and thus show themselves to be reprobate. Calvin immediately goes on to contrast that choice with the way that "we receive the doctrine of God with obedience" and thus find certainty of election.[170] Calvin discusses God's veiled will to help assure his listeners of God's disclosed disposition toward those who look to Christ by faith. Later in the sermon, Calvin again acknowledges the fact that some people do not receive the gospel and thus remain "in the general destruction of mankind," but again he immediately draws the conclusion that this only highlights God's goodness because "we are no better [*meilleurs*] than they."[171] In short, Calvin acknowledges the reality of God's veiled will toward some people but subsequently uses that fact to highlight further God's gracious electing will and emphasize the asymmetry between the two.

In summary, these two sermons from 2 Tim. 1:8–10 provide further confirmation of our findings, particularly Calvin's asymmetrical treatment of God's revealed electing will and veiled reprobating will.

Galatians (1557–1558)

After finishing a sermon series on 1 Corinthians, and prior to a series on Ephesians, Calvin preached forty-three sermons on Galatians on Sunday mornings and afternoons from November 14, 1557, to May 8, 1558.[172] As one might expect from the text, a few of the recurring themes in the sermons are human depravity, justification by faith, law and grace, holiness, and the errors of the Church of Rome.[173] For this survey, we have selected a central text for the Protestant understanding of justification by faith (Gal. 2:15–16) and an important text regarding Jesus' substitutionary death on behalf of sinners (Gal. 3:13–18). As expected with texts that do not explicitly address election, these two sermons include more tangential references to God's disposition toward humanity than explicit predestination texts (e.g., 2 Tim. 1:8–10). However, in these two sermons, Calvin continues to preach God's disclosed disposition of love to his undeserving listeners, while recognizing that the offer of the gospel that extends to all is not received by all.

In the Galatians 2 sermon,[174] Calvin teaches that both unbelievers and believers are equally guilty and worthy of condemnation in their flesh. He says, "When it comes to our nature, we are only evil [*mal*] within."[175] Thus, justification is an expression of God's disclosed disposition of love and electing will as the "favor which God bestows upon us when we become his children and he our Father."[176] Similarly, in the sermon on Gal. 3:13–18,[177] Calvin highlights the death of Jesus for "us," again affirming God's loving disposition toward humanity.[178] He says that, because of how much the Father loves the Son, his listeners can be completely confident that God will be favorable to them as they trust in Jesus' bearing their curse.[179] Although all are unworthy,

Jesus took the curse of sin upon himself to make them into the church of God as the children of God.[180]

Calvin also here proclaims God's loving disposition toward all while recognizing that not all people will receive it. Referring to God's promises to Abraham, Calvin says that the promise that initially was extended only to the Jewish people "was made applicable to the whole world [à *toute le monde*]" in Jesus, the seed of Abraham.[181] Thus the promise to Abraham by the one who "would reveal himself as the Saviour and Father of the whole world [*tout le monde*] applies not just to Abraham's physical descendants "but to all men [*pour tous hommes*]."[182] However, alongside the universal nature of the promise of God's love, Calvin says that Jesus bore the curse of "all those he would call to salvation [*ceux lesquels il devoit appeler à salut*]" and points out that some people will hear about the Son of God bearing the human curse and reject that proclamation as foolishness.[183] In other words, God's loving call (disclosed disposition) goes out to all, but only some receive the gift of God's love revealed in Christ. This echoes Calvin's commitment to the fact that the crucifixion of Jesus Christ is sufficient for the redemption of all people but only efficient in redeeming the elect.

In summary, Calvin's sermons on Galatians again affirm our findings, this time highlighting the deserved condemnation of every human being and Jesus' gracious death on the cross that extends the merciful promise of Abraham to all who would receive it by faith, while acknowledging that not all people will receive it, according to God's veiled will toward humanity.

Conclusion

Like our previous case studies, this survey of sermons from across the textual and chronological spectrum of Calvin's extant sermons confirms our findings regarding God's disposition toward humanity in Calvin's preaching. Calvin proclaims God's loving disposition revealed in Jesus Christ to all his listeners and hopes for the salvation of all while acknowledging the reality of God's veiled will toward some people displayed in the fact that not all people receive the gospel by faith. He also sees this twofold but asymmetrical expression of God's will in election and reprobation as somehow cohering in God's one righteous will.

SUMMARY

Consistent with the example from 1 Tim. 2 at the beginning of this chapter, in a survey of a wide range of Calvin's sermons from 1549 to 1560, we find that Calvin is consistent in his preaching of God's disposition toward humanity. Calvin persistently preaches the gospel of Jesus Christ to all his listeners, hoping and praying for the salvation of all and calling the congregation to do the same, thus emphasizing God's disclosed disposition and revealed nature that directly correspond to God's electing will. His sermons also display an acknowledgment of God's veiled reprobating will by recognizing that God does not enable every person to receive God's offer of salvation in Jesus Christ but leaves some in their hardness of heart, blinded by evil. However, Calvin also affirms the drastic asymmetry between God's disclosed electing will and God's veiled reprobating will in a variety of ways, including the manner that Calvin repeatedly extends the offer of God's love and grace to all his listeners while rarely discussing God's veiled reprobating will. Calvin also affirms the epistemological asymmetry in the way that God's disclosed disposition and electing will directly reflect God's nature while his veiled reprobating will is chiefly inscrutable to humans, only partially understandable as corresponding to God's just judgment and as highlighting God's unmerited mercy toward the elect. At the same time, Calvin asserts the fact that these two asymmetrical movements of God are united within God's one righteous will. Finally, Calvin clearly exhorts his listeners to trust in God's merciful and just nature revealed in Jesus Christ, finding assurance in God's fatherly love for them in life and in death.

This study of Calvin's preaching confirms the findings from our study of Calvin's theological teaching. In short, Calvin unapologetically preaches God's love to his listeners, exhorting them *all* to trust in God's grace revealed in Jesus Christ and persevere in that faith. He can do that because he is proclaiming the only God that can be truly known, the God who has revealed himself in creation, in Scripture, and in Jesus Christ. Scripture and experience show that for some unknown reason God does not enable every person to respond to the gospel with faith. For Calvin, this does not prevent him from preaching God's love. Instead, he preaches it all the more, longing for all who hear to receive the fatherly love of God that he has come to know through faith.

Calvin notably does not add any disclaimers to his proclamation of God's love. He does not say, "God loves you if you respond in faith" or "God loves you if you show signs of election." He also does not address parts of his preaching to the elect and other parts of his preaching to the reprobate. Instead, he preaches as if all are loved by God and redeemed in Jesus Christ. He does not believe that every person receives the gift of God's love in the end, but that tragic reality does not limit his proclamation of God's loving disposition toward all, of which he is convinced. Instead, he simply accepts by faith that somehow the fact that God does not provide the gift of faith for all people corresponds with the loving, just, righteous nature of the God revealed in Jesus Christ according to God's secret will.

This final step has been difficult for some people to accept since Calvin's time, and it is the task of contemporary believers to continue to wrestle with Scripture and what God has made known about himself in Jesus Christ to determine how to proclaim best God's disposition toward humanity in their contexts. With that task in mind, having established Calvin's teaching on God's disposition toward humanity and tested our findings in his preaching ministry, in the next two chapters, we explore, respectively, key secondary literature on Calvin and the teaching of a few other important theological voices in the Reformed tradition regarding God's disposition toward humanity and the doctrine of predestination as we begin to engage in more critical reflection of Calvin's teaching.

NOTES

1. *Selected Sermons from the Pastoral Epistles*, 1 Tim. 2:3–5, p. 103; *CO* 53:153.

2. *Selected Sermons from the Pastoral Epistles*, 1 Tim. 2:3–5, p. 105; *CO* 53:154. Translation mine.

3. *Selected Sermons from the Pastoral Epistles*, 1 Tim. 2:3–5, p. 101; *CO* 53:151.

4. The sermon, preached on October 28, 1554, was part of a series of fifty-four sermons on 1 Timothy that Calvin preached during a particularly tumultuous time in Geneva. See "2 Timothy (1555)" below for more details.

5. Chronologically, the work researching Calvin's theology of God's disposition toward humanity came prior to this survey of Calvin's preaching.

6. *Selected Sermons from the Pastoral Epistles*, 1 Tim. 2:3–5, pp. 96–98, *CO* 53:147–149.

7. *Selected Sermons from the Pastoral Epistles*, 1 Tim. 2:3–5, p. 101; *CO* 53:151. Translation mine.

8. *Selected Sermons from the Pastoral Epistles*, 1 Tim. 2:3–5, pp. 102–3; *CO* 53:152.

9. *Selected Sermons from the Pastoral Epistles*, 1 Tim. 2:3–5, p. 110; *CO* 53:160.

10. *Selected Sermons from the Pastoral Epistles*, 1 Tim. 2:3–5, p. 110; *CO* 53:160.

11. He also was committed to training good preachers, as seen in the establishment of the Academy in 1559. Cf. T. H. L. Parker, *Calvin's Preaching* (Louisville, KY: Westminster/John Knox Press, 1992), 38–39. Cf. Gordon, *Calvin*, 299.

12. *Inst.* 1.7.1, p. 74; *CO* 2:56.

13. For example, Calvin regularly acknowledges textual issues (e.g., copyist errors), the styles of various authors, and the historical settings of various books of the Bible.

14. *Comm. 2 Tim.* 3:16; *CO* 52:383.

15. Parker, *Calvin's Preaching*, 22.

16. Parker, *Calvin's Preaching*, 25–27.

17. Parker, *Calvin's Preaching*, 28–29. Cf. Calvin's sermon on Deut. 3:12–22; *CO* 26:67.
18. Parker, *Calvin's Preaching*, 31.
19. *CO* 54:287. Translation from Parker, *Calvin's Preaching*, 11–12.
20. Parker, *Calvin's Preaching*, 93.
21. Parker, *Calvin's Preaching*, 103.
22. For four examples from his sermons on 1 and 2 Timothy, see Parker, *Calvin's Preaching*, 94–101.
23. *CO* 54:288–289. Translation from Parker, *Calvin's Preaching*, 12.
24. Parker's summary is, "The gracious self-revelation of the hidden God and man's grateful acceptance and submission to it" (*Calvin's Preaching*, 107).
25. Parker, *Calvin's Preaching*, 79. Cf. *Sermons on 2 Tim.* 3:16–17; *CO* 54:289.
26. Calvin averaged approximately 2.5–7 verses per sermon, typically lower for New Testament books than Old Testament books (McKee, *The Pastoral Ministry and Worship in Calvin's Geneva*, 929–35).
27. Other Reformed churches often used the lectionary or *loci communes* to guide sermon series. With the exception of one series on the Psalms, Calvin only deviated from *lectio continua* for Christmas, Easter, Pentecost, and Holy Week (McKee, *The Pastoral Ministry and Worship in Calvin's Geneva*, 453).
28. For a catalogue of dated sermons and Scripture texts from 1549 through 1564, see McKee, *The Pastoral Ministry and Worship in Calvin's Geneva*, 875–921.
29. Calvin to Somerset, 22 October 1548 (*Selected Works of John Calvin: Tracts and Letters,* trans. David Constable [Albany, OR: Books for the Ages, 1998], 203); *CO* 13:71.
30. Parker, *Calvin's Preaching*, 149. Cf. McKee, *The Pastoral Ministry and Worship in Calvin's Geneva*, 524–27.
31. Parker, *Calvin's Preaching*, 139–49.
32. McKee, *The Pastoral Ministry and Worship in Calvin's Geneva*, 524–26. He explicates the details in his commentaries and theology lectures.
33. Parker, *Calvin's Preaching*, 86. Parker points out that English translations (e.g. Golding's) sometimes add "Hebrew" or "Greek" when all Calvin said was "the word means."
34. Calvin to Somerset, 22 October 1548 (*Selected Works of John Calvin: Tracts and Letters*, 203); *CO* 13:71.
35. Parker, *Calvin's Preaching*, 57–58.
36. McKee, *The Pastoral Ministry and Worship in Calvin's Geneva*, 483–89. McKee also confidently hypothesizes sermon series on Jude, Genesis, Habakkuk, Haggai, Zechariah, Malachi, and Hebrews. She more tentatively suggests Philippians, 1 Peter, and 1 John in an unaccounted year and a half in 1546 to 1547.
37. Parker, *Calvin's Preaching*, 57–64.
38. Although many sermons are still extant, sadly many of the recorded sermons were accidentally sold for the weight of old paper from the Geneva library in 1805. Less than one third of the forty-three volumes has been recovered (*The Pastoral Ministry and Worship in Calvin's Geneva*, 501–2).

39. Parker, *Calvin's Preaching*, 65–67. Cf. McKee, *The Pastoral Ministry and Worship in Calvin's Geneva*, 501.

40. Cf. Raguenier's catalogue in Parker, *Calvin's Preaching*, 153–56.

41. Parker, *Calvin's Preaching*, 65. The only set of sermons that Calvin did edit was the early "Four Sermons" (*Quatre Sermons* published in French in 1552) in which Calvin addresses the problem of Reformed Christians worshipping in the Roman Catholic church. Calvin uses them as a type of treatise on the topic, in contrast with the rest of his sermons that were published in their extempore form (McKee, *The Pastoral Ministry and Worship in Calvin's Geneva*, 542–43).

42. McKee points out that Calvin was quite reticent to publish his sermons because they were intended for a specific congregation at a specific time. They were not rhetorically and stylistically polished (as they would have been if Calvin had written them), and they were much longer than a commentary on those books needed to be. Various publishers over the years convinced him that publishing them would be beneficial (McKee, *The Pastoral Ministry and Worship in Calvin's Geneva*, 544, 556).

43. McKee, *The Pastoral Ministry and Worship in Calvin's Geneva*, 908–9.

44. *CO* 48:585–664 and *SC* 8.

45. As noted above, Raguenier's stenography work began on September 29, 1549. Cf. Parker, *Calvin's Preaching*, 65–75.

46. *Sermons on Acts*, 6:1–6, pp. 318–19; *SC* 8.206–207.

47. *Sermons on Acts*, 3:17–19, p. 102; *SC* 8:68.

48. *Sermons on Acts*, 7:51, pp. 586–87; *SC* 8:373.

49. For example, *Sermons on Acts*, 7:51, p. 593; *SC* 8:377. Cf. *Sermons on Acts*, 7:58–60, p. 638; *SC* 8:406.

50. Muller, *Calvin and the Reformed Tradition*, 60–61.

51. In his sermon on Acts 7:9–16, Calvin grieves over the fact that some of God's human creatures will go to hell (p. 414); *SC* 8:266.

52. *Sermons on Acts*, 3:17–19, p. 108; *SC* 8:72. It is noteworthy that for Calvin, the language of "peoples and nations" can at times refer to all people groups and all classes of people in society, not necessarily every individual. For an example, see *Comm. 1 Tim.* 2:4; *CO* 52:268. Cf. *Sermons on Acts*, 5:17–21, p. 246; *SC* 8:156. Cf. 5:30–32, p. 273; *SC* 8:178. Cf. McKee, *The Pastoral Ministry and Worship in Calvin's Geneva*, 507.

53. *Sermons on Acts*, 4:5–12, p. 135; *SC* 8.88.

54. See "God's Revealed Will and Veiled Will in Christian Mission" in chapter 2 above. Cf. *Inst.* 3.23.14, p. 964; *CO* 2:711.

55. *Sermons on Acts*, 7:51, p. 595; *SC* 8:378.

56. Parker notes Calvin's conviction that the preacher was always also being addressed by the text himself is another reason that he utilized the first person plural pronouns. He was preaching to himself as well as his listeners (*Calvin's Preaching*, 116–17).

57. *Sermons on Acts*, 7:37–38, pp. 515–16; *SC* 8:330. Italics mine.

58. *Sermons on Acts*, 7:45–50, p. 570; *SC* 8:364. Cf. *Sermons on Acts*, 2:41–42, p. 57; *SC* 8:39. Cf. *Sermons on the Saving Work of Christ*, Acts 1:1–4, pp. 198–99; *CO* 48:587.

59. *Sermons on Acts*, 2:39–40, p. 42; *SC* 8:28. Cf. *Sermons on Acts*, 7:20–22, p. 444; *SC* 8:285. Cf. *Sermons on the Saving Work of Christ*, Acts 2:22–24, p. 280; *CO* 48:655.

60. *Sermons on Acts*, 5:30–32, p. 269; *SC* 8:174.

61. *Sermons on Acts*, 5:13–16, p. 221; *SC* 8:141.

62. *Sermons on Acts*, 7:52–56, p. 607; *SC* 8:385.

63. See above, chapter 3, "The Call to All, Faith as a Gift to Some."

64. *Sermons on Acts*, 3:17–19, p. 102; *SC* 8:68. Cf. pp. 96–97; *SC* 8:64. Cf. p. 106; *SC* 8:71. Cf. 2:41–42, p. 56; *SC* 8:38.

65. *Sermons on Acts*, 7:35–37, p. 496; *SC* 8:318.

66. *Sermons on Acts*, 7:31–35, p. 470; *SC* 8:301.

67. *Sermons on Acts*, 5:33–35, 38–39, p. 276; *SC* 8.179. Cf. 7:42–43, p. 542; *SC* 8:347.

68. *Sermons on Acts*, 7:52–56, p. 608; *SC* 8:385.

69. *Sermons on Acts*, 5:25–32, pp. 248–49; *SC* 8:158.

70. *Sermons on Acts*, 7:42–43, p. 539; *SC* 8:345.

71. *Sermons on Acts*, 7:31–35, p. 476; *SC* 8:305. Cf. *Sermons on Acts*, 7:35–37, p. 496; *SC* 8:318.

72. *Sermons on Acts*, 7:35–37, p. 499; *SC* 8:320.

73. *Sermons on Acts*, 7:38–42, p. 527; *SC* 8:337.

74. *Sermons on Acts*, 7:15–19, p. 427; *SC* 8:274.

75. *Sermons on the Saving Work of Christ*, p. 202; *CO* 48:589.

76. Of the 262 sermons, we have extant records of 113 of them (McKee, *The Pastoral Ministry and Worship in Calvin's Geneva*, 933–35).

77. "Treze Sermons de M. I. Calvin Traitans de l'Election Gratuite de Dieu en Iacob, et de la Reiection en Esau," *CO* 58:ix–198. They were translated by John Field into English and published in 1579, the same version that was reprinted in 1996 (John Calvin, *Sermons on Election and Reprobation*, trans. John Field [Willow Street, PA: Old Paths Publications, 1996]). Only ten other sermons from the Genesis series were published in the sixteenth century: three sermons concerning Abraham's encounter with Melchizedek (Gen. 14:13–16, 18–24), four on Abraham's justification by faith (Gen. 15:4–7), and three on Abraham's obedience in the command to sacrifice Isaac (Gen. 21:33–22:14) (John Calvin, *Sermons on Melchizedek and Abraham*, trans. Thomas Stocker [Willow Street, PA: Old Paths Publications, 2000]). Two volumes of extant sermons from Genesis 1–20 have recently been translated into English and published by Banner of Truth (John Calvin, *Sermons on Genesis 1–11*, trans. Rob Roy McGregor [Edinburgh: Banner of Truth, 2009]; John Calvin, *Sermons on Genesis 11–20*, trans. Rob Roy McGregor [Edinburgh: Banner of Truth, 2012]).

78. McKee, *The Pastoral Ministry and Worship in Calvin's Geneva*, 933.

79. *Sermons on Election and Reprobation*, no. 4, Gen. 25:24–28, p. 72; *CO* 58:59.

80. *Sermons on Election and Reprobation*, no. 5, Gen. 25:29–34, p. 106; *CO* 58:80.

81. Calvin says that when God brings us into his church, "let us walk in purity, and labor to make sure [*ratifier*] our election, and to have the testimony thereof in

our hearts, by the Holy Ghost" (*Sermons on Election and Reprobation*, no. 2, Gen. 25:21–22, p. 27); *CO* 58:33.

82. *Sermons on Election and Reprobation*, no. 2, Gen. 25:21–22, p. 34; *CO* 58:36.

83. *Sermons on Election and Reprobation*, no. 3, Gen. 25:21–22, p. 55; *CO* 58:49.

84. *Sermons on Election and Reprobation*, no. 3, Gen. 25:21–22, p. 58; *CO* 58:51.

85. Cf. *Sermons on Election and Reprobation*, no. 9, Gen. 26:23–25 p. 205; *CO* 58:138.

86. *Sermons on Election and Reprobation*, no. 6, Gen. 26:1–5, p. 134; *CO* 58:97. Cf. no. 12, Gen. 27:13–21, p. 270; *CO* 58:176–177.

87. *Sermons on Election and Reprobation*, no. 13, Gen. 27:31–38, p. 298; *CO* 58:193.

88. *Sermons on Election and Reprobation*, no. 9, Gen. 26:23–25 p. 209; *CO* 58:141.

89. McKee, *The Pastoral Ministry and Worship in Calvin's Geneva*, 507.

90. *Sermons on Election and Reprobation*, no. 13, Gen. 27:31–38, p. 304, *CO* 58:198.

91. *Sermons on Election and Reprobation*, no. 7, Gen. 26:6–10, p. 165; *CO* 58:116.

92. *Sermons on Election and Reprobation*, no. 8, Gen. 26:11–21, p. 188; *CO* 58:130.

93. *Sermons on Election and Reprobation*, no. 12, Gen. 27:13–21, p. 281; *CO* 58:184.

94. *Sermons on Election and Reprobation*, no. 6, Gen. 26:1–5, p. 142; *CO* 58:102.

95. *Sermons on Election and Reprobation*, no. 5, Gen. 25:29–34, p. 98; *CO* 58:75. "And therefore, as it is said unto us, that God is the author of our salvation" (*Sermons on Election and Reprobation*, no. 2, Gen. 25:21–22, p. 46). Cf. *Sermons on Election and Reprobation*, no. 4, Gen. 25:24–28, p. 74; *CO* 58:61.

96. *Sermons on Election and Reprobation*, no. 6, Gen. 26:1–5, p. 134; *CO* 58:97.

97. *Sermons on Election and Reprobation*, no. 4, Gen. 25:24–28, p. 74; *CO* 58:61.

98. *Sermons on Election and Reprobation*, no. 5, Gen. 25:29–34, p. 106; *CO* 58:80.

99. *Sermons on Election and Reprobation*, no. 13, Gen. 27:31–38, pp. 294–96; *CO* 58:191–192.

100. *Sermons on Election and Reprobation*, no. 3, Gen. 25:21–22, p. 63. Cf. no. 11, Gen. 27:3–9, 253; *CO* 58:167.

101. *Sermons on Election and Reprobation*, no. 12, Gen. 27:13–21, pp. 271–72; *CO* 58:177.

102. *Sermons on Election and Reprobation*, no. 10, Gen. 26:26–27:2, p. 224; *CO* 58:150.

103. *Sermons on Election and Reprobation*, no. 3, Gen. 25:21–22, p. 63; *CO* 58:54.

104. "We see here how God hath laid open the beastliness [*brutalité*] of Esau, and hath showed that he was already forsaken [*delaissé*] of him, and was not governed by his holy spirit [*sic*]" (*Sermons on Election and Reprobation*, no. 5, Gen. 25:29–34, p. 105; *CO* 58:79). Cf. p. 98; *CO* 58:75. Cf. p. 104; *CO* 58:79.

105. *Sermons on Election and Reprobation*, no. 9, Gen. 26:23–25, p. 204; *CO* 58:138.

106. *Sermons on Election and Reprobation*, no. 9, Gen. 26:23–25, p. 193. Cf. p. 197. Cf. no. 6, Gen. 26:1–5, p. 132; *CO* 58:95. Cf. no. 8, Gen. 26:11–21, pp. 166–88; *CO* 58:115–130. Cf. no. 9, Gen. 26:23–25, pp. 204–5; *CO* 58:138–139.

107. *Sermons on Election and Reprobation*, no. 9, Gen. 26:23–25, pp. 204–5; *CO* 58:139.

108. *Sermons on Election and Reprobation*, no. 7, Gen. 26:6–10, pp. 160–61; *CO* 58:112. Cf. *Sermons on Election and Reprobation*, no. 8, Gen. 26:11–21, p. 186; *CO* 58:127.

109. Cf. *Sermons on Election and Reprobation*, no. 2, Gen. 25:21–22, p. 37; *CO* 58:38.

110. *Sermons on Election and Reprobation*, no. 2, Gen. 25:21–22, p. 29; *CO* 58:34.

111. *Sermons on Election and Reprobation*, no. 2, Gen. 25:21–22, p. 30; *CO* 58:34. Cf. no. 3, Gen. 25:21–22, p. 53; *CO* 58:48. Cf. pp. 56–57; *CO* 58:50.

112. *Sermons on Election and Reprobation*, no. 2, Gen. 25:21–22, p. 37; *CO* 58:38.

113. Although it does not appear that Calvin preached in this manner every year during Holy Week, McKee records five other occurrences of this practice between 1549 and 1562 (*The Pastoral Ministry and Worship in Calvin's Geneva*, 907–21).

114. *Sermons on the Saving Work of Christ*, Sermon 2, Matt. 26:40–50, p. 76; *CO* 46:855. Cf. p. 80; *CO* 46:858.

115. *Sermons on the Saving Work of Christ*, Sermon 7, Matt. 27:45–54, p. 157; *CO* 46:920.

116. *Sermons on the Saving Work of Christ*, Sermon 7, Matt. 27:45–54, p. 155; *CO* 46:919.

117. *Sermons on the Saving Work of Christ*, Sermon 8, Matt. 27:55–60, p. 183; *CO* 46:942. Cf. p. 172; *CO* 46:933.

118. *Sermons on the Saving Work of Christ*, Sermon 1, Matt. 26:36–39, p. 52; *CO* 46:833–834.

119. *Sermons on the Saving Work of Christ*, Sermon 5, Matt. 27:11–26, p. 128; *CO* 46:897.

120. *Sermons on the Saving Work of Christ*, Sermon 1, Matt. 26:36–39, p. 52; *CO* 46:824.

121. *Sermons on the Saving Work of Christ*, Sermon 2, Matt. 26:40–50, p. 74; *CO* 46:853.

122. *Sermons on the Saving Work of Christ*, Sermon 7, Matt. 27:45–54, p. 153; *CO* 46:917.

123. *Sermons on the Saving Work of Christ*, Sermon 9, Matt. 28:1–10, p. 193, *CO* 46:951.

124. *Sermons on the Saving Work of Christ*, Sermon 1, Matt. 26:36–39, p. 65; *CO* 46:846.

125. *Sermons on the Saving Work of Christ*, Sermon 1, Matt. 26:36–39, pp. 61–62; *CO* 46:842.

126. *Sermons on the Saving Work of Christ*, Sermon 5, Matt. 27:11–26, p. 133; *CO* 46:901.

Sadly, this type of commentary on the events of the crucifixion have been used to justify anti-Semitic sentiments. That would be an incorrect use of Calvin for many reasons, including the fact that he was often criticized for being too sympathetic in his approach to the Jewish people in his exegesis of the Old Testament. Cf. G. Sujin Pak, *The Judaizing Calvin: Sixteenth-Century Debates over the Messianic Psalms* (Oxford: Oxford University Press, 2009).

127. *Sermons on the Saving Work of Christ*, Sermon 4, Matt. 26:67–27:10, p. 108; *CO* 46:881.

128. *Sermons on the Saving Work of Christ*, Sermon 8, Matt. 27:55–60, p. 173; *CO* 46:934.

129. *Sermons on the Saving Work of Christ*, Sermon 9, Matt. 28:1–10, p. 190; *CO* 46:948.

130. *Sermons on the Saving Work of Christ*, Sermon 4, Matt. 26:67–27:10, p. 110; *CO* 46:883. Calvin then highlights the fact that his listeners should be particularly grateful for God's goodness and grace in rescuing them from their natural fate. Acting in his typical pastoral manner, Calvin sees God's wrath enacted as an occasion to comfort and encourage the faithful in the abundance of God's unmerited love.

131. *Sermons on the Saving Work of Christ*, Sermon 5, Matt. 27:11–26, p. 123; *CO* 46:891.

132. *Sermons on the Saving Work of Christ*, Sermon 3, Matt. 26:51–66, pp. 87–88; *CO* 46:864.

133. *Sermons on the Saving Work of Christ*, Sermon 3, Matt. 26:51–66, pp. 87–88; *CO* 46:864.

134. *Sermons on the Saving Work of Christ*, Sermon 5, Matt. 27:11–26, pp. 125–26; *CO* 46:895. Translation mine.

135. For example, in the midst of the Perrinist conflict, Calvin's sermons on 2 Timothy and Deuteronomy provide no notable divergence in regard to Calvin's preaching of God's disposition toward humanity. Because of space limitations, we are not able to engage significantly with the political and social context surrounding each set of sermons. For two excellent biographies on Calvin that enlighten those events, see Selderhuis, *John Calvin*, and Gordon, *Calvin*. Cf. Parker, *Calvin's Preaching*, 114–28.

136. The sermons were selected out of each series based on their applicability to our topic of God's disposition toward humanity, either in the biblical text or in content of the sermon itself.

137. Saturday, December 27, 1550. Throughout his Genevan preaching career, Calvin commonly continued his weekday OT series on Saturdays.

138. Saturday, January 10, 1551.

139. *Sermons on Micah*, 6:6–8, p. 336; *SC* 5:190.

140. *Sermons on Micah*, 6:6–8, p. 336, *SC* 5:190. For more on Calvin's preaching on this topic, see my chapter, "Pietas and Caritas: John Calvin's Preaching on Love for Neighbor," in Karin Maag and Arnold Huijgen (eds), *Calvinus Frater in Dominus: Papers of the Twelfth International Congress on Calvin Research* (Göttingen: Vandenhoeck & Ruprecht, 2020).

141. *Sermons on Micah*, 7:10–12, pp. 410–11; *SC* 5:231.

142. *Sermons on Micah*, 7:10–12, p. 411; *SC* 5:232.

143. *Sermons on Micah*, 7:10–12, p. 413; *SC* 5:233.

144. As observed above, this is a doctrinal decision that some may not be able to affirm, but this is how Calvin saw it. He trusted God's revealed nature, disclosed disposition, and electing will and had faith that anything that did not seem to fit with God's revealed nature would be seen differently when viewed from a heavenly perspective instead of a limited human perspective.

145. Following the acrostic structure of the psalm, Calvin preached one sermon for each letter of the Hebrew alphabet, addressing the appropriate eight verses each week.

146. McKee, *The Pastoral Ministry and Worship in Calvin's Geneva*, 910.

147. *Sermons on Ps. 119*, v. 41–48, p. 94; *CO* 32:549.

148. *Sermons on Ps. 119*, v. 121–128, p. 232; *CO* 32:669. Cf. *Sermons on Ps. 119*, v. 41–48, p. 94; *CO* 32:549.

149. For example, *Sermons on Ps. 119*, v. 81–88, p. 170; *CO* 32:615.

150. *Sermons on Ps. 119*, v. 121–128, pp. 235–36; *CO* 32:671–672.

151. For example, *Sermons on Ps. 119*, v. 81–88, p. 171; *CO* 32:616.

152. McKee, *The Pastoral Ministry and Worship in Calvin's Geneva*, 881–85.

153. *Sermons on Job*, 1:1, p. 3; *CO* 33:21.

154. *Sermons on Job*, 1:1, p. 4, *CO* 33:22–23.

155. Wednesday, March 20, 1555 to Wednesday, July 15, 1556. This series immediately followed the Job sermon series (McKee, *The Pastoral Ministry and Worship in Calvin's Geneva*, 885–91).

156. The first sermon is on Deut. 4:44–5:3, and the final sermon is on Deut. 6:1–4. These sixteen sermons were first published as a group in French in 1557 and first in English in 1579 (de Greef, *The Writings of John Calvin*, 182–92).

157. *Sermons on the Ten Commandments*, Deut. 5:28–33, p. 284; *CO* 26:417.

158. *Sermons on the Ten Commandments*, Deut. 5:28–33, p. 275; *CO* 26:410.

159. As mentioned at the close of chapter 3, this analysis brings up two potential weaknesses of Calvin's approach. First, he assumes that not everyone comes to faith, an assumption that seems clear to human eyes but one that ultimately only God in his secret counsel knows. Secondly, he seeks to defend logically God's actions when it would arguably be better to be silent.

160. McKee, *The Pastoral Ministry and Worship in Calvin's Geneva*, 911–13.

161. In Calvin's first sermon on 2 Timothy, he says, "As for me, I know that this epistle has profited me more than any other book in Scripture—and still profits me every day" (*CO* 54.5). Translation from Parker, *Calvin's Preaching*, 83.

162. The election of the Little Council in February 1555 marked a significant decision point for Geneva in determining whether the church or the city council held the power to excommunicate. Calvin thought the church should hold that power.

After Calvin supporters won the majority, the Perrinist revolt arose on May 16, which could have had horrific results, especially for the French refugees in Geneva (Parker, *Calvin's Preaching*, 123). Cf. Selderhuis, *John Calvin*, 208–10.

163. See "Introduction" in this chapter above.

164. *Selected Sermons from the Pastoral Epistles*, 2 Tim. 1:8–9, p. 39; *CO* 54:46.

165. *Selected Sermons from the Pastoral Epistles*, 2 Tim. 1:8–9, p. 41; *CO* 54:48.

166. *Selected Sermons from the Pastoral Epistles*, 2 Tim. 1:9–10, p. 50; *CO* 54:55.

167. *Selected Sermons from the Pastoral Epistles*, 2 Tim. 1:9–10, p. 49; *CO* 54:55.

168. *Selected Sermons from the Pastoral Epistles*, 2 Tim. 1:9–10, p. 55; *CO* 54:60.

169. *Selected Sermons from the Pastoral Epistles*, 2 Tim. 1:9–10, p. 57; *CO* 54:62.

170. *Selected Sermons from the Pastoral Epistles*, 2 Tim. 1:9–10, p. 50; *CO* 54:55.

171. *Selected Sermons from the Pastoral Epistles*, 2 Tim. 1:9–10, p. 54; *CO* 55:59.

172. McKee, *The Pastoral Ministry and Worship in Calvin's Geneva*, 916–17.

173. Kathy Childress, "Introduction," in *Sermons on Galatians* (Edinburgh: Banner of Truth, 1997), x.

174. Sunday afternoon, December 26, 1557 (McKee, *The Pastoral Ministry and Worship in Calvin's Geneva*, 216).

175. *Sermons on Galatians*, 2:15–16, pp. 183–84; *CO* 50:425–426.

176. *Sermons on Galatians*, 2:15–16, p. 178; *CO* 50:420.

177. Sunday morning, January 23, 1558 (McKee, *The Pastoral Ministry and Worship in Calvin's Geneva*, 217).

178. Once again, it is important to note that Calvin does not assume to know that everyone listening has placed faith in Christ.

179. *Sermons on Galatians*, 3:13–18, p. 287; *CO* 50:512. Cf. p. 284; *CO* 50:510.

180. *Sermons on Galatians*, 3:13–18, p. 294, *CO* 50:518.

181. *Sermons on Galatians*, 3:13–18, p. 288; *CO* 50:513.

182. *Sermons on Galatians*, 3:13–18, pp. 291–92; *CO* 50:516.

183. *Sermons on Galatians*, 3:13–18, p. 284; *CO* 50:509.

Chapter Six

Predestination and God's Love in Recent Calvin Scholarship

Although the volume of Calvin scholarship on predestination is more than could be comprehensively addressed here, in this chapter we shall provide a brief overview of significant recent scholarship addressing the question of Calvin's teaching on predestination and God's disposition toward humanity. We shall note the ways these scholars' assertions concur or conflict with our findings, and we shall also begin our explicit critical evaluation of Calvin's doctrine by acknowledging a few of the important strengths and weaknesses of Calvin's account throughout.

This secondary literature is organized according to relevance to the topic at hand, from more general to more specific.

CHARLES PARTEE

Charles Partee, in his brief exposition regarding Calvin's teaching on predestination, seeks to clarify Calvin's teaching by refuting three typical misunderstandings regarding predestination. He first asserts that predestination for Calvin is not about speculation but about exalting God's unmerited care for his chosen ones.[1] Second, Partee refutes the central dogma thesis regarding the place of Calvin's doctrine of the divine decrees in his broader theological project. In a more doubtful assertion, Partee contends that Calvin's theology is comprehensive and integrated while centering on the confession of Jesus Christ as Lord and union with Christ.[2] Third, Partee discusses eternal reprobation. Reprobation reminds us of God's grace in election; the identity of the reprobate is not able to be ascertained by people; and no believer is reprobate.[3] Partee primarily draws from the *Institutes* but sporadically utilizes other sources as well.

Although his assertions are not particularly novel, Partee's contribution to this conversation is his refutation of three commonly held misinterpretations of Calvin's doctrine of predestination. Although I do not agree with his claim to place union with Christ as a new central dogma for Calvin interpretation, the rest of his analysis aligns with our conclusions.

WILHELM NEUSER

In his essay on Calvin's doctrine of predestination, Wilhelm Neuser provides a critical and developmental overview of the doctrine and concludes by asserting that Calvin describes the doctrine of predestination very differently in a sermon compared with his dogmatic exposition. After an historical overview of the development of Calvin's doctrine of predestination, Neuser compares Calvin's *Congregatión* sermon on predestination from December 18, 1551 with Calvin's description of predestination in the 1559 *Institutes*.[4] In his analysis, Neuser concludes, "Calvin taught two doctrines of predestination that vary in their approach. In the sermon we have election by grace, and in the *Institutio* we find double predestination." The sermon limits its substantial teaching to election, mentioning the reprobate only to stir gratitude in the hearts of the elect. In contrast, in the *Institutes*, Calvin "presents opposing arguments and does not shy away from an investigation of the consequences."[5] In the essay, Neuser utilizes a broad spectrum of texts, including the 1536, 1539, and 1559 *Institutes*; the catechism of 1538; the occasional *Consensus Genevensis* of 1552; and Calvin's *Congregatión* of 1551.

Although Neuser's thesis based on one (albeit important) sermon is interesting, it requires modification in light of Calvin's long preaching ministry, as displayed in the broader cross-section of preaching analyzed in this study. As demonstrated in chapter 5, Calvin does focus on God's loving disposition toward humanity in his preaching, but he is still apt to preach regarding God's veiled reprobating will. More importantly, we found that Calvin's doctrine is actually quite consistent across his corpus, even though different occasions do engender different emphases. Neuser rightly acknowledges the asymmetrical nature of Calvin's teaching of God's twofold will, but the one *Congregatión* sermon does not provide enough data to justify his assertion that Calvin in practice teaches two distinct doctrines of predestination.

CHRISTIAN LINK

In his essay on election and predestination, Christian Link takes a similar approach to Neuser, highlighting two distinct but not conflicting approaches that Calvin takes when describing predestination. One approach starts with God and God's eternal purposes as manifest in the decrees and God's secret counsel, primarily explicated in the *Institutes* and *de aeterna Dei praedestinatione*. The other approach starts with elect humanity as observed in Calvin's *Congregatión* sermon in December 1551.[6] When addressing predestination from the perspective of the elect, Calvin focuses on the perseverance of grace and the assurance of God's loving care now and eternally.[7] One of Link's helpful contributions is his acknowledgment of Calvin's commitment to maintain the apparent contradiction that double predestination puts forth. As Link says, "It speaks well of Calvin that he resisted the temptation to find a solution or an understandable intellectual, rational means to diffuse this dilemma." Instead of contemplating the abstract, mysterious, eternal decrees, Calvin calls us to look upon Christ to contemplate our own election in him alone.[8] In his brief work, Link draws upon a relatively broad cross-section of Calvin's work, including commentaries, a sermon, and the *Institutes*.

Although Link utilizes the same sermon as Neuser, his observations correspond better to the data examined in our study, acknowledging Calvin's embrace of the mystery of God's twofold will and urging people to find assurance in Christ, not in the decrees or human understanding of God's secret will. Link's thesis about two different starting points in Calvin's explication of predestination is interesting, but I do not see in Calvin any justification for thinking that he has a varied understanding of the doctrine based on a different starting point. Instead, I think Link is helpfully identifying the way that Calvin's teaching takes different tones based on the occasion and the intended audience.

WILHELM NIESEL

In his chapter on "God's Eternal Election," Wilhelm Niesel expounds the doctrine of predestination in light of what Niesel asserts is the primary theme of Calvin's theology, the revelation of God through Jesus Christ who is God incarnate. Niesel thus frames his discussion around two main questions: (1) can predestination fit within a theology of revelation of the incarnate God? and (2) does Calvin teach that assurance of salvation comes through works as seen in the Practical Syllogism? To the first, Niesel answers that far from a starting point of metaphysical speculation, Calvin's teaching on predestination arises from his obedience to the witness of Scripture and the experience that not everyone equally receives the Word of God when it is preached.[9] Predestination is not Calvin's a priori central dogma but a revealed doctrine that teaches God's unmerited grace and the believer's assurance of salvation according to the righteous but mysterious will of God. To the second question, after examining the *Institutes* and two relevant sections of the commentaries, Niesel emphatically concludes that Calvin does not teach any sort of Practical Syllogism to ground one's assurance of faith in the works produced in one's life. Assurance comes not from looking at humans but from Jesus Christ alone as he has been revealed to us.[10] As noted, Niesel primarily utilizes the *Institutes* along with a few relevant commentaries.

Niesel's analysis has a weakness and a few strengths. A weakness is his choice of a central theme of Calvin's theology that he uses as a basis to analyze other doctrines. As we have asserted and observed, Calvin is primarily a theologian of the Bible. While it is true that Calvin sees the person and work of Jesus Christ as the center of the biblical witness and even his hermeneutical lens for proper biblical interpretation,[11] choosing any central dogma will inevitably undermine the interpreter's ability to let Calvin's specific teaching rightly speak for itself.

Niesel's account is strong in his eschewing of predestination as a central dogma for Calvin and in his rejection of the Practical Syllogism in Calvin's teaching of assurance. As we have seen, for Calvin, ultimate assurance comes by looking to the mirror of election, Jesus Christ. However, regarding the Practical Syllogism, a good Calvin interpreter will also recognize that in the same way that Calvin does not separate justification and sanctification as gifts of grace, he does not conceptualize a genuine faith in Christ that is not accompanied by the works of faith (*pietas* and subsequent *caritas*).[12] The works do not establish salvation or assurance in themselves, but they are logically inseparable from a genuine faith in Christ.

WILLEM VAN 'T SPIJKER

Willem van 't Spijker provides interesting insight in his brief analysis of predestination. Drawing primarily from the 1536, 1539, and 1559 *Institutes* (along with a much broader background knowledge of Calvin and his theology), van 't Spijker points out the pastoral nature of the doctrine and its relation to the church. First, he says that the doctrine of predestination is "situated in the context of pastoral care," particularly regarding the necessity of sanctification and the assurance of salvation based on a firm foundation outside of ourselves. The Holy Spirit brings about sanctification for those who already find assurance of their election in the mirror of God's free grace, Jesus Christ. Van 't Spijker also posits a connection between the doctrine of election by grace and ecclesiology. In the 1536 *Institutes*, Calvin placed election (positive only) in the section on the church; in Calvin's 1559 version his discussion of predestination is immediately followed by Book IV, "The

External Means or Aims by Which God Invites Us into the Society of Christ and Holds Us Therein,"[13] where he affirms that the "foundation of the church is [God's] secret election" and that all the elect are united in Christ.[14]

Van 't Spijker's analysis is a helpful complement to other secondary literature listed here. He affirms Calvin's connection between free justification and God's sanctification (mentioned above regarding the Practical Syllogism in Niesel's work) and helpfully elevates the important connection between ecclesiology and election. It is often forgotten that the longest section in the *Institutes* is Book 4. Highlighting the communal and ecclesial element of election brings forth the fact that for Calvin salvation in Christ (and thus election) is always both individual and communal. Van 't Spijker's assertion of the pastoral nature of Calvin's doctrine of predestination also aligns with our findings and helpfully reminds readers not to forget Calvin's primary identity as a pastor as they encounter his teaching or preaching. Calvin self-identifies and works as a pastor-scholar, in that order.

CORNELIS VAN DER KOOI

Cornelis van der Kooi, in his careful and extensive study of Calvin's and Barth's teachings on knowing God, provides an important perspective within Calvin scholarship regarding our question of God's disposition toward humanity in that he moves away from an emphasis on historical theology or theological retrieval and instead provides a critical and constructive analysis in dialogue with modern concerns. For example, after acknowledging the legitimate worry that Calvin's doctrine of predestination can make God appear to be a tyrant in modern eyes, van der Kooi criticizes Calvin's response to Jerome Bolsec, calling Calvin's approach "bitter, harsh and disproportionate" as one who saw Bolsec's different opinion "as a revolt against God."[15] He also explores the question of whether God has a completely arbitrary will, eventually concluding that Calvin "fences off reflection on God's being" and instead focuses on "the effect that God wants to produce" in people through his actions toward humanity,[16] namely the mirrors that God gives to provide real knowledge of himself, primarily faith that is aimed at Christ. "In these sources [God] provides trustworthy knowledge, in human language and metaphors, acting as a father who out of his own love gives Christ and adopts men as his children."[17] God can be known as he graciously makes himself known.

Utilizing sources from across Calvin's corpus in his work, he affirms the commonly held fact that the heart of the doctrine of election is God's unmerited grace. He proceeds by asserting Calvin's three main justifications for double predestination: Scripture teaches it, experience confirms it, and it provides a solid anchor of assurance for the salvation of believers.[18] However, going further than most, he also contends that Calvin went beyond the clear Scriptural witness by extending the doctrine of election to all of its rational conclusions in reprobation.[19]

Besides his sound and well-researched account of Calvin's teaching, van der Kooi's critical analysis is refreshing because he holds Calvin to the standards Calvin sets for others. Calvin asserts the importance of love for neighbor and enemy yet is known to lambast rhetorically his theological opponents, including name calling. Calvin also decries any speculation beyond Scripture, but van der Kooi points out that some of Calvin's rational conclusions regarding predestination extend beyond the clear scriptural witness and also have little usefulness for helping believers develop faith and piety, one of Calvin's tests of good theological reflection. Van der Kooi's helpful reflections provide a starting point for us that will continue in chapters 7 and 8 as we critically engage Calvin's teaching and seek to measure his teaching based on his own standards.

RICHARD MULLER

Richard Muller is arguably the most important voice in Calvin scholarship over the past fifty years. Although his work has been broad and diverse, one of his primary contributions has been to refute a number of myths about Calvin and the development of the Reformed tradition. Three of these myths are: (1) predestination as the center of Calvin's theology; (2) covenant as an alternative to predestinarian Calvinists; (3) Calvin as neo-orthodox and Christocentric against the predestinarian Calvinists (or Calvin focused on union with Christ against the Calvinists who want a strict *ordo salutis*).[20] In various works, a number of which have been utilized throughout this analysis, he has sought to refute these three myths and, in the process, has shed light upon "a variegated Reformed tradition that drew variously and eclectically on the patristic and medieval backgrounds, that does not rest on the theology of a single founder but was diverse from its beginnings, and that developed in dialogue and debate during the early modern era."[21] In other words, he has helped Calvin scholarship appreciate the general continuity of Calvin's theology with those prior to, contemporary with, and after him.

In his 1986 book, *Christ and the Decree*, Muller asserts his scholarly opposition to the "Calvin against the Calvinists" mentality by examining the theology of a number of Calvin's contemporary and successive Reformers, but before doing so, he provides a careful description of Calvin's doctrine of predestination. He asserts that Calvin's doctrine is linked to Christology and based on Scripture. Just as it is the eternal Son who brings about redemption as the incarnate Son, the decrees of predestination cannot be separated from the execution of the decree in time. As a result of this inexorable connection between Christology and predestination, Muller contends there should be no concern about a *Deus nudus absconditus* because there is no way to consider the decrees abstractly "apart from a sense of the Trinitarian economy and the effecting of salvation in the work of the Son of God incarnate."[22] For example, Christ's work of redemption is sufficient for all but is applied through his priestly office only to the elect, again highlighting the interdependence of Christology and predestination.[23] In other words, Muller does not perceive predestination as undermining one's ability to know and trust God because it is always the merciful God who has become incarnate in Christ who is the source and the executor of the decrees.

Muller also helpfully points out that Calvin's teaching on predestination is not novel but is in accord with a long line of Augustinian interpreters of Paul.[24] Like Dowey, Holmes, and Jacobs, he also asserts that although Calvin taught that both election and reprobation were fully determined by God, "in view of Calvin's emphasis on knowledge of God, reprobation does not appear the exact coordinate of election. It occurs apart from Christ and therefore apart from any mediated knowledge of God."[25]

Beyond Muller's important work establishing Calvin's general continuity with his contemporary theological tradition, Muller's affirmation of the link between Christology and predestination is insightful. Muller rightly asserts that recognizing Christ's role in executing the decree prevents the fear of a *Deus nudus absconditus* in predestination, but his further assertion that reprobation occurs apart from Christ partially undermines his first claim. Christ executes God's electing will, so that the God made known in election directly corresponds to the God revealed in Jesus Christ, just as we found in our study of Calvin's theology. However, reprobation's occurring "apart from any mediated knowledge of God" actually promotes the idea of a *Deus nudus absconditus*; the God of reprobation is an (at least somewhat) unknown God. Therefore, the link between Christology and predestination is completely assuring for believers, just as Calvin would assert, but it provides no comfort for persons who are concerned that they might be reprobate. As we shall see in chapters 7 and 8, this is a major problem for Calvin's doctrine, namely that what he considered completely assuring does not have the same consoling effect on all people.

DAVID GIBSON

Another important contribution to recent Calvin scholarship regarding God's disposition toward humanity is David Gibson's *Reading the Decree: Exegesis, Election, and Christology in Calvin and Barth*. Gibson draws from across Calvin's corpus but focuses primarily on the *Institutes* intentionally as Calvin's hermeneutical guide to reading Scripture (according to Calvin's words in his introductory letter to King Francis). In the book, Gibson compares Calvin's and Barth's approaches to understanding Scripture and subsequently predestination. Drawing upon terminology coined by Muller,[26] Gibson develops the argument that both Calvin and Barth are "Christocentric" theologians but in different ways. Calvin's *soteriological Christocentrism* means that Christ is at the center of God's work of redemption and salvation history. This understanding of salvation by the grace of Christ informs and shapes how Calvin reads all of Scripture and redemptive history in light of Christology. That contrasts with Barth's *principial Christocentrism* that privileges Jesus Christ as the ground and content of all theological doctrine.[27] In other words, according to Gibson, Calvin can speak of Christ *and* the decree, whereas Barth contends that Christ *is* the decree. This distinction between Calvin's soteriological Christocentrism and Barth's principial Christocentrism contributes to the consideration of Calvin's continuity or discontinuity with the teaching of contemporary and successive Reformers, many of whom exercised a similar soteriological Christocentrism to Calvin, but arguably none of whom practiced Barth's principal Christocentrism.[28]

Besides this valuable distinction, Gibson's key contribution to the discussion of Calvin's teaching on predestination is his emphasis on Christ's economic work as the mediator of election in time. For Calvin, Christ is the representative elect one, the perfect human upon whom God looks when he is electing.[29] Jesus Christ is therefore the object of election as God's beloved human but also the object of saving faith.[30] Gibson repeatedly emphasizes that for Calvin, contra Barth, Christ's mediatorial work does not provide substantial insight into the triune God's immanent life,[31] but focuses on his "temporal-economic" work in time as the object of saving faith throughout the history of the covenant.[32] However, Christ as mediator, subject, and object of election in time does reveal some of what God is like for us, enough for us not to be afraid of a *deus absconditus* because of the *deus manifestatus in carne*, Jesus Christ.[33]

One other important note from Gibson's study is his assertion that assurance of salvation in Christ for Calvin is inseparable from the witness of Scripture. The written Word of God reveals God's election, and believers appropriate that election by clinging to the Living Word (Jesus) by faith.[34]

Gibson's project, which could be seen as an elaboration on Muller's work in the area of Barth studies and Biblical exegesis, provides many helpful insights into Calvin's teaching on predestination and Calvin's focus on the economic work of Christ as the electing and elect one. Particularly his elaboration on the distinction between Calvin's and Barth's Christocentrism is an important contribution to Calvin studies because it provides a conceptual framework that affirms Calvin's version of Christ-centered theology without reading Calvin's works through the lens of Barth's style of Christ-centered dogmatics. In other words, in Calvin's theological method, "christology reaches out to and touches on other doctrines which nevertheless can be given coherent description in themselves without the language of christological description."[35] As we have seen, Gibson is also right to assert that Calvin guards against substantial knowledge of God's essence or immanent life. Calvin is not concerned about knowing God's essence but about knowing God's unchanging nature through his works. According to Calvin, believers can know what God is like *for* them with confidence and assurance.

A final important strength of Gibson's project is his affirmation of Scripture as central for Calvin's understanding of any doctrine, including election. However, Gibson is misguided in his assertion that Scripture is "truly the source of the revelation of election."[36] Instead, as foundational as Scripture is for understanding one's election, this assertion based only on a reading of the *Institutes* ignores Calvin's clear elevation of Christ as the ultimate source of assurance of salvation as the mirror of our election that we have observed across Calvin's corpus.

PAUL JACOBS

The most influential and comprehensive modern study of Calvin's doctrine of predestination is Paul Jacobs's study, *Prädestination Und Verantwortlichkeit Bei Calvin* (Predestination and Responsibility in Calvin), published in 1968, in which Jacobs demonstrates that instead of seeing double predestination as the central dogma of Calvin's theology, a proper reading of Calvin recognizes the integration of Christ throughout Calvin's project and the trinitarian, soteriological, and ecclesiological thrust of predestination. Unfortunately for the non-German-speaking world, Jacobs's work is still only available in German and thus inaccessible to many. Although a complete summary of Jacobs's findings is beyond the scope of this overview, we shall highlight a few of his most relevant assertions as they relate to our question of God's disposition toward humanity.

First, in accordance with the title (and in agreement with van 't Spijker), Jacobs primarily establishes the relationship between election and responsibility, asserting them as inseparably linked in the trinitarian act of election in which Christ provides for the elect both justification and sanctification, both revelation of God's love and the subsequent love for neighbor as empowered by the Spirit.[37] Jacobs describes Calvin's determinism as "willing necessity" in which the will of the human person is not disabled but brought to its creaturely flourishing through the miraculous work of Christ's moving God's will of sanctification through that person. In other words, instead of a tension between or need to synthesize artificially election and responsibility, they are unified in an analytic sense as the *one* integrative act of the *one* triune God.[38]

In regard to reprobation, Jacobs provides some of his most insightful observations, particularly regarding the asymmetry of election and reprobation and the asymmetry of Calvin's substantial teaching of the two poles of predestination. For example, Jacobs points out the way that reprobation, although typically mentioned alongside Calvin's teaching on election, has no integral place in Calvin's theological project. Jacobs says, "Whereas the teaching of election in language as in content has interwoven all of Calvin's teaching and it takes up itself a place in the *Institutio*, which could not be vacated [*geräumt*], without which the complete structure thereafter would suffer, indeed would become wreckage [*Wrack*], the teaching about reprobation remained almost completely isolated."[39] Reprobation is a doctrine that has no grounding or connection in Christ, a statement that is unthinkable regarding election. Jacobs further asserts that Calvin, stirred on by his battles against Pelagianism, extended his teaching on predestination from the rightful teaching of election by Christ's free grace with a *boundary-marking* element of reprobation to an actual *teaching* of reprobation. This, according to Jacobs, made sense in Calvin's historical battles but was not justified theologically. In other words, what should have been a boundary line in Calvin's theology is breached when Calvin puts forth a substantial "*teaching* of reprobation" (*Reprobations l e h r e*).[40]

Jacobs also asserts that Calvin's teaching on reprobation is polemic and isolated, as seen in the lack of teaching on reprobation in other loci in the *Institutes*. He sees Calvin only providing substantial teaching on reprobation in the systematic works of the *Institutes* and the polemic occasional writings (like his reply to Pighius). However, he contends that Calvin's teaching on reprobation is almost completely lacking in the commentaries and even more vacuous in his sermons.[41] A broader examination of sermons would be necessary to establish fully Jacobs's claim here. Jacobs assesses a large spectrum of sermons and commentaries, not least the commentaries on the Gospels and Calvin's sermons on Job, noting a number of texts that naturally relate to reprobation but did not lead Calvin to provide substantial teaching on reprobation.[42] However, Jacobs does not assess Calvin's so-called *Sermons on Election and Reprobation* from Gen. 25–27 that we examined in chapter 5. Three of the thirteen sermons do explicitly address reprobation, and it is clear that Calvin is not averse to mentioning reprobation in his sermons or his commentaries elsewhere. However, as we have seen, Calvin consistently speaks of election more commonly and with significantly more material teaching than reprobation, including in the Gen. 25–27 sermons. This is another striking example of the asymmetry of these doctrines and the way that reprobation is typically a boundary or shadow doctrine for Calvin relative to election.

Similarly, Jacobs further demonstrates the incongruity of election and reprobation in the fact that God is the direct *causa-fundamentum* of election and sanctification but is not the *causa-fundamentum* of reprobation. Instead, sin, which does not find its source in God, has a synthetic relationship to reprobation. In other words, although all people are stained by sin, not all people are reprobate in the end; we thus observe a relationship between human sin and reprobation, but it is not an analytic relationship in the way that Christ-Election-Responsibility are integrally connected.[43]

In short, Jacobs provides an in-depth and comprehensive look at Calvin's doctrine of predestination and its relation to human responsibility before God. Jacobs rightly recognizes the central importance of election in Calvin's teaching and the tangential significance of reprobation. To use our language, we can have fleshed out, material knowledge of election but only limited, skeletal knowledge of reprobation, and as a result, we can confidently know God's loving disposition and revealed will alongside limited knowledge of God's veiled reprobating will. We shall further explore Jacobs's assertion of Calvin's overstepping of boundaries in his substantial teaching of reprobation in chapter 8.

CONCLUSION

In the foregoing overview of some of the relevant scholarship regarding Calvin's doctrine of predestination, a few key themes have arisen as well as a few gaps in the scholarship. First, we have seen themes of predestination as a doctrine of grace and assurance, the asymmetry of election and reprobation, and the way that election alone occurs in and through Christ. Predestination as a doctrine of unmerited grace and assurance is not a novel concept, but it is worth noting that for all of these scholars, this is foundational to their depiction of predestination in Calvin's teaching. Many of these scholars also recognize and highlight the incongruence of election and reprobation; they are not two sides of the same coin. Their asymmetry is observed in a variety of ways, including the relative frequency of their being addressed across Calvin's corpus, their relative prevalence in sermons, what can be known about the doctrines, what can be known about who is elect or reprobate, and the ways that God is responsible for them. Finally, many of these authors point out the fact that election occurs as a trinitarian reality in and through Jesus Christ. Election is not a speculative idea but a reality of grace directly affected by the Father through the Son by the Spirit.

This overview also reveals a few gaps in the scholarship. First, no one has directly asked the question of God's disposition toward humanity. Our world today needs to know what can be said about God's attitude toward humanity in general. Second, there is a lack of analysis that engages carefully with sources from across Calvin's entire corpus and seeks to integrate the findings into a cohesive account. Although Jacobs's account sought to do so fifty years ago, he did not seem to have access to all the sermonic material, his account is still limited to German readers, and he was asking a different question than we are asking (perhaps the question of human responsibility was more germane in his time and context). Third, missing is an attempt to integrate the scholarly shift of the past thirty-five years that acknowledges Calvin's continuity with his theological forebears, contemporaries, and successors into a study of Calvin's theology that does not assume complete continuity or discontinuity with the tradition but lets Calvin speak for himself.

The present work is an attempt to fill those gaps, providing a theological retrieval of *Calvin's* specific understanding of God's disposition toward humans by engaging broad-ranging sources across his corpus, including significant analysis of his sermons. We now begin to examine critically Calvin's understanding of predestination and God's disposition toward humanity by comparing his doctrine with those of a few other important theologians in the Reformed tradition.

NOTES

1. Partee, *Theology of John Calvin*, 243, 251.
2. Partee, *Theology of John Calvin*, 247. In my view, any attempt at choosing a "central dogma" in Calvin is ill-advised because Calvin's primary aim is to interpret the whole of Scripture in a cohesive manner.
3. Partee, *Theology of John Calvin*, 249.
4. Neuser points out that the 1559 version includes all of the 1539 teaching on predestination, with extra embellishment and documentation. Calvin's core understanding of predestination changed very little from 1539 ("Predestination," in *The Calvin Handbook*, ed. H. J. Selderhuis [Grand Rapids: Eerdmans, 2009], 316).

5. Neuser, "Calvin Handbook," 322.
6. Link, "Election and Predestination," 112.
7. Link, "Election and Predestination," 118–20.
8. Link, "Election and Predestination," 121.
9. Niesel, *Theology of Calvin*, 168.
10. Niesel, *Theology of Calvin*, 180–81.
11. See below regarding David Gibson's thesis of Calvin's "christologically extensive hermeneutical approach."
12. Cf. McKee, *John Calvin on the Diaconate*. Cf. Mckee, *Calvin: Writings on Pastoral Piety*. Cf. my chapter, "Pietas and Caritas: John Calvin's Preaching on Love for Neighbor" in Karin Maag and Arnold Huijgen (eds), *Calvinus Frater in Domino: Papers of the Twelfth International Congress on Calvin Research* (Göttingen: Vandenhoeck & Ruprecht, 2020).
13. *Inst.* 4, p. 1011; *CO* 2:745.
14. *Inst.* 4.1.2, pp. 1013–14; *CO* 2:747.
15. van der Kooi, *As in a Mirror*, 162.
16. van der Kooi, *As in a Mirror*, 175–76.
17. van der Kooi, *As in a Mirror*, 185.
18. van der Kooi, *As in a Mirror*, 164–65.
19. van der Kooi, *As in a Mirror*, 419.
20. Muller, *Calvin and the Reformed Tradition*, 17–18.
21. Muller, *Calvin and the Reformed Tradition*, 10.
22. Muller, *Christ and the Decree*, 18.
23. Muller, *Christ and the Decree*, 34.
24. Muller, *Christ and the Decree*, 22. We shall engage with a few of those interpreters in chapter 7.
25. Muller, *Christ and the Decree*, 25.
26. Richard Muller, *After Calvin: Studies in the Development of a Theological Tradition* (Oxford: Oxford University Press, 2003), 97–98.
27. Gibson, *Reading the Decree*, 5–6. Gibson also differentiates between Calvin's "christologically extensive hermeneutical approach" from Barth's "christologically intensive hermeneutical approach." For Calvin, "christology reaches out to and touches on other doctrines which nevertheless can be given coherent description in themselves without the language of christological description." Whereas for Barth, "Christology draws everything else to itself so that all other doctrinal loci cannot be read in Scripture apart from explicit Christological reference" (*Reading the Decree*, 15).
28. See chapter 7 for examples in dialogue with Calvin.
One example of those who interpret Calvin in stark discontinuity from his contemporaries and successors is R. T. Kendall (*Calvin and English Calvinism*). Cf. Rolston, *John Calvin versus the Westminster Confession*. Cf. Armstrong, *Calvinism and the Amyraut Heresy*. Cf. Partee, *Theology of John Calvin*.
29. Gibson, *Reading the Decree*, 65.
30. Gibson, *Reading the Decree*, 58.
31. Gibson, *Reading the Decree*, 76, 88, 152.

32. Gibson, *Reading the Decree*, 177.
33. Gibson, *Reading the Decree*, 57, 83–84.
34. Gibson, *Reading the Decree*, 177.
35. Gibson, *Reading the Decree*, 15.
36. Gibson, *Reading the Decree*, 177. "If one hand is grasping Christ himself, the other hand grasps his words in the Word" (p. 177).
37. Jacobs, *Prädestination*, 122–30.
38. Jacobs, *Prädestination*, 132–39.
39. Jacobs, *Prädestination*, 145–46. Jacobs also points out the asymmetry of the fact that election is directly grounded in Christ whereas reprobation is not directly grounded in Satan.
40. Jacobs, *Prädestination*, 147.
41. Jacobs, *Prädestination*, 157.
42. Jacobs, *Prädestination*, 148–52.
43. Jacobs, *Prädestination*, 156. Jacobs identifies but does not attempt to solve Calvin's problematic overassociation of sin and reprobation in his systematic teaching on reprobation.

Chapter Seven

Calvin in Dialogue

Placing the Mystery

Having completed our study of Calvin's teaching on God's disposition toward humanity, tested our conclusions in Calvin's sermons, and examined key secondary literature, we now critically engage Calvin's perspective by placing his approach alongside the work of a few other theologians in the Reformed tradition. However, first we shall establish the framework for the dialogue, namely the presence of mystery in one's doctrine of predestination.

Matthew Levering, in his book on the biblical and historical development of the doctrine of predestination, comes to the conclusion that interpreters of Scripture must face the tension of two assertions: (1) "God's eternal and redemptive love for his rational creatures has no deficiency, limitation, or stinginess," and (2) "yet from eternity God's plan of election allows some of his rational creatures freely to remain in their sins."[1] Levering's criterion for a good doctrine of predestination is one that can maintain both of these biblically derived assertions without letting one overpower the other.

Levering approaches the question through biblical, historical, and theological research to examine how faithful exegetes of Scripture have addressed this question over the past two millennia. Although a closer look at Levering's thoughtful work is beyond the scope of this project, his conclusions provide a helpful framework for our critical engagement with Calvin's doctrine of predestination. Levering concludes that Catherine of Siena (1347–1380) and Francis de Sales (1567–1622) offer the two best models for a doctrine of predestination that rightly balances the two poles of his biblical definition because they both affirm the tension that exists in the co-held beliefs that God seeks the salvation of every creature, that salvation is a free gift from God, and that God allows some creatures permanently to reject his love.[2] They both hold this tension while acknowledging the mystery of it instead of seeking systematically to resolve it.[3] Levering concludes that this tension must be left unresolved, just as Paul did in Romans 11:33; instead of resolution, the tension should lead us to worship.[4]

What Levering asserts is the fact that a biblical doctrine of predestination will inevitably include an element of mystery. A sound doctrine of predestination rightly holds this inherent tension, thus embracing the breadth of the biblical witness and submitting to God in worship. In sum, any biblical account of the doctrine of predestination will include a locus of mystery somewhere. In this section, we shall explore various theologians whose accounts locate the mystery differently.

INTRODUCTION TO THE DIALOGUE

Calvin was not abnormal among Reformed theologians of his time in his articulation of God's gracious predestination to eternal life. Common to all of the key Reformers' teaching was the emphasis on the predestination of God apart from human merit and inseparable from the doctrine of justification by grace alone.[5] If humans do not merit salvation through works, they must be chosen by God via grace. However, the Reformers were not unanimous in their explication of predestination, including where it most logically fit in their broader theological system, the detail with which they articulated the doctrine of reprobation, their emphases, and more. As they sought to explicate Scripture as faithfully as possible in their specific contexts, they all faced the paradox of God's love for all humanity alongside the biblical and experiential evidence that God only elects to salvation a subset of that humanity. As a result, they all included a locus of mystery in their accounts of predestination, some more explicitly than others.

This study obviously cannot provide a similar depth of analysis for the others that we have provided for Calvin, but here we briefly examine Martin Luther's, Huldrych Zwingli's, Heinrich Bullinger's, Jacobus Arminius's, and Karl Barth's teachings regarding predestination and God's disposition toward humanity, particularly noting the locus of mystery and respective strengths and weaknesses in each of their accounts. Luther and Zwingli provide examples of the generation of Reformers that preceded Calvin. Bullinger is a contemporary of Calvin, and Arminius is a seventeenth-century theologian whose teaching raised the ire of many of Calvin's Reformation successors. Barth is arguably the most influential Reformed theologian of the twentieth century whose (widely embraced) development of the Reformed doctrine of predestination provides a valuable comparison with Calvin's doctrine.

One commonality among these faithful theologians and exegetes[6] is an elevation of the person and work of Jesus Christ as the foundation for describing God's disposition toward humanity. They are convinced that God has graciously made himself known in the person and work of Christ. Placing Calvin in context of others illuminates the necessity of making hermeneutical, exegetical, theological, and logical priority decisions that result in specifically assigning the locus of mystery in the doctrine of predestination and influence God's corresponding disposition.

We begin with a brief recapitulation of Calvin's doctrine and an assessment of his locus of mystery.

CALVIN: MYSTERY IN GOD'S SECRET COUNSEL

> The cause of eternal reprobation is so hidden [*abscondita*] from us, that we can do nothing else but wonder at the incomprehensible counsel [*consilium*] of God.[7]

The mystery in Calvin's teaching on predestination lies in God's secret counsel to elect some to salvation and to pass over others who remain in their state of alienation from God. Calvin is utterly confident of God's nature that has been made known in God's works as Creator and Ruler of creation, in Scripture, and most clearly in Jesus Christ. This loving, righteous, and judging God directly and openly brings about unmerited election by grace according to his power, goodness, and mercy. For reasons beyond the limits of human cognition, God chooses to leave some people in their sin and deserved condemnation. For Calvin, this act of passing over the reprobate does not change his view of God. Instead, he assumes that the God who reprobates is acting according to his character and nature that has been clearly revealed. It is for this reason that, contra Luther as we shall see next, the mystery for Calvin lies not in God but in God's secret counsel. Calvin is confident of who God is.

When speaking of this mystery, Calvin appeals to a spectrum of related phrases to emphasize that the explanation is only available to God—for example, God's secret counsel (*arcanum consilium*) or God's secret good pleasure (*arcanum beneplacitum*). Thus, commenting on Paul's exclamation in Romans 11:33–36 ("O the depth of the riches and wisdom and knowledge of God! How unsearchable are his judgments."), Calvin says, "Whenever then we enter on a discourse respecting the eternal counsels [*consiliis*] of God, let a bridle be always set on our thoughts and tongue, so that after having spoken soberly and within the limits of God's word, our reasoning may at last end in admiration [*stuporem*]."[8] Similarly, he often warns people not to seek reasons for reprobation beyond God's hidden will lest they find themselves lost in a labyrinth. In short, Calvin places the mystery in his doctrine of predestination in God's secret counsel from which God determines from eternity to pass over the reprobate and to leave them in their deserved state of condemnation.

The major weakness of Calvin's approach has been manifest in the reception history and development of Calvin's theology. Clearly, although Calvin did not see it as a serious concern, his placement of the mystery in God's secret counsel has commonly led to an undermining of assurance of salvation for believers and a depiction of God as a tyrant. Barth's critique describes this weakness well, "The electing God of Calvin is a *Deus nudus absconditus*. It is not the *Deus revelatus* who is as such the *Deus absconditus*, the eternal God."[9] By placing the mystery of such a heinous act as creating people for eternal damnation in God's secret counsel, Calvin unintentionally weakened the ability of some to know and trust the God of Jesus Christ about whom Calvin so passionately preached and taught.

We now look to Martin Luther and find a similar approach to Calvin, albeit with a slightly different locus of mystery.

LUTHER: MYSTERY IN GOD

German Reformer Martin Luther (1483–1546) placed the mystery in his doctrine of predestination directly in God. We begin by examining Martin Luther's teaching on God's disposition toward humanity in his doctrine of predestination before commenting on the locus of mystery in his project in relation to Calvin's approach.

In his book *Luther on Predestination: The Antinomy and the Unity between Love and Wrath in Luther's Concept of God*, Fredrik Brosché broadly explores Luther's teaching on predestination, asking a question very similar to ours. I shall summarize Brosché's exposition of Luther's teaching before comparing Luther's and Calvin's approaches. In the end we find that Luther and Calvin had dramatically similar approaches to understanding and teaching about God's disposition toward humanity in predestination but a slightly different locus of mystery.

In regards to predestination, Luther, like Calvin, ascribes election fully to God's free grace in rescuing the elect from their just condemnation. Contrary to the way that Lutheran orthodoxy later softened the doctrine to single predestination, Luther himself takes the logic of election to its conclusion and asserts that reprobation (like election) is also a work of the omnipotent God. At the same time, Luther recognizes the apparent contradiction in the divine being that double predestination poses. Contrary to some claims, Brosché demonstrates that the doctrine of double predestination is an integral part of Luther's doctrine of God.[10]

However, unlike Calvin, Luther does not attempt to make a rational synthesis out of the conundrum that is double predestination, instead choosing to acknowledge the paradox in his concept of God.[11] Thus as Brosché summarizes, Luther teaches that "God does good and God does that which appears to reason to be evil, and which results in reprobation."[12] Some of God's will is beyond human inquiry. In Luther's words, we know "that (*quod*) there is a certain inscrutable will in God, and as to what, why, and how far (*vero, cur et quatenus*) it wills, that is something we have no right whatever to inquire into, hanker after, care about, or meddle with, but only to fear and adore."[13] This inscrutable will of God is the will of Luther's *Deus absconditus* and something that is true of God but does not seem to us to correspond with the God who has been revealed.[14]

As a part of his theological project, Luther differentiates between two types of knowledge, *notitia* as general knowledge and *usus* as personal knowledge.[15] For Luther, believers can have *notitia* (general) knowledge that God causes all things, as linked with the *Deus absconditus*, but they are not able to have *usus* (personal) knowledge of this truth in a manner that directly attributes all occurrences to the revealed God.[16] Applying these principles to predestination, God unconditionally elects to salvation and reprobates. We cannot understand by reasoning how or why the *Deus absconditus* elects and rejects. Humans can understand the general idea (*notitia*) of predestination but they are not to speculate about it on the level of personal knowledge (*usus*).[17] To describe it further, at the conceptual or *notitia* level, God's predestination is the cause of justification and perseverance because there is no human meriting of God's grace. However, at the personal or *usus* level, justification by faith takes priority over predestination.[18]

Luther is convinced that "the God who is wholly good and just cannot diverge from goodness and justice in his actions."[19] Thus, certainty of salvation comes for Luther not from contemplating one's election but by looking with eyes of faith on the love of God revealed in the suffering Christ.[20] This personal certainty of God's love thus enables believers to obey and preach the revealed will of God and find that predestination is "spontaneously" realized.[21] Believers see God's goodness and love in such a way that no rational objections (at the *notitia* level) can undermine one's belief in them. Brosché concludes that for Luther, God's love revealed at a personal level in the justifying person and work of Jesus Christ gives believers grounds to assert confidently and proclaim that "God in all His acts is love," even in the midst of the knowledge of reprobation.[22]

Brosché's analysis of Luther's depiction of God's love and wrath in his doctrine of predestination is strikingly similar to the conclusions we reached in our analysis of Calvin's teaching. Although he uses different language, the core concepts are nearly identical: multiple levels of causality that affirm God as the cause of all things while affirming human sin and evil as the proximate causes of the fall and reprobation; bare, skeletal knowledge of reprobation but no access to God's secret reasons for reprobation; God's revealing of his nature and disposition toward humanity in Jesus Christ so clearly that God's goodness is deemed unquestionable, even in light of actions that appear unjust; and finally, God confidently known and proclaimed as the loving God revealed in Jesus Christ.

For Luther, the locus of mystery in his doctrine of predestination is in God, the *Deus absconditus* who causes reprobation who is also the the *Deus revelatus* made known in Jesus and in God's gracious electing acts.

Although Calvin uses distinct terminology, and thus is likely not drawing directly upon Luther's teaching, both Calvin and Luther build their doctrine of God's disposition toward humanity in similar ways, namely letting God's self-revelation in Jesus Christ provide the content and grounds of God's character and disposition toward humanity. Both of them acknowledge the mystery of predestination in God's secret counsel, although Luther more directly acknowledges the ways that God's mysterious reprobating actions seem to come from a different God than the God of election. Like Calvin's placement of the mystery in God's secret counsel, Luther did not attempt to avoid the teaching of a *Deus absconditus* that Barth (and many others) perceived as deeply problematic; I believe that both Calvin and Luther were utterly confident of the *Deus revelatus* in Jesus Christ. While Calvin's tradition has generally maintained his doctrine through the ages, Luther's was quickly modified toward single predestination by Philip Melanchthon and codified in the 1577 *Formula of Concord* (Article 11).

Though Luther and Calvin may have disagreed on some other important doctrines of the Reformation, on this question the two great Reformers were essentially of one accord.

ZWINGLI: MYSTERY IN GOD'S TOTAL PROVIDENCE

Swiss Reformer Huldrych (Ulrich) Zwingli (1485–1531) places the mystery of predestination in his understanding of God's direct and complete providential control over all occurrences. We begin by examining Zwingli's teaching on God's disposition toward humanity in his doctrine of predestination before commenting on the locus of mystery in his project in relation to Calvin's teaching.

Along with the Reformation emphasis on Christ's unmerited atoning work, a central focus of Zwingli's theology is the doctrine of providence. His teaching on predestination, which he developed later,[23] flows from his understanding of providence.[24] As Zwingli says, "Providence is, so to speak, the mother of predestination."[25] Along these lines, Zwingli's doctrine of predestination is primarily concerned with attributing the whole of human salvation to God. As William Stephens puts it, "The fundamental function of the doctrine of election is to deny human merit or free will. It is therefore primarily an affirmation of the sovereignty of God and of our total dependence on him that are for Zwingli at the heart of the Christian faith."[26]

Zwingli defines election as, "the free disposition of God's will concerning those who are to be saved."[27] God's election is the first cause of salvation by faith. Although Zwingli does assert God's sovereign rule over all things, including reprobation, he typically restricts predestination positively to election[28] that flows from God's goodness and wisdom.[29] Children of Christian parents are known to be elect and are thus cleansed from original sin. As a result, if they die at a young age, they are mercifully spared the evil and stain of sin.[30] As children come of age, and for adults, faith is the fruit of one's election, and that faith expresses itself in love as a sign of one's election.[31] Zwingli relates sanctification to God's providence, asserting that good works flow from faith because it is God's sovereign will to use believers as God's "instrument and vessel through which God works" by grace.[32] Also because God's providence is the primary cause of salvation, Zwingli denies the efficacy of sacraments for salvation. God's providential election is what leads to salvation, not anything people do. Although he does maintain that salvation is always through Christ, he opens up the possibility of salvation chronologically before one has faith and avails the possibility that some outside of the Christian faith (e.g., Socrates and Seneca) could be saved by election.[33]

Zwingli's approach is particularly interesting because, as Paul Helm puts it, instead of starting with Scripture as his primary source for his doctrine of providence, Zwingli

> exemplifies the case of an *a priori* theologian who attempts to deduce the Christian metaphysic about the nature of God and the creation, the law, the nature of sin and so on, from a doctrine of God as the Supreme Being that he has gained not by induction from Scripture but from an philosophical conglomerate extracted from Plato, Pythagoras, and others.[34]

One of the key results of this approach is Zwingli's eschewal of secondary causes. God is the direct cause of all that comes to pass.[35] Thus, contra Calvin and his nuances of causality, God is the primary cause of sin in the Garden of Eden and the cause of the sinful acts of all humans. This type of teaching caused Bullinger to accuse him (along with Calvin) of making God the author of sin.[36] According to Zwingli, since God is not under the law, acts of his that we would call sinful are not sin for him.[37] Thus, for the elect God brings about good from what they would perceive as good *and* evil, while leaving the nonelect to the consequences of their evil choices.[38]

In summary, Zwingli's doctrine of predestination flows from his deep commitment to the doctrine of God's direct sovereignty over all. Zwingli also tends to focus on election instead of reprobation, although God is the cause of both. Finally, like all the key Reformers, Zwingli asserts predestination in conjunction with the affirmation that the whole of human salvation depends on God's unmerited grace.

Although there is material continuity regarding Calvin's and Zwingli's commitments to God's providence and to God's unmerited grace displayed in predestination, there are three major distinctions between Calvin's and Zwingli's understandings that we shall note here. First, by the 1559 version of the *Institutes*, Calvin locates predestination primarily in relation to soteriology and Christology (and ecclesiology) instead of providence, where it was placed in Calvin's 1539 *Institutes*. This subtle distinction points to a second key divergence between Calvin and Zwingli regarding predestination and providence. For example, in eschewing secondary causes, Zwingli makes God directly and primarily responsible for evil acts and the fall in ways that Calvin does not. As we have seen, Calvin is always careful to distinguish the levels of causality in regard to the fall and reprobation, identifying the human proximate causes in sinful choices while still affirming his Augustinian commitment to God's ultimate causality of all that comes to pass in the universe. For Calvin, this upheld the logic of the biblical doctrine of God's sovereign rule without turning God into a tyrant or the possessor of an arbitrary *potentia absoluta*. Zwingli seems not as concerned with letting God be a law unto himself. A third distinction is that, even though Calvin was willing to recognize the wisdom of nonbiblical philosophers (particularly when discussing the knowledge of God available outside of special revelation),[39] Calvin's doctrine of predestination (and providence) emerge directly (and nearly exclusively) from Scripture and the person and work of Christ.

As is now clearly evident, Zwingli's locus of mystery in predestination falls within God's direct causation of everything that comes to pass. Although Zwingli asserts the goodness of God as the source of predestination, his placement of the mystery in God's providence is quite problematic pastorally. Calvin and Luther place their loci in their doctrine of God, but in a more pastorally sensitive and biblically faithful manner. Whereas Calvin and Luther both seek to find ways to distance the God revealed in Jesus Christ from the direct causing of reprobation and to protect God from being perceived as a tyrant, Zwingli does not take such measures. Instead, Zwingli's placement of the mystery leads to an account of predestination that seems to indicate two disparate (and nearly symmetrical) dispositions toward humanity in God, one to elect and the other to reprobate.

However, even though Calvin and Luther sought ways to uphold God's character revealed in Christ while affirming God's providential rule over all things, clearly (as noted above), not everyone who heard their teaching was able to do the same. In short, Calvin's, Luther's, and Zwingli's approaches to placing the mystery of predestination in the doctrine of God all opened up the possibility of undermining trust in the God revealed in Jesus Christ.

Although a more in-depth engagement with Zwingli's teaching (particularly his soteriology) would provide more clarity, it is apparent that Calvin and Zwingli had significant disparities in their approaches to predestination and God's subsequent disposition toward humanity. Zwingli's description of his sovereign, powerful, wise God who chooses some to elect and others to reprobate was not the same as Calvin's loving, righteous, judging God made known in Jesus who expressed his twofold asymmetrical will for humanity in predestination.

Perhaps some of these concerns were in Calvin's mind when he distanced himself from Zwingli in Calvin's 1552 reply to Bullinger's letter regarding the Bolsec controversy, "Zwingli's book, confidentially, is crammed with such knotty paradoxes, as to be very different, indeed, in point of moderation, from what I hold."[40] It also may be that Zwingli's placing the mystery of predestination squarely within his doctrine of providence influenced the thinking of his successor in Zurich, Heinrich Bullinger, to whom we now turn.

BULLINGER: MYSTERY IN THOSE OUTSIDE OF CHRIST

Heinrich Bullinger (1504–1575) was the Reformation successor to Huldrych Zwingli in Zurich. Although sometimes overlooked, he was a significant theologian of the Reformation, and his work was crucial to the unity and development of the Reformed church, particularly through the First and Second Helvetic Confessions that he authored.[41] He was a contemporary of Calvin's, and he directly corresponded with Calvin regarding predestination and the Bolsec controversy in the early 1550s.

In Bullinger's account of predestination, he places the locus of mystery in those who are outside of Christ. As we shall see, Bullinger seeks to avoid teaching about reprobation, but when he does speak of it, the responsibility for reprobation falls on those who are outside of Christ because of unbelief, with a slight nod to God's sovereign participation in that reality.

In Cornelis Venema's book *Heinrich Bullinger and the Doctrine of Predestination*, Venema ably describes Bullinger's doctrine of predestination from his *Oratio* in 1536 through the *Decades* of 1549–1551 and correspondence in 1551–1553 until he codified his teaching in the Second Helvetic Confession completed in 1566. In his analysis, Venema finds no substantial shift in Bullinger's teaching on predestination through his life. We shall here summarize Bullinger's doctrine of predestination and his key emphases before comparing his approach with Calvin's and revisiting his locus of mystery.

First, Bullinger defines predestination similarly to Calvin but qualifies the definition and provides unique emphases. In the *Decades*, Bullinger defines predestination as "the eternal decree of God, whereby he has ordained either to save or destroy men; a most certain end of life and death being appointed unto them. Whereupon also it is elsewhere called a foreappointment."[42] Although this rare definition is similar to Calvin's, Luther's, and Zwingli's descriptions of predestination, Venema points out that his definition is still "quite moderately stated by contrast."[43] For Bullinger, contra Zwingli, predestination is most closely related with the doctrines of Christ and salvation in Christ, not providence.[44] Similarly, election and reprobation find their center "in Christ" in the sense that the end of predestination to life is communion with Christ and predestination to death results in not trusting Christ and therefore being outside of Christ.[45] Like Calvin, Bullinger teaches that Christ is the mirror of our election, and that assurance of salvation comes through faith in the gospel. In his mature teaching in the Second Helvetic Confession, what Venema calls the best summary of Bullinger's theology,[46] Bullinger directly identifies predestination and election; there is no mention of God's act of reprobation.[47] Those who are rejected (*reprobi*) are simply those who are outside of Christ because of their unbelief. For Bullinger, faith is God's gift and the sign of election, but unbelief, not God, is the occasion for reprobation.[48]

Overall, Bullinger emphasizes God's goodwill toward all people in his teaching and opposes any doctrine that might implicate God in evildoing. Therefore, as Venema says, "Bullinger eschews any investigation of the connection between the will of God and the non-salvation of the reprobate."[49] For example, in contrast to most theologians of his time, he does not elaborate his doctrine of reprobation in terms of God's efficient and deficient willing or God's decision to pass over the reprobate. He never goes beyond his skeletal, formal definition that some people, because of unbelief, end up outside of Christ.[50] Thus, unlike Calvin, Luther, and Zwingli, Bullinger avoids placing the mystery of predestination in God alone but places it vaguely in those who end up "outside of Christ."[51]

Venema describes Bullinger's teaching on predestination as "homiletical Augustinianism." Bullinger teaches the Augustinian doctrine of sovereign and gracious predestination but does so "within the framework of a keen awareness of its pastoral and homiletical implications." He places predestination in relation to God's saving purposes in Christ, particularly God's gracious answer to the complete need of sinners unable to turn to God on their own. Denying synergism or foreknowledge, Bullinger teaches that God is the one who graciously enables faith through the preaching of the gospel.[52] Venema describes Bullinger's homiletical emphasis on God's grace and kindness toward sinners revealed in Christ, "Fearful that the grace of God in Christ might be overshadowed by the specter of an implacable decree of reprobation, Bullinger accents throughout his presentations of the doctrine of predestination the theme of God's goodwill in Christ toward sinners, as this is announced in the preaching of the gospel."[53] In this way, he avoids the accusations of God's tyranny that Calvin's teaching occasionally generated.

Bullinger's approach has many similarities to and a few divergences from what we have observed in Calvin's teaching. Similar is the centrality of Christ, the completely gracious nature of election, election occurring in Christ, assurance by looking with faith to Christ as the mirror of election, the call to proclaim the gospel to all people in hope for the salvation of all, and a clear asymmetry between God's electing will and reprobating will. There are differences as well. Regarding providence, Bullinger is slightly less concerned to stress God's causality of all. Instead, again taking a pastorally sensitive approach, he focuses on God's governance of the world as a comfort for believers and includes a doctrine of God's permissive will that allows for occurrences that God allowed but abhorred.[54] Second, for Bullinger, some of Calvin's logical conclusions regarding predestination result in a distortion of the gospel and an undermining of the trustworthiness of God. Accordingly, Bullinger intentionally seeks to avoid teaching about reprobation. As such, in his correspondence with Calvin, Bullinger repeatedly asserts that any teaching on predestination must not assign sin to God or imply that God blinds people through the preaching of the gospel.[55] Similarly, Bullinger strictly opposes locating the mystery of predestination in his doctrine of God and thus putting a stumbling block in the way of those who might hear the gospel and respond in faith.

These different foci led to divergent emphases in their teaching of predestination, even though Calvin and Bullinger largely agreed on the content of the doctrine, as evinced by their correspondence and their mutually ratified *Consensus Tigurinus*.[56] Based on his responses to Bullinger (and others who accused him of making God a tyrant), Calvin clearly did not perceive in his teaching anything that would ascribe sin to God or make God into an unpredictable tyrant. Based on our study, I believe that Calvin truly felt that he was already perspicuously proclaiming and teaching about the merciful, judging, and righteous God revealed in Jesus Christ whose disposition toward humanity is love. At the same time, in light of nearly five hundred years of reception history, it seems Calvin might have been wise to have listened more closely to Bullinger's concerns and thus recognize that some people would not be able to apprehend in Calvin's doctrine of predestination the loving God so evident to him.

In Bullinger's account of predestination, he seeks to minimize focus on the tension by de-emphasizing God's role in reprobation. When forced to place the mystery, he locates it primarily in those who are outside of Christ, leaving unexplained how or why they are there. Instead, he quietly sets that mystery aside and loudly invites all to know and trust the good and loving God revealed in Jesus Christ.

ARMINIUS: MYSTERY IN HUMAN REJECTION OF GOD'S GRACE

Jacobus (Harmenzoon) Arminius (1559–1609) was a Dutch Reformed pastor who studied under J. J. Grynaeus and Theodore Beza and read widely in the patristic, humanist, Reformed, and scholastic traditions. He sought unity in the church and boldly advocated for church reform in his day, both against abuses in the Roman Catholic Church and against what he perceived as theological missteps in the Reformed churches.[57] Although Arminius is sometimes characterized as a theologian of "free will" or "anti-predestinarianism," William den Boer has made a compelling case that the driving concern in Arminius's theology is the justice of God. In sum, "At every level Arminius's theology shows itself to be centered on God's justice and goodness, and on the full one-sided responsibility of humans for sin and evil."[58] After a brief overview of Arminius's relevant teaching, we shall see that the mystery of predestination for Arminius lies in a quite different place than it does for our previous subjects, namely in the question of *why* any human being would reject God's grace that has been extended to him or her.

Drawing largely on den Boer's analysis, we examine here Arminius's theological context, his account of God's justice and God's corresponding twofold love, and his specific doctrine of predestination before making a few observations regarding his relation to Calvin's theology and Arminius's locus of mystery in predestination.

First, Arminius was reacting to specific doctrines that were commonly accepted in the Reformed tradition of his time. Specifically, Calvin's theology provided the theological context in which Arminius developed his ideas. For Calvin, as we have seen, because of God's innate righteousness and the fact that human creatures cannot fully know or understand all of God's ways, people cannot measure or evaluate God's justice; they must accept it by faith. This opens up the possibility of the accusation that God is the author of sin and evil, an important debate in the sixteenth century.[59] Calvin appealed to limited human understanding and some logical distinctions to answer this question, but the subsequent early Orthodox Reformers shifted more toward various logical distinctions in their apologies, including adopting a version of Vermigli's distinctions regarding the freedom of the will that allowed sin to be both voluntary and necessary.[60] In these theological commitments, Arminius found great offense because they seemed to make God the author of sin. While still affirming God's providence over all that Scripture attributes to God, he thus rejected the unknowability of God's justice and the scholastic distinctions that did not have room for "real" free choice.[61]

Second, in this theological context, God's justice, as expressed in his doctrine of God's twofold love, became the foundation of Arminius's theology.[62] For Arminius, God's justice is "to render to each his or her due,"[63] which includes God's love for righteousness and hatred of sin.[64] God does not possess justice, but "God is justice"; thus God can only act according to justice. As Arminius says, "God cannot prescribe what is unjust, because he is justice, wisdom, and omnipotence itself."[65] This justice of God presupposes the freedom of God's subjects so that God rightly responds to what each deserves. This definition of justice is notably different from Calvin's in the fact that it has no incomprehensible or hidden elements; humans can recognize God's justice directly in his actions.[66]

Arminius's doctrine of God's twofold love follows this definition of justice and was for him the foundation of all right religion. God's twofold love is: (1) his love for justice and (2) his love for humans. The first takes precedence over the second: God cannot love humans who are not just.[67] Therefore, God cannot love people unless they are converted from their sin and approach God by sharing in the righteousness of Christ through Christ's blood shed on their behalf.[68] God opens up human access to his love through faith in Christ and repentance.

According to Arminius, the doctrine of double predestination violates the order of God's twofold love because in it God loves people before they are just and hates some without regard to their choices, thus not following God's justice in rendering either the elect or the reprobate their due.[69] Reprobation further violates God's twofold love because it does not allow the work of Christ, which is sufficient to fulfill God's justice for all, to be applied to any who would repent. Again, people are not given the opportunity to receive their due.[70] Arminius is also very concerned about the *carelessness* (antinomianism) that results from people knowing that they are elect regardless of their actions and about the *despair* that comes from knowing that no matter what certain people do, God will not show mercy to them (as reprobate ones).[71] For him, once God's twofold love is rightly understood, both carelessness and despair will be alleviated.[72]

In light of God's justice and twofold love, Arminius created his own account of predestination ("the gospel") in a four-decree structure. First, God decrees that Christ should be Mediator, Savior, Redeemer, Priest, and King and thus obtain salvation and communicate righteousness to humanity by his death. Second, God decrees to receive in Christ all who repent and believe and to condemn all those who do not. Third, God decrees to "administer *in a sufficient and efficacious manner* the *means* which were necessary for repentance and faith," according to God's wisdom (in his mercy and severity) and executed according to God's justice. Fourth, God decrees to save some whom he knew through his foreknowledge would believe (via prevenient grace) and persevere in belief (by grace). God likewise decrees to damnation those whom God knew would not believe and persevere.[73]

This account of predestination includes a universal call to salvation for all,[74] a rejection of unconditional predestination (and thus an affirmation of "real" freedom of human choice),[75] and a rejection of Pelagianism. Arminius seeks to protect the doctrine of God's unmerited grace and avoids synergism in salvation through his doctrine of middle knowledge that appropriates salvation for those whom God foreknows will repent, believe, and persevere.[76]

With this overview in place, we can now see where the mystery lies in Arminius's account, namely in the human refusal of God's freely given grace. According to his justice, God has provided all people with everything necessary for salvation, including the power to repent and persevere by grace. It is inexplicable that any human being created for communion with God, and for whose sins Christ died on the cross, would reject God's grace. Yet, somehow it happens, and God therefore does not enable repentance in those whom he foreknew would reject his grace, leaving them in their deserved state of condemnation. Humans mysteriously reject God's grace.

As already noted, Arminius's position contrasts significantly with Calvin's, particularly in regard to God's unconditional election by grace and God's sovereign role in the appropriation of salvation. Although Arminius thought he was avoiding synergism, I believe that Calvin would assert that Arminius's logic breaks down in his assumptions about the human response to God. What is it that allows anyone to respond to God's grace with faith? For Calvin, according to Arminius's account, because of the utter fallenness of every human, no one would be elect! God would foreknow that no one would be accounted worthy of God's enabling grace. Another significant difference is their teaching on human ability to know and assess God's justice. In addition, their divergence on the understanding of God's sovereignty over all that comes to pass undergirds many of the visible differences that occur in their theological conclusions.

There are also a few key similarities in Arminius's and Calvin's approaches. First, both are deeply convinced of and committed to God's justice. Although Calvin does not allow the Creator God's justice to be judged by limited humans, he is adamant that God is not a possessor of an arbitrary *potentia absoluta*; God's character and nature have been made known! Second, both believe in the sufficiency of Christ's death for the redemption of all who would respond in faith. Third, they both agree that God's enabling grace is necessary for people to repent (even though this is manifest in a different manner for each).

Calvin and Arminius differ in regard to their doctrines of God's providential rule, human agency in salvation, and human knowledge of God, but they are quite similar in their foundational convictions about God's character and the person and work of Christ.

In summary, we see in Arminius's description a reaction to expositions of predestination that place the mystery of predestination in God and thus expose God to the accusation of causing sin or evil and also reduce human agency and responsibility. Via his commitment to God's twofold love of justice first and humanity second, Arminius provides a doctrine of predestination that protects God's justice while providing humans with "real" freedom of choice. In so doing, he relocates the mystery in the inexplicable fact that some people choose to reject God's grace and receive condemnation. This is the mystery of Arminius's position.

We now turn to consider another Swiss Reformed theologian, this time from the twentieth century.

BARTH: MYSTERY IN HUMAN REJECTION OF THE REALITY OF REDEMPTION

In his book *Deviant Calvinism*, which seeks to broaden the boundaries of what should be considered "Reformed theology," Oliver Crisp includes a chapter entitled "Barthian Universalism?." There Crisp points out that although Karl Barth (1886–1968) explicitly denies teaching universalism,[77] there has been much disagreement among Barth scholars regarding Barth's actual stance on the extent of salvation.[78] In light of the confusion, Crisp applies the tools of analytic theology to "the letter" of Barth's teaching on election in *Church Dogmatics* II/2 (and elsewhere) and concludes that Barth's teaching is either inconsistent or that he teaches a species of universalism.[79] However, contrary to his previous analyses,[80] Crisp does not cease his explorations of Barth's doctrine there. Instead, he proceeds to provide an account of what he describes as "the spirit" of Barth's teaching on election, subsequently drawing a different conclusion.[81] Crisp makes three key observations: (1) All humanity is derivatively elect in the Father's election of the Son; (2) because of this election in Christ, "all humans are born elect, but *remaining in this state is conditional upon each human's not finally opting to reject Christ*;" and (3) the church's mission of evangelism is to awaken people to their status as elect in Christ.[82] In short, there is eschatological *hope* for the salvation of all people but no declaration of universal salvation. Crisp acknowledges that this "spirit-not-letter" account makes better sense of Barth's broader teaching and direct denials of universalism, but Crisp asserts that this account still necessitates ignoring a few of Barth's claims in *CD* II/2 that directly identify all of humanity as unconditionally elect in Christ.[83]

Besides the general benefits of drawing upon Crisp's clear analysis of Barth's teaching on election, we highlight Crisp's work here because it directly illustrates where Barth places the mystery in his account of predestination, namely how it could be that humans who have been objectively and decisively redeemed in Christ could not be eternally saved.

Although one could write at length on this topic, we shall briefly expand upon Crisp's account to further clarify Barth's stance and show that for Barth, the mystery of predestination exists in the "impossible possibility" of rejecting the reality of one's redemption accomplished in Christ. We shall first glance at Barth's teaching on predestination before touching on Barth's account of reconciliation, clearly identifying Barth's locus of mystery, and briefly comparing Barth's approach with Calvin's.

First, Barth teaches that God reveals his one life-giving will in his election of the incarnate Son as the elect and reprobate One. In his critique of Calvin's doctrine of predestination, he accuses Calvin (and the rest of the Reformed tradition) of separating the predestinating God from the God revealed in Jesus Christ. As we have seen, Barth says, "The fact that Calvin in particular not only did not answer but did not even perceive this question is the decisive objection which we have to bring against his whole doctrine of predestination. The electing God of Calvin is a *Deus nudus absconditus*. It is not the *Deus revelatus* who is as such the *Deus absconditus*, the eternal God."[84] In other words, Barth identifies the locus of mystery that we observed above in Calvin's, Luther's, and Zwingli's accounts and concludes that a mystery in the doctrine of God inevitably undermines one's assurance of faith and grounds for worship.

Barth sets forth his account of predestination as an important correction to this perceived Reformed misstep, contending that an account of predestination that is founded upon God's *hidden decision* in eternity to elect by *hidden means* in time results in a dual unknown: both God and the elect. This leaves humanity without assurance and without a known God to adore with proper humility.[85] Thus, instead of the Reformed divines' (including Calvin's) accounts of the hidden will of God's secret good pleasure, Barth declares that God's will has been made known to us: in Jesus Christ, God and humanity are unconditionally united in a covenant of grace.[86] Human sin is the rejection of God's will, but God's will does not change. His wrath is therefore the expression of his rejection of the human spurning of God. To use Barth's terminology, God has said "Yes" to humanity, but humanity has replied with a "No." God responds with an emphatic "Yes" to his eternal purposes for humanity by becoming incarnate in Christ, thus uniting God and humanity in the person of Jesus Christ. By assuming sinful humanity in the incarnation, Jesus Christ becomes the reprobate One, taking upon himself the guilt of the human contradiction of God.[87] God's one will is for humanity to be united with him.

Second, Barth's specific teaching on Christ's reconciling work further clarifies Barth's teaching on predestination. In *CD* IV/1, Barth describes the root of human sin as the desire to judge good and evil apart from God who is the true Judge. Therefore, in Christ's fourfold act of reconciliation for humanity, (1) Christ the true Judge (2) takes the deserved judgment of fallen humanity upon himself and (3) enacts judgment on humanity at the cross, (4) thus establishing the righteousness (justice) of God again in humanity.[88] In the cross and resurrection, God fulfills his purposes of life for humanity, saying "*Yes* to man and the world, even in the No of the cross which it includes."[89]

This reconciliation with God is an objective reality completed in Christ on behalf of all humanity. Thus, the grace of Jesus Christ is "the grace in which God from all eternity has chosen man [*den Menschen*] (all men) in this *One*, in which He has bound Himself to man—before man ever existed—in this *One*."[90] Therefore, as Crisp notes, conversion is simply awakening to the reality of one's reconciliation with God in Christ. It does not bring about a new ontological reality as if the act of believing made one into a forgiven child of God. Instead, "We believe that we are because we are,"[91] and the church lives in the freedom of God's "Yes" of covenant love and life while inviting those outside the church to recognize that same reality for themselves.

Finally, one concept that helps clarify Barth's stance on predestination and the scope of salvation is his phrase, "the impossible possibility" (*die unmögliche Möglichkeit*). For Barth, the impossible possibility describes both the initial human choice to sin and the general (non)existence of evil or "nothingness" (*das Nichtige*). Barth describes the person of sin, both before and after Christ's work of redemption, as an "impossible possibility, which as such is not amenable to rational presentation. It is simply a brute fact."[92] Thus, just as evil "exists" as an impossible possibility in a universe created by an all-good God, and just as humanity chose the impossible possibility to sin instead of trusting God in the beginning, so the impossible possibility remains that some people might reject the reality of their redemption by rebelling against God's "Yes" to them in Christ.[93] This is unthinkable and inexplicable, but as witnessed to by the presence of evil and sin in the world, such rejection of God and his purposes could still occur.

This impossible possibility is the locus of mystery in Barth's account of election and salvation. It also makes sense of the ambiguity regarding Barth's scope of salvation that has caused Crisp and others so much confusion. It is unthinkable that any who are elect in Christ could not be saved, and yet the tragic fact remains that some may "impossibly" reject God's gracious covenant love.[94]

Although Barth and Calvin both provide accounts that recognize Christ as the center of God's self-revelation and the center of God's redeeming work in the world, their methodologies are distinct, particularly in relation to the knowledge of God. For Calvin, Christ is the supreme accommodation of the God who dwells in unapproachable light. This incarnational accommodation aligns with and clarifies God's accommodation in creation and providence and in Scripture's broader witness. God is made known in Christ, but no limited human could ever know God fully. For Barth, in contrast, Christ provides direct knowledge of God's being and is thus the lens through which one examines all of Scripture and all of God's works. In short, "The one God is revealed to us absolutely in Jesus Christ. He is absolutely the same God in Himself."[95] Because God in himself has been made known in Christ, Barth's theology (including his account of predestination) leaves no doubt about God's disposition toward humanity; in light of God's assuming flesh in Christ, God's word to humanity is always "Yes." In another contrast, Calvin places election within the economy of salvation while Barth situates it within the doctrine of God. For Calvin, election is something God does in and through Christ, while for Barth, "Christ is the decree" as electing God and elected man.[96] In other words, Barth would extend Calvin's description of God's disclosed merciful disposition toward humanity as univocally expressing God's *only* will toward humanity. For him, there is no space in the God of Jesus Christ for a twofold will for humanity (per Calvin). Instead, God has made known his single disposition and will for humanity, namely God's will of electing love.

One major strength of Barth's account is his grounding of reprobation in his doctrine of God. Instead of the Christ-less doctrine that reprobation is in Calvin's teaching, Barth's account of Jesus as the reprobate One who receives God's wrath on behalf of humanity definitively removes the undermining problem of a hidden God choosing to reprobate unidentified people.

A few weaknesses in Barth's approach are the speculative nature of his doctrine of election (and lack of explicit biblical support for it), the biblical indicators of damnation of some human beings (e.g., the wide and narrow road of Matt. 7, the sheep and the goats of Matt. 25, and various parables of Jesus), the human experience of people's rejecting God's grace extended in Christ (although, as noted elsewhere, it is only God who knows in the end how each person responds to Christ), and the potential in his approach for limited humans to assert more comprehensive knowledge of the transcendent God than can be justified by Scripture and the incarnation. Although Barth was committed to founding his theology on sound biblical exegesis, he seems forced to stretch the biblical witness to fit his magnificent portrayal of Jesus' reconciling work. Regarding the final weakness, the central question is whether human knowledge of God is comprehension of God's essence or simply confident knowledge of God's nature and character. Barth claims essential knowledge, but I believe that Calvin arrived at similar confidence in God without needing to reduce so drastically the Creator-creation distinction by claiming such significant human knowledge of God's essence.

To summarize, Barth's account of predestination places the mystery in the impossible possibility that any human being who has already been graciously redeemed in Jesus Christ would somehow reject God's love. This is quite similar to Arminius's account. Both theologians believe that God has one, openly disclosed will of communion with all humanity in accord with his goodness. Both believe that God's grace precedes any human response to God. The key difference lies in the application of Christ's work. For Arminius, Christ's redemptive work is applied only to those who God foreknows will receive his grace, but for Barth, Christ's redemptive work is an *objective reality* for all people, as they are already elect in Christ. For him, only those who fight against Christ's redemption will experience the fiery wrath of God's love. In short, the mystery for Barth is how it could be that people could reject the reality of their gracious redemption in Christ.

CONCLUSION

In this chapter, we followed Levering's criteria of a good doctrine of predestination that holds together the mysterious tension of God's superabundant love and God's permission for some creatures to be eternally lost.[97] We examined Calvin's account and five other descriptions in the Reformed tradition of where the mystery might be located in a biblical doctrine of predestination. Every biblical account of predestination will necessarily include a mystery somewhere. Following Calvin's example, faithful pastors, scholars, and church members must evaluate the scriptural faithfulness and the pastoral usefulness of the different approaches in light of their context and the contemporary challenges of their communities.

All five of the accounts studied had significant similarities to Calvin's as well as some key differences. One key commonality across all of the accounts (possibly weakest in Zwingli) is the deep confidence all of the theologians had in God's character as revealed in Scripture and most clearly in Jesus Christ. Many of the distinct theological moves were made in accordance with this deep conviction of who God is (e.g., Arminius's move to defend God's justice, Luther's attempt to distinguish the *Deus absconditus* from the *Deus revelatus*, and Calvin's own careful and consistent depiction of God's one loving disposition toward humanity and asymmetrically twofold will).

Among the differences, the most important observation is what happens when the locus of mystery is placed in the doctrine of God. Although Calvin (and Luther) clearly did not think their exposition would or should undermine anyone's ability to trust God and find assurance of God's love in Christ, they were wrong.[98] Still today, many find Calvin's doctrine abundantly assuring while others fearfully cower before or angrily accuse the unknown God behind the decrees. I believe that one primary difference between those who find Calvin's account assuring and those who do not is whether a person comes to be utterly convinced of God's character revealed in Jesus Christ logically prior to a consideration of predestination. Those who find themselves certain of God's character may be able to accept by faith with Calvin that God's acts in the "black box"[99] of predestination somehow will be seen in the eschaton to correspond to God's loving, righteous, and just nature revealed in Jesus Christ. However, other people of faith may not be able to make that step without an irrevocable erosion of one's ability to trust in and worship God.

I find myself with Calvin in the former camp, able trust that the bare fact of (some sort of) reprobation will be seen to correspond somehow to God's revealed nature in the end. However, I know and respect many faithful Christian brothers and sisters who are not able to set aside the doctrine of reprobation so easily. I believe that our different experiences, backgrounds, cultures, and personalities all impact the ways that we process certain Christian doctrines, especially in the case of a challenging doctrine like double predestination.

Therefore, in light of our findings, and in my setting, I think that Bullinger's account provides the best option for broad Christian teaching and preaching. As mentioned above, Bullinger's account is almost identical to Calvin's in his focus on God's gracious and unmerited election in Christ and on God's nature revealed in Scripture and Christ. However, his careful eschewal of any accounts that seemed to assign responsibility for sin or evil to God allow him to minimize the problems of the mystery of predestination by leaving the mystery as undefined as possible in those who somehow are "outside Christ." Bullinger capitalizes on the best of Arminius in his defense of God's justice but does so while affirming the biblical witness to the inability of any fallen human being to receive God's grace based on his or her own inclinations. Bullinger's account also arrives at a similar end as Barth's in his affirmation of God's nature and abundant grace extended to all in Jesus Christ, but he does so without needing to construct a doctrine of reconciliation that so significantly stretches the biblical witness and reduces the human regard for God's holy otherness. In regard to Barth's account, Bullinger's description also makes better sense of human experience and biblical witness that both seem to suggest that people who are yet to trust in Christ are not already reconciled to God and are thus living (tragically) in alienation from God.[100]

I shall return to Bullinger's account briefly in chapter 8 after we critically evaluate Calvin's approach discerned in this study and draw some practical conclusions for today.

NOTES

1. Levering, *Predestination*, 34–35.

2. Levering, *Predestination*, 90–95, 117–127. Levering also includes a brief analysis of Calvin's teaching on predestination, concluding that it is wanting because Calvin overtly ascribes the causality of damnation to God. I believe that a closer and more broad reading of Calvin (beyond the *Institutes*) demonstrates that his account of predestination fulfills Levering's criteria in a manner similar to, but superior to, Catherine and de Sales. In particular, attention to Calvin's teaching on the nuances of causality as they relate to reprobation and Calvin's assertion of real human agency alongside his affirmation of God's sovereignty alleviate Levering's key criticisms of Calvin. Going further, Calvin's account as we have discerned it does exhibit God's "superabundant love for every creature" in God's one disclosed disposition. Calvin's account also evinces God's all-encompassing providence that allows for permanent rebellion according to God's veiled, reprobating will. I believe Calvin's account is actually stronger than Levering's exemplars because of the careful systematic coherence of Calvin's doctrine in the midst of the mystery.

We further examine a number of the weaknesses of Calvin's argument in this and the subsequent chapter.

3. Levering, *Predestination*, 68, 127. Levering concludes that de Sales's position thus "fails in terms of logical clarity," but, like Catherine, it "crucially succeeds in affirming both aspects of the biblical witness" (*Predestination*, 127).

4. Levering, *Predestination*, 198.

5. Muller, *Christ and the Decree*, 74.

6. With the possible exception of Zwingli, as we shall examine below.

7. *Comm. Rom.* 11:7; *CO* 49:216.

8. *Comm. Rom.* 11:33; *CO* 49:230.

9. *CD* II/2, pp. 110–11; *KD*, p. 119.

10. Fredrik Brosché, *Luther on Predestination: The Antinomy and the Unity between Love and Wrath in Luther's Concept of God* (Stockholm, Sweden: Almqvist & Wiksell International, 1978), 131.

11. Brosché, *Luther on Predestination*, 120.

12. Brosché, *Luther on Predestination*, 117.

13. *Bondage and Liberation of the Will; WA* 18.686, quoted from Brosché, *Luther on Predestination*, 129.

14. For more on Luther's *deus absconditus*, see B. A. Gerrish, ""To the Unknown God": Luther and Calvin on the Hiddenness of God," *The Journal of Religion* 53, no. 3 (1973).

15. Brosché, *Luther on Predestination*, 47.

16. Brosché, *Luther on Predestination*, 131.

17. Brosché, *Luther on Predestination*, 142.

18. Brosché, *Luther on Predestination*, 158–59.

19. Brosché, *Luther on Predestination*, 204.

20. Brosché, *Luther on Predestination*, 209.

21. Brosché, *Luther on Predestination*, 141.

22. "Faith is so convinced of the innermost goodness of the divine being that not even a universal reprobation could undermine it!" (Brosché, *Luther on Predestination*, 204–5).

23. He first explicitly wrote about it in 1526 and described the doctrine most fully in 1530, the year prior to his death (William Peter Stephens, "The Place of Predestination in Zwingli and Bucer," in *Reformiertes Erbe: Festschrift Fur Gottfried W. Locher Zu Seinem 80. Geburtstag. Band 1*, ed. Heiko A. Oberman, et al. [Zurich: Theologischer Verlag, 1992], 393).

24. According to Stephens, Zwingli's *De Providentiae Dei* is "the least biblical and most philosophical of all of Zwingli's writings" (*The Theology of Huldrych Zwingli* [Oxford: Clarendon Press, 1986], 93). As Dong-Joo Kim puts it, he describes predestination from the logical reflection on divine supremacy ("Luther and Zwingli on Predestination," *Korean Journal of Christian Studies* 42 [2005], 149).

25. Quoted from Gottfried W. Locher, *Zwingli's Thought: New Perspectives* (Leiden: Brill, 1981), 124.

26. Stephens, *The Theology of Huldrych Zwingli*, 105–6.

27. Quote from Locher, *Zwingli's Thought*, 130.

28. Stephens, "The Place of Predestination in Zwingli and Bucer," 410.

29. William Peter Stephens, "Election in Zwingli and Bullinger: A Comparison of Zwingli's *Sermonis De Providentia Dei Anamnema* (1530) and Bullinger's *Oratio De Moderatione Servanda in Negotio Providentiae, Praedestinationis Gratiae Et Liberi Arbitrii* (1536)," *Reformation & Renaissance Review* 7, no. 1 (2005), 43–44.

30. Stephens, "Election in Zwingli and Bullinger," 46–47.

31. Stephens, *The Theology of Huldrych Zwingli*, 103–4.

32. Locher, *Zwingli's Thought*, 140.

33. Stephens, *The Theology of Huldrych Zwingli*, 103. Cf. Locher, *Zwingli's Thought*, 137.
34. Paul Helm, "Calvin (and Zwingli) on Divine Providence," *Calvin Theological Journal* 29 (1994), 404.
35. Helm, "Calvin (and Zwingli) on Divine Providence," 404.
36. Venema, *Heinrich Bullinger and the Doctrine of Predestination*, 61.
37. Stephens, "Election in Zwingli and Bullinger," 44.
38. Stephens, *The Theology of Huldrych Zwingli*, 104.
39. For example, *Inst.* 1.3–1.4.
40. *CO* 14:252. Quoted from Calvin, *Selected Works of John Calvin: Tracts and Letters*, 343–44.
41. Venema, *Heinrich Bullinger and the Doctrine of Predestination*, 18.
42. Quoted in Venema, *Heinrich Bullinger and the Doctrine of Predestination*, 44.
43. Venema, *Heinrich Bullinger and the Doctrine of Predestination*, 49.
44. Venema, *Heinrich Bullinger and the Doctrine of Predestination*, 53.
45. Venema, *Heinrich Bullinger and the Doctrine of Predestination*, 45.
46. Venema, *Heinrich Bullinger and the Doctrine of Predestination*, 99.
47. *Reformed Confessions of the 16th and 17th Centuries in English Translation: Volume 2, 1552–1566* (Grand Rapids: Reformation Heritage Books, 2010), 826. Cf. Venema, *Heinrich Bullinger and the Doctrine of Predestination*, 98.
48. Venema, *Heinrich Bullinger and the Doctrine of Predestination*, 68.
49. Venema, *Heinrich Bullinger and the Doctrine of Predestination*, 55.
50. Venema, *Heinrich Bullinger and the Doctrine of Predestination*, 105.
51. *Second Helvetic Confession*, Article 11,
52. Venema, *Heinrich Bullinger and the Doctrine of Predestination*, 101–3.
53. Venema, *Heinrich Bullinger and the Doctrine of Predestination*, 106.
54. Venema, *Heinrich Bullinger and the Doctrine of Predestination*, 65.
55. Venema, *Heinrich Bullinger and the Doctrine of Predestination*, 60–62. Cf. *CO* 14:208–210. Cf. *CO* 14:289–290. Calvin's response is that he was simply defending the free grace of God against Bolsec's synergistic distortions and that his approach should be considered moderate, *CO* 14:251–254.
56. The accord primarily addresses concerns regarding the Lord's Supper, but it does include a vague reference to (positive) election in a statement regarding adoption that occurs through being ingrafted into Christ "by the agency of the Holy Spirit" by a "free imputation of righteousness" (*Reformed Confessions of the 16th and 17th Centuries in English Translation: Volume 1, 1523–1552* [Grand Rapids: Reformation Heritage Books, 2008], 540).
57. Thomas H. McCall and Keith D. Stanglin, *Jacob Arminius: A Theologian of Grace* (Oxford: Oxford University Press, 2012), 25–36.
58. William den Boer, *God's Twofold Love: The Theology of Jacob Arminius (1559–1609)*, trans. Albert Gootjes (Göttingen: Vandenhoeck & Ruprecht, 2010), 326. Cf. McCall and Stanglin, *Jacob Arminius*, 13. Cf. Richard Muller, *God, Creation, and Providence in the Thought of Jacob Arminius: Sources and Directions of Scholastic Protestantism in the Era of Early Orthodoxy* (Grand Rapids: Baker, 1991), 281.

59. William den Boer, "Jacobus Arminius: Theologian of God's Twofold Love," in *Arminius, Arminianism, and Europe: Jacobus Arminius (1559/60–1609)*, ed. Th. Marius van Leeuwen, Keith D. Stanglin, and Marijke Tolsma (Boston: Brill, 2009), 27–28.

60. den Boer, "Jacobus Arminius," 29–30.
61. den Boer, "Jacobus Arminius," 31, 34.
62. den Boer, "Jacobus Arminius," 39.
63. den Boer, "Jacobus Arminius," 34.
64. den Boer, "Jacobus Arminius," 41.
65. James Arminius, "A Modest Examination of Dr. Perkins's Pamphlet," in *The Works of James Arminius, Vol. 3* (Grand Rapids: Baker Book House, 1986), 358. Cf. McCall and Stanglin, *Jacob Arminius*, 113–14.
66. McCall and Stanglin, *Jacob Arminius*, 92.
67. den Boer, "Jacobus Arminius," 40.
68. den Boer, "Jacobus Arminius," 42.
69. den Boer, "Jacobus Arminius," 43.
70. den Boer, "Jacobus Arminius," 45.
71. den Boer, "Jacobus Arminius," 45.
72. As we have seen, Calvin (and others in the Reformed tradition) also perceived these concerns and held theological positions that addressed them. For Calvin, these were, respectively, the double grace of justification and sanctification (expressed in piety and charity) and the mirror of our election, Jesus Christ. Jacobs brilliantly illuminates Calvin's inherent link between predestination and responsibility (*Prädestination*).
73. den Boer, "Jacobus Arminius," 49.
74. Muller, *God, Creation, and Providence*, 234.
75. McCall and Stanglin, *Jacob Arminius*, 111. Cf. James Arminius, "A Declaration of the Sentiments of Arminius," in *The Works of James Arminius, Vol. 1* (Grand Rapids: Baker Book House, 1986), 623.

By "real," I mean Arminius's version of human choice in which God has no causal role.

76. den Boer, *God's Twofold Love*, 179ff. Cf. McCall and Stanglin, *Jacob Arminius*, 140.
77. Throughout this account, I refer to the species of universalism that definitively asserts all human beings will be saved. This is in contrast to other species like "hopeful universalism." Cf. Crisp, *Deviant Calvinism*, 151–52.
78. Crisp, *Deviant Calvinism*, 152.
79. Crisp, *Deviant Calvinism*, 169–70.
80. Oliver Crisp, "On the Letter and Spirit of Karl Barth's Doctrine of Election: A Reply to O'Neil," *Evangelical Quarterly* 79 (2007). Cf. Oliver Crisp, "On Barth's Denial of Universalism," *Themelios* 29 (2003).
81. In his "spirit-not-letter" account, Crisp seeks to tell charitably the story of the breadth of Barth's account without becoming overly focused on the details of some specific statements Barth makes, particularly in *CD* II/2 (*Deviant Calvinism*, 170–74).
82. Crisp, *Deviant Calvinism*, 170–72. Emphasis orig.

83. Crisp, *Deviant Calvinism*, 173.

84. *CD* II/2, pp. 110–11; *KD*, p. 119. Berkouwer similarly asks, "For although we do not attempt to penetrate into that which, according to God's revelation, must remain hidden for us, the fact of that hiddenness remains known to us and we wonder whether out of this hiddenness—this *deus absconditus*—a shadow is not also cast where the *deus revelatus* is preached with emphasis" (*Divine Election*, 12). For more on Luther's *deus absconditus*, see Gerrish, "'To the Unknown God': Luther and Calvin on the Hiddenness of God."

85. *CD* II/2, pp. 146–47; *KD*, pp. 157–59.

86. *CD* II/2, p. 157; *KD*, p. 171.

87. *CD* II/2, pp. 164–67; *KD*, pp. 179–83.

88. *CD* IV/1, pp. 211–83; *KD*, pp. 231–311.

89. *CD* IV/1, p. 347; *KD*, p. 383. Emphasis in German.

90. *CD* IV/1, p. 91; *KD*, p. 97. Emphasis in German.

91. *CD* IV/1, p. 357; *KD*, p. 394.

92. *CD* IV/3, p. 463; *KD*, p. 553.

93. As noted earlier, for Barth, God's wrath is God's opposition to anyone and anything that opposes his loving purposes for humanity. As an expression of his love, God rejects human rejection of him. This opposition to human opposition is "the scorching fire of the love of God," *CD* IV/1, p. 173; *KD*, p. 189. Cf. Wynne, *Wrath among the Perfections*. For those who tenaciously say "No" to God, God's even more insistent "Yes" will be received as eternal wrath.

94. One further clarification to Crisp's "spirit-not-letter" account (particularly point 2) is the way that for Barth, the rejection of Christ does not change one's ontological status (e.g., from elect to reprobate), even though it results in the wrath of God, as seen in the previous footnote.

95. *CD* II/1, p. 297; *KD*, p. 334. Cf. *CD* I/1, p. 165; *KD*, p. 171. Cf. Alan J. Torrance, "The Trinity," in *The Cambridge Companion to Karl Barth*, ed. John Webster (Cambridge: Cambridge University Press, 2000), 83–84. It is worth noting that Barth, like Calvin, still does not teach that God can be comprehensively known by humans. Barth affirms God's mystery, transcendence, and freedom but sees them as actually expressed in God's self-revelation in Christ.

96. Gibson, *Reading the Decree*, 4.

97. Outside of unconditional universalist accounts, one standing in the Reformed tradition *can* still hope that somehow God will rescue *all* people from their sins according to his grace. Cf. Oliver Crisp, "Augustinian Universalism," *International Journal for Philosophy of Religion* 53, no. 3 (2003).

98. Cf. Zachman, *Assurance of Faith*.

99. See chapter 4.

100. I say this with hesitation because as Calvin says, Scripture, not experience, should be our primary foundation for our theological positions. However, I believe that experience (held loosely) can add confirmation to biblical doctrines, as in this case.

Chapter Eight

Predestination in the Key of Jesus Christ

As we conclude, we begin with Calvin's words from one of his Genesis sermons:

> We know that by hearing the promises of the forgiveness of our sins and of the free adoption of God, we hear that he inviteth us to him, that he openeth the door unto us, to the end that we might have familiar access to call upon him.[1]

Can someone who is following Calvin's interpretation of Scripture stand in front of a group of people and proclaim, "God loves you!" without adding an explicit or implicit qualification such as, "if you respond in faith" or "if you are elect"? Can a preacher confidently preach and teach God's trustworthy and loving character? Can followers of Jesus trust God's love, justice, goodness, and power for themselves? Do Christians have an obligation to regard all people as loved by God?

According to Calvin's theology, the answer to these question is affirmative—the God of love revealed in Jesus Christ can be known, trusted, and proclaimed, and he is the only God who can be known, trusted, and proclaimed, even in light of God's mysterious twofold will.

SUMMARY OF FINDINGS

We have considered this question of God's disposition toward humanity by particularly examining Calvin's teaching on the knowledge of God and predestination, discerning what can be known and proclaimed about God. In sum, we found that according to Calvin's exposition of the breadth of Scripture, God has one disposition toward humanity and one, secret, and righteous will that is expressed in a twofold, patently asymmetrical manner toward humanity. God's disclosed, merciful disposition corresponds to God's revealed electing will and to God's unchanging, loving, righteous, wise, powerful, good, and judging (of evil) nature. That disclosed disposition is extended to all and appropriated by the elect as they are enabled by God to trust the gospel of Christ according to God's electing will. God inscrutably leaves some people in their state of rebellion against God and ensuing just condemnation according to God's veiled reprobating will, an element of God's one will that is only humanly known to relate to God's nature in part.

For Calvin, this twofold will does not lead to insecurity regarding the knowledge of God primarily because of who God is, but also because of the drastic asymmetry between the revealed and veiled parts of God's will. God has made his unchanging nature known to believers through his works, so Calvin wholeheartedly espouses trust in and proclamation of the God revealed in creation, in Scripture, and most of all in the person and work of Jesus Christ through whom he expresses his love for the world and judgment of evil. Election itself confirms God's merciful, powerful, and righteous nature via God's gracious electing will toward his children. Another part of God's one, secret will is his veiled reprobating will, but the electing and reprobating elements of God's will are asymmetrically related in regard to how they relate to God's revealed nature, how much can be known about them, and how much they inform proclamation about God. For Calvin, God's veiled reprobating will, though factual, does not undermine trust in God and in God's disclosed disposition toward humanity.

To expand upon a metaphor introduced earlier, in creation, Scripture, election, and most clearly in Jesus Christ, God has openly made himself and his disposition toward humanity known, as if someone were looking out over a beautiful vista from an elevated lookout on a clear, sunny day. The beauty, power, and goodness are directly apparent. This is God's nature, electing will, and disposition toward humanity that God has expressly made known. God's reprobative will is like a large black shed in the field below that catches the observer's eye as it disrupts the magnificent viewing experience. Upon closer inspection, the observer peaks through a crack in the shed and can see a few shapes in the shadows that indicate a connection with what had been observed of the beautiful vista in the sunlight, but nothing observed in the dark shed can change or erase what the observer saw and experienced in the warmth of the sun on the viewing platform. For Calvin, God has made himself and his disposition toward humanity known. Reprobation is an inscrutable fact (who let someone build a black shed in the middle of a beautiful natural landscape anyway?), but it does not change what is known, trusted, and proclaimed of God.

After synthesizing Calvin's teaching regarding God's disposition toward humanity, we tested our findings by examining Calvin's preaching. There our theoretical conclusions were confirmed in practice: Calvin applied his theoretical approach in his preaching, explicitly and implicitly preaching God's disclosed disposition toward humanity while acknowledging the two, drastically asymmetrical parts of God's one, righteous, and hidden will.

In this project, we sought to let Calvin primarily speak for himself as we discerned his understanding of God's disposition toward humanity. In the past five hundred years, developments in theology and biblical studies have provided many other options for answering this question. Calvin himself would encourage pastors and theologians today to keep searching the Scriptures, learning about the world of Jesus, and considering how to best proclaim the good news of Jesus in the contemporary world. To this end, we brought Calvin in brief dialogue with five other theologians in the Reformed tradition as a means to learn about how the doctrine of predestination necessitates a decision regarding the placement of the inevitable locus of mystery. In so doing, we observed similarities and differences, including strengths and weaknesses of Calvin's approach vis-á-vis the others, and I concluded with a brief explanation of my preference for Heinrich Bullinger's approach alongside my appreciation for Calvin's teaching. Having seen how the thorough and passionate pastor, theologian, and Christian John Calvin explicated God's witness to himself in predestination, I hope that readers will be equipped to evaluate critically and to appropriate constructively other options that may arise, adhering to Calvin's example of faithfully trusting in, preaching about, and teaching regarding the God of the Bible revealed in Jesus Christ. However, in spite of Calvin's sincerity and effort, he was still a limited human being serving in a specific time and place whose teaching deserves critical reflection, to which we now turn.

CALVIN'S MISSTEPS

In addressing a topic that has historically been quite problematic and a person who is often stereotyped or misconstrued, I have attempted to give Calvin a thorough and fair reading in this project of retrieval. Having let Calvin primarily speak for himself throughout and having given him the benefit of the doubt regarding his assumptions and philosophical moves, I am now compelled to address four key weaknesses that I see in Calvin's account. Some of these have been mentioned at the end of chapter 3 or in notes, but here we bring them together with accompanying critical remarks. We shall discuss Calvin's violation of his prescribed theological methodology, his letting experience overly inform his teaching, his ignorance of election as mission, and his lack of empathy for the reprobate. All four of these doctrinal missteps are important, but the first is the most significant.

Violating His Scriptural, Nonspeculative, Pastoral Methodology

First, and most importantly, Calvin violates his own scriptural, nonspeculative, and pastoral methodology in his teaching of reprobation. Calvin is clear that he expects dogmatic conclusions to find their source in Christian Scripture, not to arise from speculation,[2] and to be pastorally useful for believers. In my view, Calvin's doctrine of reprobation does not sufficiently meet any of these three criteria. Calvin believes that the doctrine is based in Scripture, and he finds some relevant passages to support that claim; however, upon closer reflection the biblical basis for God's active reprobation is relatively weak. For example, Romans 9–11 is Calvin's key passage for reprobation, but its text allows for many different interpretations, as witnessed in a brief survey of any contemporary commentaries. Further, many of the prophecies of condemnation in the Old Testament can be read as *warnings* of coming judgment, not necessarily God's intentional purposes or plans. In addition, Jesus' parables (e.g., the parable of the weeds in Matt. 13:24–30, the parable of the net in Matt. 13:47–50, and the parable of the wedding banquet in Matt. 22:1–14) clearly speak of a coming judgment, but upon closer inspection they do not explicitly include God's reprobating actions. There are other proof texts, but many of those also have debatable interpretations. In sum, contrary to what could be said about God's positive election in Christ, there is not an indisputable or widespread biblical witness indicating God's intentional reprobation of people to eternal damnation.

Instead of being explicitly and consistently included in the biblical witness, reprobation is primarily a logical deduction from the (clearly biblical) doctrine of unmerited election and the belief in God's sovereign reign over all things. The doctrine of reprobation is bolstered by human experience that seems to confirm the fact that not all people come to faith in Christ. In other words, if God must actively rescue people from their state of sinful rebellion against him and if not all people come to put their faith in Christ (as the Bible seems to indicate and experience seems to confirm), then clearly God passes over some people and leaves them in their state of deserved condemnation. This may be logically true, but it is what Jacobs calls a boundary-line (*Grenzlinie*) doctrine or van der Kooi calls a shadow doctrine. Biblically, reprobation is not a doctrine that has enough backing to be taught with substance.

Building upon that conclusion, I believe that Calvin's teaching on reprobation also violates Calvin's commitment to nonspeculative theology. Although

Calvin is quick to affirm the epistemological limits of humans trying to decipher God's secret counsel, he regularly claims knowledge of God's reprobating actions and motives. As we observed above,[3] Calvin defines speculation as impious inquiry that ignores God's gracious self-witness in Scripture and results in cold and worthless knowledge. Does not the doctrine of reprobation fall within Calvin's definition of speculation, as it reaches outside of Scripture's clear witness to something about which humans have little to no epistemic access? As such a speculative topic, it should not be commonly pursued or taught.

Calvin's doctrine of reprobation also fails Calvin's test of being pastorally useful. Although Calvin thought the doctrine would be useful, Bullinger's letter (quoted in chapter 1) and Barth's accusation of a *Deus nudus absconditus* both point out the pastoral problem that has recurred countless times over the past five hundred years as a result of the doctrine.[4] Even though Calvin did not think it should, reprobation undermines some people's ability to trust God and his goodness and love. Although for Calvin reprobation does not substantially reveal God's nature to us (besides affirming his judgment of evil), Calvin regularly highlights the doctrine's primary usefulness in the way that it increases the elect's gratitude for God's mercy on them; the contrast between God's gracious election of some and God's passing over of others in reprobation supposedly leads the elect to a deeper sense of gratitude.

I disagree with that approach for two reasons. First, Calvin is ignoring the proper Christian reaction to someone else's misfortune, namely empathy. Instead of immediately engendering gratitude for themselves, elect ones who are being empowered by the Spirit to love their neighbors as themselves should immediately be moved to mourn over the reprobate. (We shall comment further on empathy below.) Secondly, we need not understand reprobation to be exceedingly grateful for our own rescue from our deserved state of condemnation. Scripture's abundant witness to God's unmerited covenant faithfulness to sinners engenders deep gratitude and worship in and of itself. In addition, as the lives of the saints through the ages have consistently witnessed, when people develop as Christian disciples, they become more and more aware of their own sinfulness and the judgment they deserve. If they are not already overwhelmed by God's gratuitous grace, people need only to look within themselves to recognize the depths out of which God has rescued them and be led to increased gratitude. The doctrine of reprobation is not significantly useful pastorally and thus should not be regularly taught.

Although Calvin thought his exposition of the doctrine of reprobation was necessary to provide assurance of salvation and to defend his doctrine of election by grace alone, I agree with Jacobs and van der Kooi that Calvin overstepped his exegetically defensible grounds in his material teaching on reprobation.[5] I think Calvin himself generally recognized the boundary-marking character of reprobation, as witnessed to in the drastic asymmetry between God's electing will and God's reprobating will in his teaching. Perhaps, as Jacobs contends, it was the many attacks on Calvin's doctrine that led him to articulate it and defend it so substantially at times. In addition, maybe Calvin's logical mind and training as a lawyer made the deduction of the doctrine of reprobation seem obvious to him and therefore worthy of substantial teaching. Regardless of the reasons, Calvin should have left reprobation a shadow doctrine, like Bullinger sought to do, and instead focused on what is exceptionally clear in Scripture, namely God's goodness and God's gracious redemption offered to all in Christ.

Overly Influenced by Experience

Second, Calvin lets experience overly influence his teaching on predestination. As many scholars have observed, experience was a major factor in Calvin's teaching of predestination.[6] Calvin sought to explain why it is that not all people seem to respond with faith to the preaching of the gospel. This was a natural question for Calvin the pastor and for the pastors whom Calvin was training as they sought to integrate their theology into their lived experience. Good theological reflection should be understood and applied in the lives of real human beings. However, Calvin made two major errors here, both of which are rooted in his overvaluing of experience.

First, Calvin assumed that people's visible reaction to the preaching of the gospel in a certain setting indicated the eternal state of their heart. In fact, only God knows how a person is responding to his grace in a moment or how one will respond in the future. The visible response is only a single part of a larger story of a person's engagement with the gospel, and Calvin should have allowed God to be sole judge of people's souls.

Secondly, when Calvin began to suggest specific numbers of elect and reprobate, he overstepped his bounds and again moved into the realm of speculation. By suggesting that (depending on the day), only 1 to 20 percent of a group of people listening were elect because only that number responded in faith, Calvin claimed knowledge that only God can have. Calvin himself knew this, as he repeatedly affirmed the fact that no one can know another person's status as elect or reprobate. However, in Calvin's zeal to provide comfort for discouraged preachers (perhaps including himself), he let experience overly inform his teaching. Unfortunately, this type of claim (alongside a few biblical texts that can be interpreted to indicate a small number of elect—for example, the narrow door) was a seed in the Reformed tradition that germinated and further undermined the assurance of the faithful as they doubtfully wondered, "Am I really one of the few whom God has elected?"

Bullinger again provides a helpful example of a more pastorally useful approach in the Second Helvetic Confession when he responds to the question of whether few are elect. Bullinger there (citing Luke 13:24) encourages the believer not to speculate curiously about the number of the saved but "rather to endeavor that you may enter into heaven by the straight way" yourself.[7] Bullinger, in clear accordance with Calvin's pastoral and nonspeculative theological methodology, directs believers away from empty speculation about the salvation of others toward faithful obedience to and trust in Christ. Calvin should have followed his own advice and done the same regarding the varied reception of the preaching of the gospel.

Election as Escape

Third, Calvin clearly misses the inherent missional nature of biblical election. As mentioned at the close of chapter 3, Calvin's apparent ignorance of the ways that Abraham was blessed to be a blessing (Gen. 12:2), that Israel was chosen to be a "light to the nations" (Is. 42:7, 49:6), and that the disciples are chosen to be sent (John 20:21, Matt. 28:18–20, Acts 1:8) leads to a distorted understanding of election. If election is only about God's love for *me* (or my tribe) and God's rescue of *me* from this fallen and damnable world, my attitude toward others can quickly become one of proud snobbery ("I'm better than you") or one of strict separatism ("I want nothing to do with you").[8] Neither of these attitudes reflects the biblical call for disciples of Jesus Christ. The eternal Son incarnate was the supreme elect One who was *sent* into the world with a mission from God to serve and bring restoration. The model of the incarnate Son is the ultimate example of how a disciple's election is meant to launch him or her in the power of the Spirit to participate in Christ's ministry of reconciliation in the world (as a part of God's people). Through Spirit-led evangelism and the pursuit of justice, God's elect community is selected to be a faithful witness to God's kingdom reign in Jesus Christ. Calvin did not recognize the fact that God consistently elects *for the sake of the world*.

Lack of Empathy for the Reprobate

Fourth, Calvin does not acknowledge God's empathy for the reprobate nor does he personally show sufficient empathy for them. One reason for his aversion to God's empathy is likely Calvin's assumption that God is acting according to his innate justice and goodness in his doctrine of reprobation.

He assumes that even though it does not look good and righteous to limited humans, it must be good and right because God is causing it according to his sovereign plan. Therefore, neither God nor humans need mourn. That attitude fits with Calvin's broader project, at least regarding God's nature and actions.

However, another likely factor in Calvin's aversion to describing God's empathy is rooted in Calvin's sixteenth-century assumptions about God's changelessness and subsequent inability to experience human emotions.[9] For Calvin, since God does not have human emotions, God cannot feel empathy. However, if God has accommodated himself to us in Scripture and in Jesus Christ in such a way that the Bible characterizes God as one who weeps at the judgment of his people (Jer. 14:17) and depicts Jesus lamenting over Jerusalem with tears (Luke 19:41–44), there should be space in our theology for God to lament[10] over the condemnation of people who bear his image and for whom Christ died.[11]

Calvin himself also does not commonly express sorrow over the state of the elect, instead typically regarding the reprobate as God's enemies. Once again, Calvin is engaging in a type of speculation, claiming (as a limited human) to have God's perspective. Instead of speculating about God's attitude toward the reprobate, Christians should focus on the clear commands they have received. Therefore, faithful believers, who are commanded to love their neighbors as themselves and love their enemies, ought to lament when harm comes upon another, even if that harm mysteriously fits within God's sovereign plan; they would want the same from others for them. Calvin's own sermons abound with exhortations to neighbor-love as an inseparable element of Christian piety before God.[12] As one example, in his first sermon on Job, Calvin points out that neighbor-love extends beyond abstaining from hurtful actions toward others but seeks others' well-being, promotes equity, and pursues the common good.[13] A lack of empathy toward the reprobate also causes decay in the hearts of those who look on their neighbor with contempt instead of love. On top of that, a lack of empathy for others is a terrible Christian witness. How are we to witness to God's love if we do not look with sadness upon those who are far from God?

Fortunately, this lack of empathy has not reverberated through the Reformed tradition to the extent that some of Calvin's other missteps have. Perhaps this is because Calvin himself experienced this tension. We get a glimpse of this in Calvin's sermon on Micah 7:10–12, where Calvin wrestles with the question, "Ought we not demand the salvation of the entire world?" Calvin there first asserts that believers are able to rejoice in reprobation when they see it from God's perspective as God's condemnation of evil included in God's kingdom purposes. However, Calvin quickly qualifies these statements in recognition that it is extremely difficult for anyone to have God's perspective, truly setting aside worldly affections and the carnal desire for vengeance. He concludes that our call is to "strive to procure the salvation of all as best we can, and let us implore God to have mercy on those whom he has redeemed by the blood of his Son. That is what we must do. And that is why the Scripture admonishes us not to judge anyone hastily. Although we may deem a person wicked, we do not know whether God may rescue them in the end."[14]

Calvin should have taught more about God's compassion toward the reprobate, and he should have modeled the proper Christian attitude toward someone who is alienated from God, namely love and empathy.

Although other missteps could be mentioned, these are the four most important corrections that I would have for Calvin regarding his doctrine of predestination.

CALVIN'S PARADOXES

I now proceed to two paradoxes in Calvin's teaching of predestination and God's disposition toward humanity, concerning which I offer the following clarifying expositions. We first examine why Calvin's doctrine of predestination does not substantially inform his teaching on the nature of God before discussing how Calvin could teach believers to hope for the salvation of all people when he did not believe that all people would come to a saving knowledge of Christ.

Reprobation and the Knowledge of God

First, it could be said that Calvin violates his methodology regarding the doctrine of God by substantially ignoring the ways reprobation impacts his understanding of God's nature. As we saw in chapter 2, Calvin believes God's nature is best known through his works in creation and providence, in Scripture, and most of all in Jesus Christ. However, Calvin only tangentially includes reprobation as revealing God's nature in the way that it provides witness to God's judgment of evil. Why doesn't reprobation as one of God's works more significantly inform his depiction of God's nature?

Calvin's move here is in fact consistent with his broader theological project. As we have seen, reprobation for Calvin is a Christ-less doctrine, and in much of his teaching and preaching,[15] he treats it as the boundary-line doctrine that it should be. Reprobation is not meant to provide substantial direct information about God because it is hidden within God's secret counsel and veiled reprobating will. Humans do not know how God's veiled reprobating will relates to his nature, merciful disclosed disposition, or electing will. What God has kept hidden, exegetes should allow to remain undisclosed. Therefore, Calvin is being consistent by not letting reprobation materially change his doctrine of God.

However, as we noted above, this oversight by Calvin did at times have nefarious effects on those who learned from him theologically. People (theologians and lay members alike) in the Reformed tradition instinctively let God's actions in reprobation inform their doctrine of God in the same manner that God's actions in election did. At times, they lost sight of the asymmetry between election and reprobation along with the distinction between God's disclosed electing will and God's veiled reprobating will that Calvin so consistently delineated. As a result, many in the Reformed tradition were deprived of confidence in God's merciful, righteous, and judging (of evil) nature, and were left unsure of whether God loved them or hated them. Barth's identification of the *Deus absconditus* explicitly identifies this phenomenon.

In sum, Calvin was consistent in his application of his theological method regarding reprobation and the knowledge of God. However, this paradox resulted in seeds in his theological project that at times led to a distorted depiction of a God who is equally glorified and revealed in election and reprobation.

Hope for All While Acknowledging Reprobation

In a second paradox, Calvin is right to commend the preaching of the gospel to all and hoping for the salvation of all alongside his belief that God has chosen to leave some people in their sinful state. Once again, a natural question occurs as one encounters Calvin's teaching: how does one hope for the salvation of all people via preaching and prayer while believing that some people are not chosen for salvation? It speaks well of Calvin that he did not succumb to temptation to fall on one side or the other of the binary dilemma. Instead, he trusted his theological priorities and held both at the same time, walking the narrow ridge between the two. A brief review of our findings makes sense of this claim.

As we have found, Calvin is convinced that God has one disposition toward humanity, one of lovingkindness that corresponds to God's nature and revealed electing will. The God revealed in election and Jesus Christ is the only God who can be proclaimed and known. Therefore, Calvin is compelled to proclaim God's mercy in the gospel to all and hope for the salvation of all in accordance with God's nature. At the same time, Calvin affirms the existence of God's veiled reprobating will that witnesses to the bare fact that for reasons known only to him, God chooses to pass over some people and leave them in their state of sinful condemnation. Since this veiled reprobating will does not directly provide insight into God's nature and thus God's working in the world, it is right for Calvin to set it aside in his preaching of the gospel and in his praying and hoping for the salvation of all people. Calvin still trusts in God's sovereign hand over the results of his preaching, praying, and hoping, but he does so according to the appropriate asymmetry of God's revealed electing will and God's veiled reprobating will.

Calvin was faithful to his theological commitments in his hope for the salvation of all alongside his trust in God's sovereign reign over the reception of the gospel proclaimed. This paradox is faithful to the biblical witness of God's love for all people, God's unmerited grace, and God's sovereign rule.

This concludes our cross-examination of Calvin, having identified four significant missteps and clarifying two paradoxes. I now finish our study with my own convictions regarding predestination in light of this study.

CONCLUSION: PREDESTINATION IN THE KEY OF JESUS CHRIST

Both of my daughters currently play the violin. Whenever one of them starts a new piece of music, the first question that I ask is, "What key is it in?" No matter how ready she is to try out the new song, my daughter must first determine where the sharps and flats are and what clef is defining the notes on the page. After obtaining clarity regarding the key, violin playing can commence.

When considering the question of God's disposition toward humanity and the doctrine of predestination, I believe that the first and most important step is to determine the "key" of the conversation. This key will guide and influence every subsequent decision. In Calvin's case, and then witnessed to in the work of Luther, Bullinger, Arminius, and Barth,[16] the key of the teaching on predestination is clearly *Jesus Christ*. If we first and foremost establish God's gracious self-revelation in the person and work of Jesus Christ as the cornerstone of the doctrinal development, predestination can actually be parsed in a variety of biblically faithful and God-honoring ways, as the Christian tradition has clearly displayed. As we observed in chapter 7, the locus of mystery may shift, but the merciful, righteous, judging (of evil), good, holy, glorious, and powerful God will stay in view. This grants us freedom in our doctrinal wrestling, as long as we keep playing in the correct key.

As I have engaged in this study of Calvin's teaching on God's disposition toward humanity, I have come to discern my own priorities in a doctrine of predestination. I list them here not because I believe that every Christian should or will agree, but I hope that they will be a helpful model of one more attempt to "play" predestination in the key of Jesus Christ in our contemporary world. These are in no certain order except the primacy of the first.

A biblical doctrine of predestination:

- First of all asserts the primacy and centrality of God's revelation in the person and work of Jesus Christ revealed in Scripture (in congruence with God's self-revelation in the whole biblical witness). This is the foundation for knowing God's unchanging nature and being able to trust confidently in him. For me, it is not important whether I can say that God's disclosed characteristics are revelatory of God's essence or not. I am confident that God has revealed with integrity what we need to know of his unchanging character.
- Is a doctrine of grace from first to last.[17] There is no place for human merit. God graciously rescues unworthy humans from their rebellion against him and alienation from him in accordance with God's nature and according to God's will, apart from any human contribution. Through God's grace in creation, humans still have real agency in their choice to trust Christ, even while this response is enabled by grace.[18]
- Affirms the drastic asymmetry between the clearly biblical doctrine of election and the shadow doctrine of reprobation. Election by grace is essential to the good news of the gospel of Jesus Christ. It provides assurance of salvation and affirms the unmerited nature of justification. Reprobation, on the other hand, is biblically and dogmatically best left as a shadow or boundary doctrine; it is the shadow of the clear biblical doctrine of election and the boundary around election by grace. The preacher or exegete must take great care not to read logical inferences about reprobation into biblical texts that do not explicitly indicate God's reprobating acts. We do not know enough about reprobation to teach it materially, and it does not provide enough pastoral benefit to the church to proclaim it broadly.[19] I believe we should follow Bullinger's example (and Calvin's principles that he did not adhere to!) by leaving reprobation in the secret counsel of God and focusing on the good news of God's reconciling love revealed in Jesus.
- Is individual and communal. As van 't Spijker noted above, Calvin linked his teaching on election to the church. His teaching on baptism and the Lord's Supper confirm this. Predestination should be taught in a way that both affirms God's gracious love for individual people and affirms election as the entryway into the Body of Christ as part of the elect people of God (throughout the world and time).
- Lets God be God. Calvin taught me this. He is very clear that although God has made himself abundantly known by grace (most of all in Jesus Christ), God still dwells in incomprehensible light in such a way that creatures

will never comprehend God in all of his glory, majesty, and holiness. As a result, it is important for any doctrine of predestination to leave space for God and God's ways not to fit into a simply and cleanly constructed theological system. This is an instance in which I believe both Calvin and Barth miss the mark. Calvin systematized reprobation and explained it more than he should have. Ironically, I think Barth did the same thing on the other end of the spectrum. He was so keen to make sure nothing could undermine God's character that he (nearly) eliminated all the mystery in God via his creative account of the doctrine of reconciliation. I again believe that Bullinger provides an even better model in his determination to place the mystery of predestination in those outside of Christ while still allowing for a vague, mysterious way that God reigns over that development.
- Compels the preaching of the gospel. Because predestination in the key of Jesus Christ witnesses to God's gracious love in Jesus Christ, all who come to trust in Christ should be compelled from within themselves (by the stirring of the Spirit) to long for others to know this amazing good news of God's reconciling love in Christ. They are chosen for the sake of the world.
- Leads to a life of obedience in love for God and neighbor. Calvin taught that via the double grace of God, believers receive both their justification and sanctification in Christ. Therefore, though faith is completely unmerited, it is always accompanied by the works of faith, primarily expressed in love for God and love for neighbor. These works are demonstrated concretely in the world via obedience to God and participation in his work in the world that seeks the flourishing of all according to God's design.[20] Again, the elect are chosen for the sake of the world.

Although we could expand this list to include nearly every Christian doctrine, these key nodal points provide what I see as the core of a good, God-honoring, biblically faithful, pastorally useful doctrine of predestination that I can play in the key of Jesus Christ today.

We close with pastor John Calvin's confident promise, in the key of Jesus Christ:

> We are assured that Jesus Christ has so fought that he has won the victory not for himself but for us and we must not doubt that by means of him we can now surmount all anxieties, all fears, all dismays, and that we can invoke God, being assured that always he has his arms extended to receive us to himself.[21]

NOTES

1. *Sermons on Election and Reprobation*, no. 13, p. 298; *CO* 58:193.

2. Of course, as mentioned in chapter 2 ("No Comprehensive Knowledge of or Speculation about God's Essence"), this is in contrast with Thomas Aquinas's definition of speculation as an innately noble task. Calvin, who likely had little to no direct contact with Aquinas's work, exclusively speaks of speculation pejoratively.

3. See "No Comprehensive Knowledge of or Speculation about God's Essence" in chapter 2.

4. Cf. Zachman, *Assurance of Faith*.

5. Cf. Jacobs, *Prädestination*, 147. Cf. van der Kooi, *As in a Mirror*, 419.

6. For example, Hesselink, *Calvin's First Catechism*, 93. Cf. Niesel, *Theology of Calvin*, 168.

7. *Reformed Confessions, Vol. 2*, 826.

8. It can also lead to a separatist and elitist attitude regarding the created world in general that exploits instead of stewards God's good creation.

9. Huijgen, *Accommodation*, 273–75. Hence Calvin's explaining that God's wrath is not like human anger but simply an accommodation to our human understanding. See "Excursus on God's Wrath toward Humanity" above in chapter 2.

10. Huijgen points out that as humans experience God's changing, since they cannot know God's unchanging essence, they "should hold to God's accommodated revelation, which means that in practice God shows Himself as changing" (*Accommodation*, 275).

11. Calvin was clear in his assertions that the atoning death of Christ was sufficient for the redemption of all, even though it was efficient only for the elect (*Comm. 1 John* 2:2; *CO* 55:310). Cf. Muller, *Calvin and the Reformed Tradition*, 60–61.

12. Cf. my chapter, "Pietas and Caritas: John Calvin's Preaching on Love for Neighbor," in Karin Maag and Arnold Huijgen (eds), *Calvinus Frater in Domino: Papers of the Twelfth International Congress on Calvin Research* (Göttingen: Vandenhoeck & Ruprecht, 2020).

13. *Sermons on Job*, 1:1, p. 14; *CO* 33:21. Cf. *Sermons on Ps. 119*, no. 16, v. 121–128, p. 228; *CO* 32:665. Cf. *Sermons on Acts*, 2:39–40, p. 53; *SC* 8:36.

14. *Sermons on Micah*, 7:10–12, pp. 412–13, *SC* 5:233.

15. Jacobs asserts that Calvin only significantly develops the material teaching on reprobation when defending the doctrine against attack (including in the *Institutes*) and in his Romans commentary (*Prädestination*, 148–52).

16. I must admit that I am not familiar enough with Zwingli's theology to add him to this list, although it may be the case that he should be included. His embedding of the doctrine of predestination in the doctrine of God's providence does not seem to correspond to a Christ-centered approach to the doctrine.

17. In John Barclay's nomenclature, I mean that predestination is superabundant, has priority, is incongruous, and is effective. God's grace does not imply singularity in God (as we see in God's wrath on anyone who chooses to reject Christ and cling to sin) or noncircularity (as we see in the final bullet point) (*Paul & the Gift* [Grand Rapids: Eerdmans, 2015], 70–75).

18. For one way of parsing this, see "Causality" in chapter 3.

19. As we saw in chapter 5, Calvin's preaching typically reflects this conviction.

20. Alongside his tireless pastoral care for many, Calvin modeled this beautifully in his generous work supporting the refugees of Geneva. Cf. Jeannine E. Olson, *Calvin and Social Welfare: Deacons and the Bourse Francaise* (Selinsgrove, PA: Susquehanna University Press, 1989), 27. Cf. Robert M. Kingdon, "Social Welfare in Calvin's Geneva," in *Calvin's Work in Geneva*, ed. Richard C. Gamble (New York: Garland Publishing, 1992), 36. Cf. my chapter, "Pietas and Caritas: John Calvin's Preaching on Love for Neighbor," in Karin Maag and Arnold Huijgen (eds), *Calvinus Frater in Domino: Papers of the Twelfth International Congress on Calvin Research* (Göttingen: Vandenhoeck & Ruprecht, 2020).

21. *Sermons on the Passion of Christ*, First sermon, p. 30; *CO* 46:842.

Bibliography

Aquinas, Thomas. *Commentary on the Metaphysics of Aristotle*. Translated by John P. Rowan. Chicago: Henry Regnery, 1961.

———. *Summa Theologica*. 5 vols. Translated by the Fathers of the Dominican Province. Notre Dame, IN: Ave Maria Press, 1948.

Arminius, James. "A Declaration of the Sentiments of Arminius." In *The Works of James Arminius, Vol. 1*, 580–732. Grand Rapids: Baker Book House, 1986.

———. "A Modest Examination of Dr. Perkins's Pamphlet." In *The Works of James Arminius, Vol. 3*, 266–484. Grand Rapids: Baker Book House, 1986.

Armstrong, Brian A. *Calvinism and the Amyraut Heresy: Protestant Scholasticism and Humanism in Seventeenth-Century France*. Madison, WI: University of Wisconsin Press, 1969.

Augustine. *The City of God Against the Pagans*. Translated by R. W. Dyson. Cambridge: Cambridge University Press, 1998.

———. *Letters, Vol. 4 (165–203)*. Washington, DC: Catholic University of America Press, 1955.

———. *On Rebuke and Grace*. Translated by Philip Schaff. New York: Christian Literature Publishing, 1886.

———. "On the Predestination of the Saints." In *Saint Augustine: Four Anti-Pelagian Writings*. Washington, DC: Catholic University of America Press, 1992.

Ayres, Lewis. *Nicaea and Its Legacy: An Approach to Fourth Century Trinitarian Theology*. Oxford: Oxford University Press, 2004.

Balke, Willem. *Calvin and the Anabaptist Radicals*. Translated by William Heynen. Grand Rapids: Eerdmans, 1981.

Barclay, John M. G. *Paul & the Gift*. Grand Rapids: Eerdmans, 2015.

Barth, Karl. *Church Dogmatics*. Translated by G. F. Bromiley and T. F. Torrance. 4 vols. in 13 parts. Edinburgh: T&T Clark, 1956–1975.

———. *Die kirchliche Dogmatik*. 4 vols. in 14 parts. Zurich: Evangelischer Verlag, 1932–1967.

Basil of Caesarea. *Against Eunomius*. Translated by Mark DelCogliano, and Andrew Radde-Gallwitz. Washington, DC: Catholic University of America Press, 2011.

Battles, F. L. "God Was Accommodating Himself to Human Capacity." *Interpretation* 31, no. 1 (1977): 19–38.

Bauckham, Richard. *Bible and Mission: Christian Witness in a Postmodern World*. Grand Rapids: Baker Academic, 2003.

Bavinck, Herman. *Reformed Dogmatics*. Translated by John Vriend. Grand Rapids: Baker Academic, 2004.

Beach, J. Mark. "Calvin's Treatment of the Offer of the Gospel and Divine Grace." *Mid-America Journal of Theology* 22 (2011): 55–76.

Beeke, Joel R. "Theodore Beza's Supralapsarian Predestination." *Reformation and Revival Journal* 12, no. 2 (2003): 68–84.

Berkouwer, G. C. *Divine Election*. Grand Rapids: Eerdmans, 1960.

Beza, Theodore. *A Briefe Declaration of the Chief Points of Christian Religion*. Translated by William Whittingham. London: Tho, 1613.

Beza, Theodorus. "*Summa Totius Christianismi*." In *Tractationes Theologicae*. 3 vols. 1:170–205. Geneva: 1570–82.

Billings, J. Todd. *Calvin, Participation, and the Gift: The Activity of Believers in Union with Christ*. Oxford: Oxford University Press, 2007.

———. "The Catholic Calvin." *Pro Ecclesia* 20, no. 2 (2011): 120–34.

———. *Union with Christ: Reframing Theology and Ministry for the Church*. Grand Rapids: Baker Academic, 2011.

Blacketer, Raymond A. "Blaming Beza: The Development of Definite Atonement in the Reformed Tradition." In *From Heaven He Came and Sought Her: Definite Atonement in Historical, Biblical, Theological, and Pastoral Perspective*, edited by David Gibson and Jonathan Gibson, 121–42. Wheaton, IL: Crossway Books, 2013.

———. "The Man in the Black Hat: Theodore Beza and the Reorientation of Early Reformed Historiography." In *Church and School in Early Modern Protestantism*, edited by Jordan J. Ballor, David S. Sytsma, and Jason Zuidema, 227–41. Leiden: Brill, 2013.

Brosché, Fredrik. *Luther on Predestination: The Antinomy and the Unity between Love and Wrath in Luther's Concept of God*. Stockholm, Sweden: Almqvist & Wiksell International, 1978.

Buckner, Forrest. "Calvin's Non-Speculative Methodology: A Corrective to Billings and Muller on Calvin's Divine Attributes." In *Calvinus Pastor Ecclesiae. Papers of the Eleventh International Congress on Calvin Research*, edited by Arnold Huijgen and H. J. Selderhuis, 236–47. Göttingen: Vandenhoeck & Ruprecht, 2016.

———. "Pietas and Caritas: John Calvin's Preaching on Love for Neighbor." In *Calvinus Frater in Domino. Papers of the Twelfth International Congress on Calvin Research*, edited by Arnold Huijgen and Karin Maag, 175–88. Göttingen: Vandenhoeck & Ruprecht, 2020.

Busch, Eberhard. *Gotteserkenntnis Und Menschlichkeit*. Zürich: Theologisher Verlag Zürich, 2005.

Calvin, John. *The Bondage and Liberation of the Will: A Defence of the Orthodox Doctrine of Human Choice against Pighius*. Translated by G. I. Davies. Grand Rapids: Baker Books, 1996.

———. *Calvin's Commentaries*. 45 vols. Edinburgh: Calvin Translation Society, 1844–1855. Repr. 22 vols. Grand Rapids: Baker, 2009.

———. "Catechism 1538." Translated by F. L. Battles. In *Calvin's First Catechism*, ed. I. John Hesselink, 1–38. Louisville, KY: Westminster John Knox Press, 1997.

———. "Catechism of the Church of Geneva, 1545." In *Tracts, Vol. 2*, edited by Henry Beveridge and Jules Bonnet, Calvin Translation Society,

———. *Concerning the Eternal Predestination of God*. Translated by J. K. S. Reid. London: James Clark, 1961.

———. *The Epistles of Paul the Apostle to the Romans and to the Thessalonians*. Translated by Ross MacKenzie. Grand Rapids: Eerdmans, 1995.

———. *Institutes of the Christian Religion*. Translated by John T. McNeill and Ford Lewis Battles. 2 vols. Philadelphia: The Westminster Press, 1960.

———. *Ioannis Calvini Opera Quae Supersunt Omnia* 1–59. Edited by Guilielmus Baum, Eduardus Cunitz, and Eduardus Reuss. *Corpus Reformatorum* 29–87. Brunsvigae: Schwetschke, 1863–1900.

———. *Selected Sermons from the Pastoral Epistles*. Translated by Laurence Tomson. Vestavia Hills, AL: Solid Ground Christian Books, 2012.

———. *Selected Works of John Calvin: Tracts and Letters*. Translated by David Constable. Albany, OR: Books for the Ages, 1998.

———. *Sermons from Job*. Translated by Leroy Nixon. Grand Rapids: Eerdmans, 1952.

———. *Sermons on Election and Reprobation*. Translated by John Field. Willow Street, PA: Old Paths Publications, 1996.

———. *Sermons on Galatians*. Translated by Kathy Childress. Edinburgh: Banner of Truth Trust, 1997.

———. *Sermons on Genesis 1–11*. Translated by Rob Roy McGregor. Edinburgh: Banner of Truth, 2009.

———. *Sermons on Genesis 11–20*. Translated by Rob Roy McGregor. Edinburgh: Banner of Truth, 2012.

———. *Sermons on Melchizedek and Abraham*. Translated by Thomas Stocker. Willow Street, PA: Old Paths Publications, 2000.

———. *Sermons on Psalm 119*. Translated by Thomas Stocker. Albany, OR: Books for the Ages, 1996.

———. *Sermons on the Acts of the Apostles: Chapters 1–7*. Translated by Rob Roy McGregor. Edinburgh: The Banner of Truth Trust, 2008. Banneroftruth.org.

———. *Sermons on the Book of Micah*. Translated by Benjamin W. Farley. Phillipsburg, NJ: P&R Publishing Co., 2003.

———. *Sermons on the Epistle to the Ephesians*. Translated by Arthur Golding. Edinburgh: Banner of Truth Trust, 1973.

———. *Sermons on the Saving Work of Christ*. Translated by Leroy Nixon. Grand Rapids: Baker, 1950.

———. *Sermons on the Ten Commandments*. Translated by Benjamin W. Farley. Grand Rapids: Baker, 1980.

———. *Supplementa Calviniana: Sermones de libro Michaeae*. Edited by Jean Daniel Benoit. Vol. 5. Neukirchen-Vluyn: Neukirchener Verlag des Erziehungsvereins, 1964.

———. *Supplementa Calviniana: Sermon on the Acts of the Apostles*. Edited by Willem Balke and Wilhelmus Moehn. Vol. 8. Neukirchen-Vluyn: Neukirchener Verlag des Erziehungsvereins, 1994.

Canlis, Julie. "The Fatherhood of God and Union with Christ in Calvin." In *'In Christ' in Paul*, 399–426. Tübingen: Mohr Siebeck, 2014.

Childress, Kathy. "Introduction." In *Sermons on Galatians*, ix–xii. Edinburgh: Banner of Truth, 1997.

Crisp, Oliver. "Augustinian Universalism." *International Journal for Philosphy of Religion* 53, no. 3 (2003): 127–45.

———. "Calvin on Creation and Providence." In *John Calvin & Evangelical Theology: Legacy and Prospect*, edited by Sung Wook Chung, 43–65. Colorado Springs, CO: Paternoster, 2009.

———. *Deviant Calvinism: Broadening Reformed Theology*. Minneapolis: Fortress Press, 2014.

———. "On Barth's Denial of Universalism." *Themelios* 29 (2003): 18–29.

———. "On the Letter and Spirit of Karl Barth's Doctrine of Election: A Reply to O'Neil." *Evangelical Quarterly* 79 (2007): 53–67.

———. *Revisioning Christology: Theology in the Reformed Tradition*. Burlington, VT: Ashgate, 2011.

de Greef, Wulfert. *The Writings of John Calvin: An Introductory Guide*. Translated by Lyle D. Bierma. Grand Rapids: Baker, 1993.

den Boer, William. *God's Twofold Love: The Theology of Jacob Arminius (1559–1609)*. Translated by Albert Gootjes. Göttingen: Vandenhoeck & Ruprecht, 2010.

———. "Jacobus Arminius: Theologian of God's Twofold Love." In *Arminius, Arminianism, and Europe: Jacobus Arminius (1559/60–1609)*, edited by Th. Marius van Leeuwen, Keith D. Stanglin, and Marijke Tolsma, 25–50. Boston: Brill, 2009.

Dennison, James T. Jr. *Reformed Confessions of the 16th and 17th Centuries in English Translation: Volume 1, 1523–1552*. Grand Rapids: Reformation Heritage Books, 2008.

———. *Reformed Confessions of the 16th and 17th Centuries in English Translation: Volume 2, 1552–1566*. Grand Rapids: Reformation Heritage Books, 2010.

Dowey, Edward A. *The Knowledge of God in Calvin's Theology*. New York: Columbia University Press, 1964.

Frame, John. *The Doctrine of God*. Phillipsburg, NJ: P&R Publishing, 2002.

Gerrish, B. A. "'To the Unknown God': Luther and Calvin on the Hiddenness of God." *The Journal of Religion* 53, no. 3 (1973): 263–92.

Gibson, David. *Reading the Decree: Exegesis, Election and Christology in Calvin and Barth*. London: T&T Clark, 2009.

Gordon, Bruce. *Calvin*. New Haven, CT: Yale University Press, 2009.

Helm, Paul. "Calvin (and Zwingli) on Divine Providence." *Calvin Theological Journal* 29 (1994): 388–405.
———. "Calvin, Indefinite Language, and Definite Atonement." In *From Heaven He Came and Sought Her: Definite Atonement in Historical, Biblical, Theological, and Pastoral Perspective*, edited by David Gibson and Jonathan Gibson, 97–120. Wheaton, IL: Crossway Books, 2013.
———. *Calvin At the Centre*. Oxford: Oxford University Press, 2010.
———. *Calvin's Ideas*. Oxford: Oxford University Press, 2004.
———. "John Calvin and the Hiddenness of God." In *Engaging the Doctrine of God: Contemporary Evangelical Perspectives*, edited by Bruce L McCormack, 67–82. Grand Rapids: Baker Academic, 2008.
Heppe, Heinrich. *Reformed Dogmatics*. Translated by G. T. Thompson. Eugene, OR: Wipf & Stock, 2007.
Hesselink, I. John. *Calvin's First Catechism*. Louisville: Westminster John Knox Press, 1997.
———. "Calvin's Theology." In *The Cambridge Companion to John Calvin*, edited by Donald K. McKim, 74–92. Cambridge: Cambridge University Press, 2004.
Holmes, Stephen R. "Calvin on Scripture." In *Calvin, Barth, and Reformed Theology*, edited by Neil B. MacDonald and Carl Trueman, 149–62. Colorado Springs, CO: Paternoster, 2008.
———. *Listening to the Past: The Place of Tradition in Theology*. Grand Rapids: Baker Academic, 2002.
Holtrop, Philip C. *The Bolsec Controversy on Predestination, From 1551 to 1555*. Lewiston: Edwin Mellen Press, 1993.
Horton, Michael. "Knowing God: Calvin's Understanding of Revelation." In *John Calvin and Evangelical Theology: Legacy and Prospect*, edited by Sung Wook Chung, 1–31. Colorado Springs, CO: Paternoster, 2009.
Huijgen, Arnold. *Divine Accommodation in John Calvin's Theology: Analysis and Assessment*. Göttingen: Vandenhoeck & Ruprecht, 2011.
Irenaeus. *Against the Heresies*. Translated by F. R. M. Hitchcock. London: Society for Promoting Christian Knowledge, 1916.
Jacobs, Paul. *Prädestination Und Verantwortlichkeit Bei Calvin*. Darmstadt: Wissenschaftliche Buchgesellschaft, 1968.
Johnson, William Stacy, and John H. Leith. *Reformed Reader: A Sourcebook in Christian Theology*. Louisville: Westminster/John Knox Press, 1993.
Kendall, R. T. *Calvin and English Calvinism to 1649*. Oxford: Oxford University Press, 1979.
Kim, Dong-Joo. "Luther and Zwingli on Predestination." *Korean Journal of Christian Studies* 42 (2005): 143–58.
Kingdon, Robert M. "Social Welfare in Calvin's Geneva." In *Calvin's Work in Geneva*, edited by Richard C. Gamble, 22–41. New York: Garland Publishing, 1992.
Kristanto, Billy. *Sola Dei Gloria: The Glory of God in the Thought of John Calvin*. Frankfurt: Peter Lang, 2011.
Lane, A. N. S. *John Calvin: Student of the Church Fathers*. Edinburgh: T&T Clark, 1999.

Levering, Matthew. *Predestination: Biblical and Theological Paths*. Oxford: Oxford University Press, 2011.

Link, Christian. "Election and Predestination." In *John Calvin's Impact on Church and Society: 1509–2009*, edited by Martin E. Hirzel and Martin Sallmann, 105–121. Grand Rapids: Eerdmans, 2009.

Locher, Gottfried W. *Zwingli's Thought: New Perspectives*. Leiden: Brill, 1981.

Luther, Martin. "On the Bondage of the Will." In *Discourse on Free Will*, New York: Ungar, 1961.

McCall, Thomas H., and Keith D. Stanglin. *Jacob Arminius: A Theologian of Grace*. Oxford: Oxford University Press, 2012.

McGrath, Alister E. *Reformation Thought: An Introduction*. Malden, MA: Blackwell Publishers, 1999.

McKee, Elsie Anne. *John Calvin on the Diaconate and Liturgical Almsgiving*. Geneva: Librairie Droz, 1984.

———. *John Calvin: Writings on Pastoral Piety*. Edited by Elsie Anne McKee. New York: Paulist Press, 2001.

———. *The Pastoral Ministry and Worship in Calvin's Geneva*. Geneva: Librairie Droz S.A., 2016.

McKenna, Michael. "Compatibilism." *The Stanford Encyclopedia of Philosophy* (2009). http://plato.stanford.edu/archives/win2009/entries/compatibilism/

Muller, Richard. *After Calvin: Studies in the Development of a Theological Tradition*. Oxford: Oxford University Press, 2003.

———. *Calvin and the Reformed Tradition: On the Work of Christ and the Order of Salvation*. Grand Rapids: Baker Academic, 2012.

———. *Christ and the Decree: Christology and Predestination in Reformed Theology from Calvin to Perkins*. Durham, NC: Labyrinth Press, 1986.

———. *Divine Will and Human Choice: Freedom, Contingency, and Necessity in Early Modern Reformed Thought*. Grand Rapids: Baker Academic, 2017.

———. *God, Creation, and Providence in the Thought of Jacob Arminius: Sources and Directions of Scholastic Protestantism in the Era of Early Orthodoxy*. Grand Rapids: Baker, 1991.

———. *Post-Reformation Reformed Dogmatics: The Rise and Development of Reformed Orthodoxy, Ca. 1520 to Ca. 1725, Vol. 3*. Grand Rapids: Baker Academic, 2003.

———. *The Unaccommodated Calvin: Studies in the Foundation of a Theological Tradition*. Oxford: Oxford University Press, 2000.

———. "The Use and Abuse of a Document: Beza's *Tabula Praedestinationis*, the Bolsec Controversy, and the Origins of Reformed Orthodoxy." In *Protestant Scholasticism: Essays in Reassessment*, 33–61. Eugene, OR: Wipf & Stock, 2005.

Neuser, Wilhelm H. "Predestination." In *The Calvin Handbook*, edited by H. J. Selderhuis, 312–23. Grand Rapids: Eerdmans, 2009.

Niesel, Wilhelm. *The Theology of Calvin*. Translated by Harold Knight. London: Lutterworth Press, 1956.

Oberman, Heiko A. *The Harvest of Medieval Theology*. Grand Rapids: Baker Academic, 1983.

Olson, Jeannine E. *Calvin and Social Welfare: Deacons and the Bourse Francaise*. Selinsgrove, PA: Susquehanna University Press, 1989.

Owen, John. *Biblical Theology*. Translated by Stephen P. Westcott. Pittsburgh, PA: Soli Deo Gloria Publications, 1994.

———. *The Works of John Owen*. Edinburgh: 1850.

Pak, G. Sujin. *The Judaizing Calvin: Sixteenth-Century Debates over the Messianic Psalms*. Oxford: Oxford University Press, 2009.

Parker, T. H. L. *Calvin's Preaching*. Louisville, KY: Westminster/John Knox Press, 1992.

———. *The Doctrine of the Knowledge of God*. Edinburgh: Oliver and Boyd, 1952.

Partee, Charles. *The Theology of John Calvin*. Louisville: Westminster John Knox Press, 2008.

Pitkin, Barbara. *What Pure Eyes Could See: Calvin's Doctrine of Faith in Its Exegetical Context*. Oxford: Oxford University Press, 1999.

Richardson, Kurt A. "Calvin on the Trinity." In *John Calvin and Evangelical Theology: Legacy and Prospect*, edited by Sung Wook Chung, 32–42. Colorado Springs, CO: Paternoster, 2009.

Rolston Holmes III. *John Calvin versus the Westminster Confession*. Richmond, VA: John Knox Press, 1972.

Seitz, Christopher R. *Figured Out: Typology and Providence in Christian Scripture*. Louisville: Westminster John Knox, 2001.

Selderhuis, Herman J. *Calvin's Theology of the Psalms*. Grand Rapids: Baker Academic, 2007.

———. *John Calvin: A Pilgrim's Life*. Grand Rapids: InterVarsity Press, 2009.

Steinmetz, David C. *Calvin in Context*. Oxford: Oxford University Press, 1995.

———. *Reformers in the Wings: From Geiler Von Kayersberg to Theogore Beza*. Oxford: Oxford University Press, 2001.

———. "The Scholastic Calvin." In *Protestant Scholasticism: Essays in Reassessment*, 16–30. Eugene, OR: Wipf & Stock, 2005.

Stephens, William Peter. "Election in Zwingli and Bullinger: A Comparison of Zwingli's *Sermonis De Providentia Dei Anamnema* (1530) and Bullinger's *Oratio De Moderatione Servanda in Negotio Providentiae, Praedestinationis Gratiae Et Liberi Arbitrii* (1536)." *Reformation & Renaissance Review* 7, no. 1 (2005): 42–56.

———. "The Place of Predestination in Zwingli and Bucer." In *Reformiertes Erbe: Festschrift Fur Gottfried W. Locher Zu Seinem 80. Geburtstag. Band 1*, edited by Heiko A. Oberman, Ernst Saxer, Aflred Schindler, and Heinzpeter Stucki, 393–410. Zurich: Theologischer Verlag, 1992.

———. *The Theology of Huldrych Zwingli*. Oxford: Clarendon Press, 1986.

Thompson, John L. *Reading the Bible with the Dead: What You Can Learn from the History of Exegesis That You Can't Learn from Exegesis Alone*. Grand Rapids: Eerdmans, 2007.

Torrance, Alan J. *Persons in Communion: An Essay on Trinitarian Description and Human Participation*. Edinburgh: T&T Clark, 1996.

———. "The Trinity." In *The Cambridge Companion to Karl Barth*, edited by John Webster, 72–91. Cambridge: Cambridge University Press, 2000.

Trueman, Carl R. "Election: Calvin's Theology and Its Early Reception." In *Calvin's Theology and Its Reception: Disputes, Developments, and New Possibilities*, edited by J. Todd Billings and I. John Hesselink, 97–120. Louisville, KY: Westminster John Knox Press, 2012.

Tylenda, Joseph. "Controversy on Christ the Mediator: Calvin's Second Reply to Stancaro." *Calvin Theological Journal* 8, no. 2 (1973): 131–57.

van der Kooi, Cornelis. *As in a Mirror: John Calvin and Karl Barth on Knowing God: A Diptych*. Translated by Donald Mader. Leiden: Brill, 2005.

van Inwagen, Peter. "How to Think about the Problem of Free Will." *The Journal of Ethics* 12, no. 3–4 (2008): 327–41.

Venema, Cornelis P. *Heinrich Bullinger and the Doctrine of Predestination: Author of "the Other Reformed Tradition"?* Grand Rapids: Baker Academic, 2002.

Warfield, B. B. "Calvin's Doctrine of God." *The Princeton Theological Review* (1909): 381–436.

———. "Calvin's Doctrine of the Knowledge of God." *The Princeton Theological Review* (1909): 219–325.

Willis, E. David. "Rhetoric and Responsibility in Calvin's Theology." In *The Context of Contempory Theology*, edited by Alexander McKelway and E. David Willis, 43–64. Atlanta: John Knox Press, 1974.

Wright, N. T. *Paul: In Fresh Perspective*. Minneapolis: Fortress, 2005.

Wynne, Jeremy J. *Wrath among the Perfections of God's Life*. London: Continuum, 2010.

Zachman, Randall C. *The Assurance of Faith: Conscience in the Theology of Martin Luther and John Calvin*. Minneapolis: Fortress Press, 1993.

———. "Calvin as Analogical Theologian." *Scottish Journal of Theology* 51, no. 2 (2009): 162–87.

———. *John Calvin as Teacher, Pastor, and Theologian: The Shape of His Writings and Thought*. Grand Rapids: Baker Academic, 2006.

———. *Reconsidering John Calvin*. Cambridge: Cambridge University Press, 2011.

Index

Page references for figures are italicized.

absolute attributes of God. *See* knowledge of God, essential attributes
absolute power. *See potentia absoluta*
accommodation, 15–22, 28, 42, 198; in Christ, 21–22, 41; definition of, 15; God's wrath, 34–35, 204n9; necessity of, 16–17; levels of, *17*, 17–22; through creation, 18; through Scripture, 18–20
agency, human, 120–121, 125–126, 131, 135, 160, 178, 202
Amyraut, Moïse, 71
anagogue, 18–19
anti-Semitism, 148n126
apophaticism, 23
Aristotelian causality. *See* causality
Arminius, Jacobus, 176–179, 184, 201
assurance of salvation, 83–85, 102n199, 112, 122, 127, 138, 139, 145n81, 153, 154, 157, 158, 159, 161, 168, 174, 180, 196–197, 202, 203
asymmetry between election and reprobation. *See* will of God; asymmetry within
atonement: efficient for some, 8n16, 106, 118, 140, 157, 204n11; sufficient for all, 8n16, 118, 126, 134, 135, 140, 157, 204n11
Augustine, 65, 79

Barclay, John, 204n17
Barth, Karl, 2, 36–37, 82, 158, 179–183, 185, 195, 201, 203; impossible possibility, 181–182
Beeke, Joel, 89
Beza, Theodore, 86–89
Billings, J. Todd, 23
black box of reprobation, 107, 184, 192
Bolsec, Jerome, 58, 86, 155, 173
boundary-line doctrine, 82, 90, 156, 160, 184, 196, 199, 202. *See also* shadow doctrine
Brosché, Fredrik, 168–169
Bullinger, Heinrich, 1, 58, 173–176, 184–185, 195–196, 197, 201, 202, 203

calling, 62–64, 78, 83
Calvinist, 93n7
causality, 74–76, 95n53, 95n62, 99n136, 120–121, 169, 171–172
character of God. *See* knowledge of God, God's nature

Congregatión, 72, 152, 153,
Consensus Tigurinus, 175
Crisp, Oliver, 74, 99n135, 104n226, 179–182
critique, constructive, 193–199

den Boer, William, 176
discipline, church, 79
disclosed disposition of God, 59–60, 63–64, 107–108, 118–120, 122, 123–125, 129–130, 134, 137, 138, 139, 140–141, 161, 192, 200. *See also* will of God, revealed electing will
disposition of God. *See* God; disposition of
double grace, 32, 44, 100n145, 154, 160, 188n72, 203
Dowey, Edward, 14, 157

ecclesiology, 155, 159, 202
Edwards, Jonathan, vii
election: communal, 159, 202; general, 63, 197; in Christ, 58, 60, 63, 71, 85, 86, 123, 153, 155, 157, 159, 161, 166–167, 170, 174, 180, 188n72, 197, 201, 201; special 63. *See also* will of God, revealed electing will of God
empathy, 91, 195, 197–198
excellencies of God. *See* knowledge of God, God's nature
experience, 67–68, 90, 94n48, 153, 155, 166, 183, 196–197

faith, 15, 39–41
fatherly love of God, 7, 11, 30, 32–34, 36, 38, 39, 53n210, 78, 83–85, 119, 123–124, 127, 130, 137, 141. *See also* God, fatherhood of
Frame, John, 4–5
freedom of God, 68, 96n87

general revelation, 10–12.
Georgius of Sicily, 58
Gibson, David, 158–159

glory of God, 73, 76
God: aseity of, 25–26; creator, 29–30; disposition of, 4–5, 59–60, 202–203; excellencies of, 28–34, 41–42; fatherhood of, 32–34, 41, 51–52n176, 83, 109n4, 115–116, 127, 155, 203; grace of, 1, 3, 14, 38, 40, 61–64, 68, 77–78, 80, 83, 85, 92, 97n93, 98n122, 102n199, 119, 120–121, 126, 131, 137–138, 141, 148n130, 151, 155, 158, 160, 162, 166, 168, 172, 175, 178, 181, 185, 189n97, 195, 202–203; immutability of, 27–28, 41–42, 52n193, 198, 204n10; judgment of, 27, 29, 31–37, 41, 53n197, 54n239, 68, 80, 83, 87, 102n199, 108, 130, 134, 135–136, 141, 181, 194, 196; justice of, 1, 27, 29, 32–33, 50n149, 52n188, 66, 71–73, 97n114, 132, 135, 138, 169, 176–179, 185, 191, 198; mercy of, 11, 22, 27–29, 30–34, 35–36, 38, 39, 40–41, 51n164, 52n182, 53n210, 54n239, 61, 63, 68, 73, 75, 76, 78, 87–89, 92, 102n199, 104n225, 106, 107, 112, 128, 130, 134, 137, 195, 198, 199, 200–201, 202; omnipotence of, 26; redeemer, 30–32; will of, 4–5, 59–60; wrath of, 34–37. *See also* God, justice of; knowledge of God, God's nature; wrath
gospel, 61–63, 68, 78, 107–108, 112, 118–120, 121, 130, 178, 181, 203
grace. *See* God, grace of; God, mercy
gratitude, 195

hell, 77, 118, 121, 129, 130, 144n51
Hesselink, I. John, 39
hidden will of God, 70–71. *See also* will of God; secret will
Holmes, Stephen, 41, 82, 87, 92, 157
hope for salvation for all, 79, 118, 124, 134, 135, 179, 198–199, 200–201
Horton, Michael, 41
Huijgen, Arnold, 16–18, 24, 28

image of God, 21–22, 32, 80, 102n199, 118
inscrutability of God, 17–18, 22, 47n83, 57, 60, 70, 106, 132, 136, 169, 202–203. *See also* will of God, one secret will

Jacobs, Paul, 81–82, 90, 157, 159–161, 194–196
judgment, God's, 196, 198–199. *See also* God, judgment of. *See also* wrath

knowledge of God; essential attributes, 25–26; God's essence, 9, 15, 18, 21, 23–26, 28, 30, 40–42, 46n72, 47n83, 48n98, 49n128, 50n135, 54n245, 159, 183, 202; God's nature, 26–34, 42, 64, 72, 78, 81, 85, 90, 92, 105–106, 107–108, 122, 126–128, 130, 134, 136, 157, 159, 167, 169, 176, 182, 196, 199–200, 201, 202; God's self-revelation to humanity, 15–22; God's wrath, 34–37; human access to, 13–15; limited, 202–203; reprobation, 199–200; universal access to, 10–12; usefulness of, 38. *See also* accommodation; general revelation

labyrinth of predestination, 64, 66, 83–84, 137, 167
law of God, 31, 72, 91
Levering, Matthew, 2, 165–166, 183, 185n2
Link, Christian, 58, 81, 152–153
logical contradictions, 91, 99n130, 149n159, 155–156
love for God, 14, 203. *See also* double grace. *See also* piety. *See also* sanctification.
love for neighbor, 14, 91, 134, 137, 156, 160, 195, 198, 203, 205n20
love of God. *See* God, mercy of
Luther, Martin, 168–170, 184, 201

majesty of God, 16–17
McGinley, Phylis, vii
McKee, Elsie, 14, 113, 116–117
methodology, 194–197, 199–200
mirror of election, 85, 154, 175
mission, 78–81, 90–91, 94n45, 181, 197, 198, 203
Muller, Richard, 23, 30, 63, 71, 86–89, 156–157, 158
mystery. *See* predestination, mystery

nature of God. *See* knowledge of God, God's nature
Neuser, Wilhelm, 152
Niesel, Wilhelm, 153–154

obedience. *See* sanctification.
Owen, John, 2

paradoxes. *See* predestination, paradoxes of
Parker, T. H. L., 29, 41–42, 113–114, 116
Partee, Charles, 151–152
pastoral usefulness. *See* usefulness
personal attributes of God. *See* knowledge of God, God's nature
piety, 9, 14–15, 40, 84, 156, 188n72, 198, 203
Pighius, Albert, 58, 74, 85–87
potentia absoluta, 60, 72–73, 94n23, 98n119, 172, 179, 197–198
prayer, 80; of Calvin for all, 119, 125, 136, 144n52
preaching, 78–79, 81, 91–92, 94n42, 106, 108, 111–112, 113, 116, 152, 174–175, 191, 193, 196–197, 203; Calvin's methods of, 113–116, 144n42; Calvin's ministry of, 116–117; first person plural pronouns, 119–120, 124, 129, 135, 144n56; reprobation, 125–126, 127–128, 130–131, 133, 137, 138, 141, 152–153, 156, 160–161, 202, 204n19; to all, 78, 118–120, 123–125, 130, 141,

198–199, 200–201, 203. *See also* Chapter 5
predestination, 91n3; in the *Institutes*, 93n18, 96n71; in the key of Jesus Christ, 201–203, mystery within, 165–166, 168, 169, 173, 176, 178, 180, 185n2, 199–201, 202; paradoxes of, 199–201
providence, 65, 74–75, 99n135, 101n176, 120–121, 136, 170–172, 175, 197–198, 201

reprobation, 65–69, 168, 174, 194–195, 197–198; Christ-less doctrine, 82, 92, 157, 160, 182, 194–195, 199. *See also* will of God, veiled reprobating will
Richardson, Kurt, 15
Robinson, Marilynne, vii

sanctification, 14, 32, 40, 44n30, 83, 85, 99n135, 100n45, 154–155, 160–161, 171, 188n72, 203
scripture, 4, 12–13, 17–20, 22, 23, 24, 46n75, 47n94, 60, 66–67, 72, 78, 84, 87, 89, 111, 113–116, 155, 156, 158, 165–166, 182–183, 194, 196, 202
secret counsel of God, 4–5, 58, 60, 64–65, 69, 70–74, 82–83, 85, 90, 92, 128, 149n159, 153, 167–168, 170, 181, 195, 199, 202
seed of religion, 10–11, 13
Selderhuis, Herman, 38
sermons, Calvin's: on Acts of the Apostles 1–7, 117–122; on Galatians, 139–140; on Genesis 25–27, 122–128; on Micah, 133–135; on the passion and resurrection of Christ, 129–132; on Psalm 119, 135–137; on the Ten Commandments, 137; on 1 Timothy, 111–113; on 2 Timothy, 138–139
sin, 11, 13, 16, 34, 35–36, 41, 58, 63, 65–66, 68–69, 74–76, 87, 92,
96n82, 100n145, 104n217, 106, 108, 121, 126, 131, 134, 139–140, 161, 164n43, 169, 171, 175, 176–179, 181–182, 195, 202
shadow doctrine, 90, 107, 161, 192, 194, 196, 202. *See also* boundary-line doctrine
sola gratia, 3, 57, 61–62, 161, 168, 171, 175, 178
speculation, 24–26, 38, 83, 90, 96n77, 104n230, 151, 156, 162, 169, 183, 194–196, 197, 198
Stephens, William, 171

temporary faith, 84
Torrance, Alan, 19–20
Trinity, 25, 75, 157, 158, 159, 162
Trueman, Carl, 61
two-fold love of God, 177

unapproachability of God. *See* inscrutability of God
universal revelation. *See* general revelation
usefulness of doctrine, 24, 38, 42, 57, 66, 156, 184, 194–195, 197, 202–203

van 't Spijker, Willem, 154–155
van der Kooi, Cornelis, 32, 38, 41–42, 57, 155–156, 194, 195
Venema, Cornelis, 173–175
Vermigli, Peter Martyr, 177

Warfield, B. B., 28
will of God, 4–5, 59–60, 106, 111–113, 140–141, 153, 161, 169–170, 182; *ad intra* vs. *ad extra*, 71, 97n110; asymmetry within, 73–82, 100n145, 100n148, 107–108, 139, 152, 157, 161, 162, 164n39, 169, 172–173, 192, 201, 202; one secret will, 69–73, 106, 128, 131, 134, 136, 139, 149n144, 155, 180–181, 192; revealed electing will, 60, 63–64, 69,

94n19, 106, 120, 125, 129–130, 192, 200; veiled reprobating will, 60, 65–69, 94n20, 106, 121, 125–126, 130–131, 134, 135, 137, 139, 140, 168, 192, 199–200, 200–201
work of Christ, 31–32

wrath, 7n2, 34–37, 52n193, 53n214, 88, 96n91, 129, 130–132, 148n130, 169–170, 181–183, 189n193, 204n9
Wynne, Jeremy, 36–37

Zachman, Randall, 18–19
Zwingli, Huldrych, 170–173, 184

About the Author

Forrest H. Buckner is the Storm Family Dean of Spiritual Life, Assistant Professor of Theology, and Campus Pastor at Whitworth University in Spokane, WA, USA. He earned his PhD in systematic theology from the University of St Andrews in Scotland.

www.ingramcontent.com/pod-product-compliance
Lightning Source LLC
Chambersburg PA
CBHW050903300426
44111CB00010B/1363